The Not-Quite Child

NEW DIRECTIONS
IN SCANDINAVIAN STUDIES

Andy Nestingen / Series Editors

This series offers interdisciplinary approaches
to the study of the Nordic region of Scandinavia
and the Baltic States and their cultural connections
in North America. By redefining the boundaries of
Scandinavian studies to include the Baltic States
and Scandinavian America, the series presents
books that focus on the study of the culture,
history, literature, and politics of the North.

Liina-Ly Roos

THE NOT-QUITE CHILD

COLONIAL HISTORIES, RACIALIZATION, AND SWEDISH EXCEPTIONALISM

University of Washington Press / Seattle

The Not-Quite Child was made possible in part by grants from the Department of Scandinavian Studies at the University of Washington and the Department of German, Nordic, and Slavic+ at the University of Wisconsin–Madison.

Support for this research was provided by the University of Wisconsin–Madison Office of the Vice Chancellor for Research with funding from the Wisconsin Alumni Research Foundation.

The publication of this book was also supported by the Louis Janus Book Subvention awarded by the Society for the Advancement of Scandinavian Study.

Copyright © 2025 by the University of Washington Press

Design by Mindy Basinger Hill

Composed in Garamond Premier Pro

The digital edition of this book may be downloaded and shared under a Creative Commons Attribution Non-Commercial No Derivatives 4.0 international license (CC-BY-NC-ND 4.0). For information about this license, see https://creativecommons.org/licenses/by-nc-nd/4.0. This license applies only to content created by the author, not to separately copyrighted material. To use this book, or parts of this book, in any way not covered by the license, please contact the University of Washington Press.

UNIVERSITY OF WASHINGTON PRESS   *uwapress.uw.edu*

Cataloging information is available from the Library of Congress

LIBRARY OF CONGRESS CONTROL NUMBER 2024053085
ISBN 9780295753812 (hardcover)
ISBN 9780295753829 (paperback)

♾ This paper meets the requirements of ANSI/NISO Z39.48-1992 (Permanence of Paper).

FOR JUSTIN

CONTENTS

Acknowledgments / ix

INTRODUCTION Childhood and the Not-Quite Child in Sweden/ 1

CHAPTER ONE Imagining Racialization and Whiteness
Through the Child Who Lines Up / 32

CHAPTER TWO Failing Childhood and Rethinking
Growing Up Swedish / 67

CHAPTER THREE Unsettling the Figure of the
Not-Quite Child / 106

Conclusion / 143

Filmography / 149

Notes / 151

Bibliography / 163

Index / 175

ACKNOWLEDGMENTS

This book has taken a long time to write, and I am immensely thankful for the many people who have helped it become what it is now. I have been very lucky to have joined a virtual Nordic studies writing group (SSAWA) in 2020. Benjamin Bigelow, Amanda Doxtater, Benjamin Mier-Cruz, and Arne Lunde have provided incredibly helpful feedback, accountability for writing, and friendship that I will always cherish. I am also deeply grateful for my colleagues at the Department of German, Nordic, Slavic+ at the University of Wisconsin–Madison who have encouraged me throughout the process of writing this book, read the drafts, asked good questions, and provided another space of collegiality and friendship that can be rare in academia. Special thanks to Dean Krouk, Thomas A. DuBois, Ida Moen Johnson, Kirsten Wolf, and Claus Elholm Andersen for taking time for conversations, walks, and coffee breaks.

My thinking around the figure of the child and this project got started at the Department of Scandinavian Studies at the University of Washington. I'm grateful for Andrew Nestingen's mentorship, his thought-provoking questions as he read the drafts of my chapters, and the seminar he taught on Nordic childhood. I have always been inspired by the way he approaches cultural texts and his ability to provide advice and support, which helped me find my own independent scholarly voice. My work benefited greatly as well from Amanda Doxtater's careful reading of my work. I continue to admire her elegant writing and generosity. Thank you also to Gordana Crncovic for showing me the beauty of close analyses and navigating complex theoretical frameworks and to Guntis Šmidchens for believing in my work from day one of graduate school, when the challenges of working in another language and on another continent sometimes made me doubt myself.

As I worked on reframing some of my original material and decided to narrow the focus of this book, Amber Rose Cedeström's feedback was incredibly helpful. I'm also thankful for insightful conversations and support of Olivia Gunn, Pernille Ipsen, Maxine Savage, Karin Eriksson, Karin Nykvist, Ann Kristin Wallengren, Maarja Hollo, and Bradley Harmon during different stages of this project.

My work on this book has been supported by generous summer salary support from the Office of the Vice Chancellor for Research Committee at the University of Wisconsin–Madison, which made it possible for me to dedicate more uninterrupted time to writing in the summers. The semester-long fellowship at the Institute for Research in the Humanities at UW–Madison was invaluable for the final stages of editing this book and getting to engage with other scholars in a supportive intellectual community.

I'm also deeply grateful for the University of Washington Press and the editorial team. Huge thanks to Larin McLaughlin for taking interest in this project and for her enthusiasm about it at each stage of getting it published. Thank you also to the series editor, Andrew Nestingen, and his helpful advice on final revisions. It was also wonderfully enjoyable to read the reports of the anonymous reviewers. I'm so thankful for their kind words and smart suggestions for improvement.

I would not have been able to write this book without the unwavering support of my family and friends. Thank you, Dad, for always encouraging me with your humor and joyful resilience. Thank you, Mom, for sharing with me your passion and curiosity for literature and culture; I wish that you would have been able to see the publication of this book and I miss you a lot. Thank you, Jonelle, for always understanding me and saying the perfect words of encouragement. Thank you, Jo, for bringing so much love, light, and presence in the last few years. Finally, I am beyond-words grateful for Justin. Thank you for always believing in me, patiently listening to my rambled first ideas for these chapters and much more, and for continuously telling me that I can do it.

The Not-Quite Child

INTRODUCTION

CHILDHOOD AND THE NOT-QUITE CHILD IN SWEDEN

Two of the most famous Swedish children of the last hundred years are most likely Pippi Longstocking and Greta Thunberg. While one of them is fictional and the other a real child, these two figures illustrate the significant role that the child has had in the rhetoric and politics of the Swedish welfare state throughout the twentieth and early twenty-first centuries. Pippi Longstocking famously came to symbolize the autonomous citizen of the welfare state, and Astrid Lindgren's books about her impacted how children were thought of in Sweden: in many ways equal to adults, with a voice, rights, and responsibilities. While the Swedish welfare state has transformed by the early twenty-first century, it is no surprise that Greta Thunberg, who has often been represented in media as a young, fierce child who reprimands the adults for their ignorance and lack of action regarding the climate crisis, is from Sweden. It is also no surprise that those two children are white girls and have come to represent Swedish exceptionalism (specifically regarding progress in gender equality and environmental consciousness). Indeed, as Emily D. Ryalls and Sharon R. Mazzarella write, "Greta Thunberg is not just white; she is light-haired, light-eyed Nordic white, which may explain why the media have privileged Thunberg's rise as a celebrity girl activist and displaced attention from young Indigenous activists and those from the Global South."[1] The figure of the ideal child—a white, middle-class child who fights for justice—has come to signify a national and familial future and it has helped to articulate a normative understanding of Swedish childhood. By the same token, those who fail to live up to this norm experience feelings of invisibility or violation and exclusion or tenuous belonging in the Swedish nation and its future.

The Not-Quite Child: Colonial Histories, Racialization, and Swedish Exceptionalism examines films and novels that incorporate a child figure who disrupts and rethinks the expected trajectory of growing up as the Swedish child in order to rethink colonial histories and racial hierarchies in Sweden. More specifically, *The Not-Quite Child* focuses on works that imagine Indigenous Sámi, Tornedalian, and Finnish-speaking children in Sweden during the twentieth century. Although since 2000 these groups have been officially recognized as Sweden's national minorities and all are typically legible as white, the colonial/racial ideologies in northern Europe have historically categorized these three groups to varying extents as inferior races, as not quite white. The cultural texts I analyze in this book suggest that this colonial history and the racialization inherent in it has been relatively invisible to the majority culture throughout the twentieth century. This invisibility typically has two meanings: First, while people of these groups have in different contexts (such as educational system, cultural narratives, media) been made to feel like they are not quite as civilized/white/Nordic, they can often pass as white Nordic citizens and blend into dominant society. Second, because of colonial erasure that seeks to assimilate people into the dominant culture, the history of racialization has not always been talked about in the society. The twenty-first century has seen an increase in fictional and other texts that seek to articulate this historical racialization from new perspectives. *The Not-Quite Child* explores that phenomenon. I argue that constructing a child figure who is either expected or desires to become Nordic/Swedish/white as they grow up provides these cultural texts with an avenue to explore how becoming relates to passing, assimilating, and erasure of cultures among people who are both minoritized and have a privilege to pass and how they share a long cultural history with and within the dominant culture.

Greta and Pippi also exemplify some of the theoretical discussions about childhood. The personas and actions of both have been received as a defamiliarizing, subversive view of the society because they are children (even though Greta will have grown out of childhood by the time this book comes out, the mediations of her as a child continue to dominate the imageries of her activism). They are imagined as inherently different from adults or as in need of education and care of adults in order to be taken seriously because they are still children, adults in the making. Of course, there are also crucial differences. Pippi is a character in a children's book, constructed by an adult writer. She represents, as Maria Nikolajeva argues, a common theme in children's literature: She is a child who does not want to grow up, and just like Peter Pan and other similar literary figures, she does not grow up, does not engage in becoming adult.[2] Greta Thunberg has indicated in her famous speeches a deep concern for the future that adults have taken away from her, often emphasizing that she is a child and should not be the one telling adults about the climate crisis. While one of the main projects of this book is to analyze how cultural texts predominantly for adult audiences (thus, different from Pippi, as a children's book character, or from Greta Thunberg, who is a real person) have constructed childhoods that are not quite in line with the ideal Swedish childhood, those texts are in dialogue with the myth of the Swedish (and Nordic) child who is a competent, autonomous, and moral truth teller, taken care of by the welfare state. Susanna Alakoski's novel *Svinalängorna* (Swine rows), discussed in chapter 2, for example, makes explicit references to Pippi Longstocking and other figures from Astrid Lindgren's books that are present through cultural mediations in the everyday life of the child protagonists. In Alakoski's novel, such references create a stark contrast to the experiences of growing up in Finnish-speaking families during the 1960s and 1970s in Sweden.

This introduction situates the texts and their constructions of child figures that the following chapters analyze. It engages with theoretical frameworks in childhood studies as well as the history and scholarship on how the Swedish welfare state rhetoric incorporated the child as a symbol for the citizens of the welfare state. As it theorizes the figure that I call the *not-quite child*, the chapter is also in dialogue with scholarship on settler colonialism, whiteness, and racial hierarchies, particularly in the Swedish welfare state during the twentieth century. It discusses the implications of the always-existing tension between the abstract idea of childhood and the ways in which children have or have not performed that idea during the twentieth century. Is it possible for children who are perceived as not quite Swedish but legible as white to perform Swedish childhood or at least to perform growing up and lining up with the white Swedish nation? What if they choose not to do it? This chapter engages with Kathryn Bond Stockton's claim that the child who cannot grow up by reigning cultural definitions grows to the side of cultural ideals, and with Sara Ahmed's discussion of the expectation to line up based on what we inherit. It demonstrates that the fictional child figures provide cultural texts with unique temporal and spatial embodiment of the expectations for the migrants and minorities in Sweden to line up and reproduce likeness.

CONSTRUCTING "THE SWEDISH CHILD"

The child has been a frequent figure in literary and cinematic texts that depict problems in the Swedish welfare state and the decades following its "golden era" since the late twentieth century. One of the key reasons for the prevalence of the child figure is the tension between the cultural construction of the Swedish child taken care of by the welfare state and the experiences of children who live in Sweden but whose everyday lives are anything but carefree. This tension is not by any means unique to Sweden or the Nordic region. The instances of child figures in films or literature who resist, find troubling, or simply do not have the ability to be like the culturally idealized child likely exist in most places where the understanding of who gets to occupy childhood refers to those who are privileged; in many Western contexts this means being white, middle-class, able-bodied, and heterosexual. Robin Bernstein, for example, discusses how depictions of Black children, such as Claudia in Toni Morrison's *The Bluest Eye* or the child in the memories of scholar Ann duCille, grapple with the experience of the forcible exclusion from the white innocent American childhood.[3] Bernstein argues that the tension between real children and the cultural constructions of childhood has been a central question in the field of childhood studies, where the concept of childhood functions as abstract and disembodied, while "real children" are seen as "tangible and fleshy."[4] Instead of understanding these two as opposing sides, Bernstein suggests that historically located children and textually based childhood co-emerge and co-constitute each other through performance. This means that childhood is "best understood as a legible pattern of behaviors that comes into being *through* bodies of all ages."[5]

The juvenile body can function as an effigy of childhood, but it will always be unstable and inadequate because it is ever growing. Childhood as an abstract idea, then, functions as an "act of surrogation that compensates for losses incurred through growth."[6] Bernstein writes this in the context of American popular culture, using the example of the 2006 Screen Actors Guild (SAG) Awards ceremony, where Dakota Fanning presented Shirley Temple Black with the SAG Life Achievement Award. Fanning, who was twelve at the time, performed perfectly Shirley Temple's "particular mold of girlhood," which the grown-up Shirley Temple Black could no longer have performed the same way. At the same time, Fanning, too, was in the process of growing up; thus, as Bernstein argues, the Shirley Temple doll that she held in her hand was the only surrogate of the Shirley Temple childhood that would not change through growth. Of course, the discourse around Shirley Temple has changed throughout the twentieth century. As Kirsten Hatch argues, it is the competing notions of innocence that have shaped childhood for a long time, and while Shirley Temple has also figured in many debates and discussions of pedophilia and the sexualization of childhood, during the time of her stardom she ultimately emblematized an innocence that was "built upon the fairly stable conception of the white child's innocence as transformative, capable not only of deflecting adult sexuality but of transforming adults for the better."[7]

The abstract idea of childhood and its impact on historically located children, however, has had a special status for both the self-image and international reputation of Sweden throughout the twentieth century. The official rhetoric of the developing welfare state in the 1920s and 1930s incorporated childhood as an emblem for the citizens of the Swedish state. Before the Social Democratic Party's victory in 1932, Per Albin

Hansson, the leader of the party, said in his famous 1928 speech at the Social Democratic Congress that Sweden as a good state should be like a home for its people. He said that in this good home no one should be privileged or left behind or be seen as a stepchild.[8] Thus, in the ideal circumstances of the Swedish welfare state, the citizens would all be taken care of by the state, have equal opportunities, and no one would feel that they are better than others nor as a "stepchild." After the Social Democratic Party came to power (and stayed in power for forty-four years), they implemented significant policies to expand the welfare state, improving state pensions, introducing maternity payments and establishing two weeks' annual vacation in the 1930s. The primary mission of the emerging welfare state, as Henrik Berggren and Lars Trägårdh argue, became protecting, caring, providing for, and educating children, who were seen as "defenseless today but citizens tomorrow and the new society's best hope."[9] This included "liberating" children from the family with the help of the state as part of a larger effort "to liberate people from the unequal and unjust relations of dependency that had characterized the old class society with its authoritarian state."[10] Childhood as an abstract idea thus came to embody the people of the welfare state, but it co-emerged with addressing the circumstances of "real children," and it greatly impacted policies regarding rights and care for children in the twentieth century. Such policies include the establishment of free school lunches in 1947, the ban of corporal punishment in schools in 1957, and, in the later decades, an increased agency and voice that children have in decisions concerning their rights. Bengt Sandin brings out a gender political aspect of this, saying, "The idea that women could work and men could participate in child rearing gave extra urgency to demands for parental education and an expansion of day care" in the 1960s and 1970s, while men's share in child care did not expand as rapidly.[11] The common figurations of children in both nonfictional and fictional texts not only stood in for the abstract idea of childhood, but they also helped to further construct and mediate the image of the Swedish child.

Children figured in several influential texts of the early twentieth century that ultimately strove to better the life of the Swedish nation. Ellen

Key declared famously that the twentieth century was to be the century of the child in her *The Century of the Child* (*Barnets århundrade* 1900), which was widely read, translated and referenced.[12] In this book, Key wrote about gender roles, marriage, and other aspects of the society, and she supported relationships and child rearing also outside of marriage, arguing that it was better for both the relationships and for the children when people enjoyed being together. Her proposed changes in child rearing and education were ultimately intended to ensure that children would grow up to be better citizens who would in turn develop the Swedish nation-state further. Her philosophy regarding children was, on one hand, Romantic in that, inspired by Rousseau, she believed that children were freethinkers and could easily be corrupted by schooling. She proposed adamantly that children should be brought up as independent thinkers so that they would be able to take on the responsibility of citizenship, as she believed that childhood determines adulthood. Thus, she also saw children as not yet but becoming citizens.[13]

The idea of children as independent thinkers in Key's writing is an early example of imagining the Swedish (and Nordic) child as autonomous and competent. Helene Brembeck, Barbro Johansson, and Jan Kampmann argue that the concept of the competent child could be understood as "part of the Nordic rural tradition," where the rural child was seen as a competent worker who took care of younger siblings and engaged in a variety of chores.[14] In the early twentieth century, as Bengt Sandin points out, the experiences of childhood were by no means equal as children were distinguished between different social classes and genders, not to mention Indigenous childhoods (which are rarely mentioned in studies on Nordic/Swedish childhood).[15] It became the responsibility of the state to make sure that children, (ideally) no matter their social class or gender, would be guaranteed a safe environment, opportunities to play, and receive a good education. The establishment of the welfare state, writes Sandin, was "parallel to the establishment of images of children as independent agents, strong and oppositional moral epigones to the adult world, fighters for rights and justice for themselves but also for animals and the downtrodden."[16] While this led to seeing childhood as a "period of life with its own characteristics" in the second half of the twentieth century, the ideas of the independent children created a paradigm where they were seen as "objects created by state individualism."[17] This means that the state had a strong role in the lives of children, which was justified by referring to parents' incompetence and children's needs for protection and independence.

The perceived incompetence of parents to take care of their children properly prompted Swedish activists Gunnar and Alva Myrdal in the 1930s and 1940s to support policies of population planning that included sterilizing people who were seen as unfit to parent and give birth to children who would not be "productive" for the Swedish welfare state. The Myrdals were widely known beyond Sweden, as Gunnar Myrdal was invited to travel to the United States to study the racial discrimination of Black Americans. This study resulted in his book *An American Dilemma: The Negro Problem and American Democracy*, a supposedly objective look based in what Benjamin Mier-Cruz has called "Swedish racial innocence" that draws from "a whitewashed history of ethnic and cultural homogeneity and a perennial myth of race and colour-blindness in the Nordic world."[18] In their close analysis of the "most iconic Swedish photograph of the twentieth century," which features the Myrdal family prior to their journey, Henrik Berggren and Lars Trägårdh write that the image represents the patriotic and progressive reproductiveness, closeness and equality in the Myrdals's marriage, and the "zenith of the family as an institution."[19]

As Per Albin Hansson had proclaimed that the Swedish welfare state should be like a home where no child is inferior to others, the decisions to force sterilization on people living in poverty or with mental illness established that the child (who also represents the citizen) who is protected and equal in the welfare state should not deviate too much from what was the norm. We can see further implications of such norm-focused thinking in the establishment and work of the Swedish State Institute for Race Biology (SIRB), which was active in Sweden from 1921 to 1958. The proponents of race biology in Sweden, particularly Herman Lundborg, the head of SIRB from 1922 until 1935, worked on mapping the Nordic racial traits in the Swedish population in the 1920s and 1930s, which included large-scale photographing of the people living in Sweden. The aim of this work, as Ulrika Kjellman demonstrates, was to secure a "healthy populace" in order to decide "who was a pure Swede and who was not, as well as what eugenic strategies to implement to strengthen the Swedish race within the borders of Sweden."[20] The three race types that SIRB found dominating the Swedish population were the Nordic type (Swedes), the East Baltic type (Finns), and the Sámi type (then referred to with the pejorative term, the Lapps). Since the Nordic type gained a superior position in the rhetoric of race biology and ensuring the health of the nation, as Kjellman shows, Lundborg chose the photographs to represent the different types in a most biased way. Thus, the Sámi types and the East Baltic types were mostly of elderly people, not well dressed or healthy-looking, and often "depicted in front of a poor settlement," while the Nordic types were represented by well-dressed young people, usually positioned in "exteriors of idyllic pastoral character, or in interiors of wealthy bourgeois homes."[21] Lundborg also advised strongly against any race mixing between Swedes and those considered lower races, such as the Sámi people, Finns, or Roma, and he promoted eugenic strategies to "save the Nordic race from degeneration."[22] These early examples show us that in order to achieve the goal of the welfare state as a good home where no child is seen as better or lesser, and to provide the autonomous competent children with the necessary support, those who deviated from that ideal had to be removed.

The thinking behind sterilization laws and population planning policies functioned similarly to what Lee Edelman has called "reproductive futurism," a politics that invests all hope for the future in children and continues to be persistent in the beginning of the twenty-first century.[23] If activists for abortion rights claim that a right to reproductive choice is good for the children and therefore for the future, writes Edelman, they are still subscribing to the ideology of reproductive futurism. This articulation of the ideology of the Child (capitalized in Edelman), who is an emblem for a future, further illustrates the significance of constructing "the child." We can see this ideology in Myrdal's writing and activism, which promoted important rights for women, including contraception and abortion, but it was inspired by the idealization of the child as the future of the welfare state. Several critical accounts of Edelman's points bring out that the child in his discussions signifies a very specific privileged childhood that should not stand in for the multiple and diverse experiences of children.[24] This is an important point. Even though Edelman differentiates the symbolic Child from the experiences of real children, whom he is not attempting to write about, rejecting the Child to resist the linear time of the nation neglects discussing the ways in which the politics of reproduction continue to impact the lives of both children and adults. In her analysis of how boarding schools intervened in the sexuality of Native children in North America, for example, Mary Zaborskis argues that racialized queer children are "barred from the future, and this barring is enacted precisely through promising futurity."[25] In other words, reproduction can be meaningful for marginalized communities who have been barred from the future because they deviate from the normative image of the nation.[26] At the same time, reproduction can be experienced as oppressive by the marginalized communities if they are expected to reproduce themselves on colonizer's terms, a topic that recurs in the novels and films analyzed in the following chapters.

The theoretical implications of childhood and reproduction are thus more complex than simply promoting or resisting the linear progress narrative.[27] In order to understand how children figure in cultural imaginaries more broadly, and in narratives that depict Indigenous and minority communities more specifically, it might be more efficacious to engage traditions and futures critically rather than disavow them (as Andrea Smith proposes in her analysis of the heteronormativity of settler colonialism in North America[28]). How does the process of becoming, so often associated with childhood and with growing up, function in narratives about children who are legible as white while also perceived as not quite white? In the understanding of progress as linear, becoming means growing up physically and temporally. It means lining up with other bodies, as Sara Ahmed writes. Her point that to "inherit whiteness is to become invested in the line of whiteness" illustrates the expected trajectory of growing up for the Swedish child.[29] The inherited whiteness, as Ahmed argues further, functions as an "orientation that puts certain things within reach."[30] Of course, growing up to line up with bodies that are considered to be the correct ones is problematic and impossible for many people who for various reasons do not inherit whiteness or other aspects that support the normative (such as heterosexuality or able-bodiedness). In that case, one might instead grow sideways, to use Kathryn Bond Stockton's term that, instead of reducing the alternative to the death drive, locates queer children (in her analysis, queered by sexuality, Freud, innocence, or race) in a movement that goes back-and-forth instead of up, with energy and pleasure and without reproductive extensions.[31] Or one might nevertheless decide to follow the normative line if growing sideways is not experienced as an option because that, too, is facilitated by the settler colonial state, internalized racialization and colonization that have barred one from the future (even if that future is normative, exclusive, and attainable only in abstraction). As I will elaborate more in the following sections, while the idealized image of childhood is not a unique phenomenon to Sweden or the Nordic region, the special status that the child has in the rhetoric of the welfare state provides unique challenges and opportunities for imagining what it might mean to perform growing up and sideways.

PERFORMING "THE SWEDISH CHILD" THROUGH PIPPI LONGSTOCKING

Literature and films have had a significant role in remediating both the image of the idealized Swedish child and the children who deviate from it. Swedish children's literature specifically, as Bengt Sandin argues, can be understood to have "fed into and expressed the moral basis of the centrality of children's rights to welfare and care in the Nordic countries."[32] The depictions of children in Nordic children's books already at the turn of the century, as Åse Marie Ommundsen argues, suggested that children had much more freedom than their peers in other Western countries.[33] Thus, the image of an independent freely roaming child has been a familiar figure for a long time. However, it is Astrid Lindgren's *Pippi Långstrump* (*Pippi Longstocking*; first published in 1945) that engaged with and made the idea of the autonomous child of the 1940s Swedish welfare state more broadly known.[34] As is well known and discussed by now,

Pippi is a completely autonomous and competent child: She has financial resources, super strength, and a house but no parental oversight, and she does not usually express any need for parents or other adults. However, there have been many contradicting interpretations and responses to this figure of the child who questions social conventions.

One of the most significant contradictions that we can see in the different readings of *Pippi* is that while Pippi subverts normativity, the image of her has simultaneously come to represent a normative Swedish exceptionalism. As Eva Söderberg argues, the focus on what Pippi represents shifted during the twentieth century from seeing her as a child who challenges the traditional adult-child power relationships to emphasizing that she is a girl and making her into a feminist icon.[35] Pippi has also been read as someone who queers children's literature and the child by going beyond boundaries between adult and child, feminine and masculine, human and animal.[36] Thus, by the end of the twentieth century, Pippi had come to represent both the cultural ideals of the welfare state (autonomy, gender equality) and "growing sideways": She rejects the institutional help/oversight in her life and the idea of growing up. For example, in *Pippi Långstrump i Söderhavet* (*Pippi Longstocking in the South Seas*), she playfully invites Tommy and Annika to eat "*krumelurpiller*" (squiggle pills) that would help them to never grow up.[37] The combination of those two contrasting elements in this exemplary image of the Swedish child helps us to understand the drastically different ways that Pippi has been understood not only in the studies of children's literature but also in discussions regarding the Swedish welfare state (and how Pippi as a child figure co-emerges with, contributes to, and performs the abstract idea of Swedish childhood). Furthermore, paying attention to this combination illuminates how Stockton's concept of "growing sideways," can, in the Swedish/Nordic context, become experienced as privileged and not attainable to everyone.

Henrik Berggren and Lars Trägårdh resolve the contradictory forces in the figure of Pippi by arguing that it is the combination of two types of children that makes Lindgren's books about her so original and such a productive example of the structure of the Swedish welfare state.[38] Namely, the stories of Pippi unfold from Tommy and Annika's perspective, whose cozy and conventional nuclear family in the neighboring house is a better example of the carefree Swedish childhood. Tommy and Annika, too, are free to roam around with Pippi without much parental supervision, but they have a family who takes care of them and who guides them in the social expectations and tasks as they are on their way to become grown-up citizens of the welfare state. Thus, as Berggren and Trägårdh argue, these two childhoods together exemplify the Swedish welfare state as a combination of total individual sovereignty and the absolute necessity of a stable social order. Their discussion of Pippi as someone who children do not actually want to identify with because she is lonely (through Tommy and Annika's eyes) suggests a reading of Pippi as someone outside of the construction of the Nordic child. Berggren and Trägårdh go on to argue that Pippi's world displays most of the characteristics of Georges Bataille's "sovereign man"—"non-productiveness, idleness, excessive and meaningless consumption, criminality and disorder."[39] Nina Witoszek and Martin Lee Mueller argue against this point in their study on ecological ethics of Nordic children's tales. They bring out that Pippi is, in fact, always busy baking, embarking on quests, cleaning, and that she fights for justice instead of being a "deviant criminal."[40] Furthermore, the reading of Pippi as someone outside the construction of the Nordic child is based on trying to relate to Pippi as a "real child." Ulla Lundqvist argues that neither Pippi nor Tommy and Annika are "realistic children" and that Tommy and Annika are constructed as too stereotypical, too puppet-like to contrast Pippi's ideas and expressions.[41] Instead, Tommy and Annika function as examples of performing the exemplary idea of Swedish childhood that Pippi represents. They are inspired by Pippi to question social conventions and to become more autonomous, and they can do so because their everyday lives are relatively independent and carefree.

A particular focus of scholarship on the implications of seeing Pippi Longstocking as a model figure has been on Pippi as a feminist icon. Eva Söderberg, for example, points out that while Lindgren, in her letter accompanying her manuscript of *Pippi*, asserted that Pippi should not function as a model for ordinary children, she has increasingly become a role model, particularly for girls and women. Pippi has become a normative figure, argues Söderberg, functioning as an ambassador who can "spread Swedish gender equality around the world."[42] If the strong, autonomous Pippi is the norm, asks Söderberg, which girls and women are excluded and othered because of that norm? Söderberg does not answer this question in her chapter that focuses mostly on a comparison of Pippi and Lisbeth Salander in Stieg Larsson's Millennium series of crime novels, but it is an important question. While this and other criticisms of Pippi focus on her as a feminist, as someone who empowers girls and women or exemplifies a normative idea of a woman (a "can-do" girl/woman, for example), her image as a normative child is equally significant, particularly when the image of that childhood is closely connected to and associated with the Swedish welfare state and, by extension, Swedishness.[43]

The significant ways in which *Pippi Longstocking* changed the meaning of childhood, however, include in that normative image of the child a figure who goes against norms. Deviating from the cultural ideals that surround Pippi in her stories crosses the traditional boundaries between child and adult: Pippi presents as a child, but she also behaves as an adult in some ways, and she sees through the normative conventions of the adults and fights against them. In many ways, she "grows sideways": There are no indications that she will ever grow "up" in the traditional understanding, and her character celebrates the back-and-forth movement of childhood without any reproductive extensions. Indeed, Jimmy Olsson's mockumentary short *Valla Villekulla / Whatever happened to Ms Longstocking* provides a comedic exploration of what Pippi's life might be like if she did in fact grow up. Olsson interviews Pippi (Ann Petrén), who is in her fifties and has had a falling out with Tommy and Annika after they started a business together, her money is gone, and it turns out that being a bit *utanför systemet* (outside of the system) has not been easy as an adult. "I didn't have a social security number," says Pippi to Olsson, "and you really need those last four digits" (*Valla Villekulla*). She continues to explain that she has not received much from the proceeds of Pippi-themed merchandise, and that no one wants to have a Pippi doll that has the looks of her adult self.

Olsson's film is part of a series of mockumentary shorts that all depict beloved Swedish children's media characters who have grown up and find themselves as adults somewhat unsettled in the adult world in contemporary Sweden and reflecting on the commodification of their childhoods.[44] Through the mockumentary mode, which includes hidden camera scenes, interviews, and handheld footage, the quirks of these characters seem odd and problematic when looked at in the realistic setting of contemporary society instead of children's literature or films. In the mockumentary, Pippi is still portrayed as somewhat outside of the normative expectations of the society—she does not seem to have a job or a romantic partner (in fact, Tommy has fallen ill because of the impacts of the unrequited love he had for Pippi), and she leaves the meeting with Tommy and Annika by climbing through a window and reaching for a soda bottle from a tree on her way (referring to the story in *Pippi Longstocking* where Pippi shows Tommy and Annika that soda bottles grow inside some trees). Her life, however, is portrayed as lonely and not so enviable anymore. The mockumentary thus draws attention to the image of childhood that Pippi has been vested with; it also further locates the ability and celebration of growing sideways and standing against norms as something that children are uniquely positioned to do.

As an exemplary figure of the child, Pippi has mediated the shifting understandings of childhood as both *being* and *becoming*, and we can see the co-emergence of that change in the abstract figure of the child as well as historically located children. As Bengt Sandin delineates, beginning in the 1960s, childhood was seen increasingly as an autonomous and adult-like time, with legislation emphasizing children's parity with the rights of adults.[45] Thus, it was established that children possess civil rights as Swedish citizens. Now, as Sandin puts it, "being a child is no longer just a matter of being, of existing as a half-adult, but is transformed into life's great project, 'becoming,' for children and parents alike."[46] This understanding further constructs an autonomous child who is also competent and should therefore have more say in decisions and is a partner with adults.[47] Thus, the image of ideal Swedish childhood, mediated through Pippi Longstocking, locates "growing sideways" in the space of privilege. It expects children to go against conventions that are oppressive because children are autonomous, competent, and moral. While the policies of better care for children have, of course, had significant impact on children living in Sweden and the Nordic countries, as Brembeck, Johansson, and Kampmann argue, they have constructed "the Nordic child" that "is primarily a construction, a rhetorical figure of thought with fluid content that from time to time has been presented to serve its purpose in ideological, political contexts."[48]

DEVIATING CHILDHOODS

Focusing on the late twentieth and early twenty-first centuries, when the Swedish welfare state went through a significant transformation of the society (moving toward a neoliberal trend of privatization, individualism, and down-sizing public sector), Eva Söderberg argues that the independence and competence of Pippi have come to suggest that it is an individual decision that everyone can make to become and be a Pippi.[49] This mind-set does not, of course, consider structural inequalities and complexities that might hinder one from becoming like Pippi or from performing qualities associated with Pippi, especially when that would essentially mean becoming Swedish/white/Nordic/middle-class—something that often has not been possible for several groups living in Sweden. While the dominating attitudes in Sweden as a settler colonial state toward the Indigenous Sámi or the Tornedalian people were steeped in racial and colonial ideologies that actively othered these communities for centuries, the later decades of the twentieth century also saw a significant increase of other minority groups in Sweden as Sweden took in migrants and refugees from the non-Western world to a comparable degree with larger European countries like the UK or France.[50] Thus, by 2010, about 15 percent of the Swedish population had a non-Western background.[51]

Sweden accepted many migrants and refugees during the era that Tobias Hübinette and Catrin Lundström call the "white solidarity" period (1968–2001), when Sweden became "the leading Western voice for anti-racism."[52] The prevalence of racism regarding people of color and other not quite white people in Sweden, however, was increasingly not talked about. Instead, in a similar fashion to many other Western European locations, discussions of race were replaced by conversations about ethnicity or culture. The 1960s media narratives did discuss race and racism some, as Hübinette has brought out, and as the transnational adoption rates were growing during that time, the adopted children of color were seen by several commentators as the key to "solving the race problem" in Sweden. As commentators at the time observed, those children would be growing up in white families and make the unfamiliar more proximate and familiar to Swedes because they would become Swedes (whereas children growing up in migrant or mixed-race families would suffer from racism, feared the critics).[53] Children and childhood also figured prominently in the writings of the Swedish Romani activist and writer Katarina Taikon during the 1960s and 1970s. We can see an example of that in Taikon's popular series about a Romani child named Katitzi, who is an outcast and does not have the protection and benefits provided by the welfare state. As Olle Widhe demonstrates, Taikon's series sought to contest the idyllic portrayal of childhood in Swedish children's literature as it depicted unjustified violence and abuse of the Romani people and children in Sweden.[54] The continued prejudice against those who deviated from normative white Swedishness thus meant there was an increasing number of children who were not included in the idealized image of the Swedish childhood, which continued to mean white, middle-class, healthy children. The exclusion felt by these children resembles many other Western societies where, as Stockton argues, "it is a privilege to need to be protected and thus to have a childhood."[55] The normative and idealized meaning of autonomous childhood functions in a similar way: It is a privilege to be autonomous in a carefree protected environment. It is also a privilege to be celebrated for going against cultural conventions.

It is not surprising that as many Swedish films and novels in the late twentieth and early twenty-first centuries depicted the crumbling welfare state, they often incorporated the figure of the child to do that.[56] These works often imagine children who are autonomous but not carefree: They are dealing with difficult circumstances on their own. While this trope tends to function as a criticism of the welfare state policies, which do not always include all its residents, particularly reflected in changes to the political landscape in the end of the twentieth century, the struggles of the children are also presented as caused by adults in their lives who are incapable of providing them with a safe environment. Autonomy in these challenging experiences can still be inspired by the triumphant Pippi, however. As Amanda Doxtater argues, there are a variety of child figures in early twenty-first-century Nordic cinema who are immigrants, refugees, or not ethnically Swedish and who despite all odds remake themselves and are thus still reproducing Swedish exceptionalism.[57] Similarly, Anders Wilhelm Åberg argues in his analysis of the 2006 Swedish comedy-drama film *Förortsungar* (*Kidz in da Hood*) (dir. Ylva Gustavsson and Catti Edfeldt) that while it is an exception among the Swedish children's films, which in the early 2000s were still almost exclusively homogeneous and increasingly nostalgic, in its storytelling it tries to optimistically transcend ethnic differences in the name of "inter-ethnic solidarity."[58] In the scenes where the nonwhite protagonist Amina reads Astrid Lindgren's book, she seems to realize that Sweden and Swedishness are a cultural realm that one can enter for positive reasons and not a threat.[59] In other words, through the image of the child who is performing Swedish childhood here, the film makes visible discrimination toward the Other in Sweden and resolves it by aligning the child with the abstract idea of Swedish childhood. Åberg concludes that the film provides a contradiction where the happy ending is possible through the child being embraced by Swedes, who have so far been depicted as the antagonists. Thinking about the significance of challenging cultural ideals and constructions, particularly in the "adult world" that Pippi Longstocking represents, Amina follows that example and is successful in performing a Swedish childhood that is supposed to question adults' motives.

As a contrast to Amina in *Kidz in da Hood* and several other similar child figures in Swedish cinema, Doxtater argues that Ruben Östlund's film *Play* (2011) is an exception to reproducing Swedish exceptionalism through child figures. *Play*, writes Doxtater, depicts autonomous children who are "surviving, rather than conquering precariousness."[60] Östlund's film is a drama based on real-life court cases, and it depicts psychological games between two groups of children in Gothenburg—a group of Black children robs a group of white children. The film raised a heated debate in Sweden about whether it contributes to racist ideologies or challenges them. The eight child protagonists in this film fail to live up to the heroic individualism that Pippi represents, which causes them to suffer. Furthermore, both through plot and stylistic choices, *Play*'s use of estrangement, washed-out bystanders, long takes, and minimal camera movement, as Doxtater argues, deflates the fantasy of social critique and triumphant fight against injustice present in the Pippi figure and instead imagines the child protagonists as unexceptional.

Another cinematic portrayal of a child who is not able to perform Swedish childhood is Lukas Moodysson's *Lilja 4-ever* (2002), which depicts a Russian-speaking girl, Lilja, from an unnamed post-Soviet country (filmed in Estonia) who gets trapped in sex trafficking in Sweden and, after breaking free from an apartment in southern Sweden, commits suicide. This film has typically been analyzed as an example of a critique of the Swedish welfare state, where, despite its welfare systems and progress in gender equality, not everyone is safe and taken care of (Andrew Nestingen calls it a melodrama of demand[61]), or as an example of a common tendency in Swedish/Nordic media to depict Eastern European women as victims of sex crimes. As Mariah Larsson has argued, these images of victimized women represented the anxieties prevalent in Swedish society regarding the post-Soviet spaces and people and, therefore, further enforced the idea of Swedish exceptionalism.[62] Most of the writing on this film does not engage with the meaning of childhood in *Lilja*, probably at least in part because getting trapped in sex trafficking removes her from the innocent child status. Furthermore, as Larsson has pointed out, *Lilja 4-ever* is ultimately about "bad sex"; it shows people who choose to engage in sex work only because they are forced or because they are from less progressive states who supposedly do not yet know about gender equality. "Bad sex" is often seen as imported, and it deviates from the national construction of "good" and moral sexuality that, as Don Kulick argues, has had an integral role in the rhetoric promoting laws on gender equality or comprehensive sex education in the Swedish welfare state.[63] In this film, Lilja's experience of violence and abuse is primarily caused by the sex traffickers, who are Eastern European men, even though her clientele in Sweden represents a variety of Swedish men.[64] Lilja is, of course, not born in Sweden; doesn't speak Swedish; and is, therefore, not expected to have the same privileges as Swedish children. She is a child who represents the "problems over there (galloping capitalism, non-existing welfare systems, etc.)" that will "obstruct progress in issues of gender equality" in Sweden.[65]

It is, thus, still somewhat rare to imagine what it would look like for a literary or cinematic construction of a child in Sweden to not perform the idea of Pippi. The child who often occurs in the narratives about migrants and minorities, for example, could in many cases be interpreted as someone who, just like Pippi, overcomes their difficult experiences through autonomy, competence, and moral compass while providing the audiences with an emotional journey and healing.[66] This kind of reading suggests that these texts ultimately reproduce the idea of the autonomous Swedish child and that anyone can become like Pippi if they only want to. As the following chapters demonstrate, however, looking at how different cultural texts imagine moments (sometimes extended and prolonged moments) of impossibility, pause, delay, and hesitance to line up as the Swedish child—or, for that matter, any other kind of child that represents a rigid identity category—open up new ways of understanding how childhood figures in the histories of racialization, colonization, and not-quiteness in Sweden.

THE NOT-QUITE CHILD

While there are, then, different examples in Nordic cultural texts where children are growing sideways, the struggle between lining up and growing sideways or backward or just getting stuck provides some unique perspectives on the narratives that deal with the experiences of the minorities and migrants that share a long colonial and cultural history with Sweden. The history of Finland as part of the Swedish empire before 1809 could be called semi-colonial, and the colonial relationship between the Sápmi lands and Tornedalen and Sweden is still ongoing.[67] This has resulted in violent and traumatic histories of colonial erasure and racialization throughout the twentieth century. As mentioned above, the Swedish race scientists in the 1920s and 1930s categorized people in different racial types and saw three types dominating in the population: the Nordic type (Swedes), which was deemed superior; the East Baltic type (Finns); and the Sámi type. Both the Sámi people and the Tornedalian people (living in the northern parts of Sweden) were subject to large-scale scientific skull measuring and other colonial violence that attempted to eliminate or segregate these cultures from the Swedish nation. At the same time, as Åsa Össbo points out, Tornedalians were also early settlers to the region that had been inhabited by the Sámi people.[68] When Finland was ceded to the Russian empire in 1809 after the war between Sweden and Russia, the border that separated Finland from Sweden was drawn and it split up both the Sámi *siida* (Sámi local community) territories and the lands where Tornedalians were living. Both groups not only faced direct settler colonial violence by Sweden but also experienced the long-lasting effects of stereotypes and prejudice based in the rhetoric that both were inferior races. The concurrent idea that Finnish-speakers were less civilized and inferior extended to common misconceptions and prejudice toward the Finnish labor migrants who arrived in Sweden in large numbers during the second half of the twentieth century. Thus, while there are crucial differences, power dynamics, and racialized hierarchies between the three groups that the texts analyzed in this book focus on, there are also shared experiences of historical racialization, of experiencing oneself as almost but not quite white/Swedish, while often also having the ability and privilege to pass as white/Swedish.

Although the majority of the Indigenous Sámi, Tornedalian, and Finnish-speakers possess this ability to pass, the racial hierarchization of them as not quite white has resulted in stereotypes that have persisted to some extent to the present day. This not quite whiteness is somewhat similar to how Rosi Braidotti has analyzed Eastern Europeans as not quite, not yet white in the imagination of Western Europe, using Homi Bhabha's much-cited discussion of the colonial nonwhite subjects who are "almost the same but not quite" in their mimicry and knowledge of the colonizer.[69] Alfred J. Lopez writes that Bhabha's "not quite/not white" explains well the colonial sham that results in "a subject who simultaneously identifies with the white ideal and is radically alienated from it."[70] The temporality of the not-yet in Braidotti's discussion, of course, reminds us of a common colonialist rhetoric that sees the currently or previously colonized as temporally othered, always lagging behind modernity or other Western-centric ideas of progress.[71] Braidotti's use of "not-yet" reminds us also of the reality that most Eastern Europeans, just like most of the historically racialized minority groups in Sweden, are legible as white and that it is easier for them to pass as white than for people of color to do so. While there is no essential difference between white passing as white and non-white passing as white, writes Sara Ahmed, there is a "structural difference that demonstrates that passing involves the re-opening or re-staging of a fractured history of identifications that constitutes the limits to a given subject's mobility."[72] In many cultural texts that address the history of Finnish-speakers, Indigenous Sámi people, and Tornedalians in Sweden, we see that the close proximity of these groups of people to whiteness in the Nordic region adds an expectation of an ease of becoming white/Swedish that at the same time is not always possible, or it can happen only at the cost of erasing one's other identities. Writing about the Sámi boarding schools, for example, Rauna Kuokkanen has argued that since the Indigenous Sámi people were integrated into the Nordic nations as any other citizen, this (settler) colonialism appears benign, but it has a significant impact on the Sámi consciousness.[73]

This book is not arguing for a unified minority or Finno-Ugric identity that would simplify the complex dynamics of racialized hierarchies in northern Europe, but it makes the case for a comparative analysis of the increased archive of cultural texts that seek to make visible the experiences of these three diverse groups of people in Sweden. This increase was likely at least in part caused by the official recognition of these three groups as well as the Roma and the Jews as national minorities in Sweden (under the European Charter for Regional or Minority Languages and the Framework Convention for the Protection of National Minorities). While this new minority political situation resulted in official support from the Swedish state and functioned as empowering for the minority groups, it has still taken time for these groups and Sweden's part in the colonial histories to be fully recognized and understood by the dominant society or even by the minorities themselves. Much of the work of recognizing this history is being done concurrently with my writing this book. In November 2023 the Truth and Reconciliation Commission on Tornedalians, Kvens, and Lantalaiset handed over its report to the Swedish government. The commission outlines the history of racial discrimination and violence (including skull measuring and photographing done for race biology as well as grave plundering), forced assimilation, and erasure of the Tornedalian culture and language in Sweden during most of the twentieth century.

A similar commission for truth of the Indigenous Sámi people in Sweden made its report in 2021, asking the Swedish government to officially recognize the violence and injustice done to the Sámi people. While the former Swedish minister of Agriculture and Sámi Affairs, Annika Åhnberg, made an official apology to the Sámi people in 1998, this apology did not lead to any real political changes.[74] The representatives of both commissions emphasize the need for Sweden as a country that criticizes other countries for being racist or helps them to achieve the goals of reconciliation to work through its own "dark history."[75] Elisabet Fura, the chair of the Truth and Reconciliation Commission for Tornedalians, Kvens, and Lantalaiset, writes in the foreword to the report that "through concrete measures, the State can lay the foundations for a future where the experiences of the old multicultural and multilingual Sweden help guide us to a future modern Sweden."[76] The experiences with assimilation and reclaiming identities of the Indigenous Sámi people are in many ways also similar in the Norwegian and Finnish sides of Sápmi and, as Harald Gaski and other Sámi scholars argue, Sámi identity is not bound by nation-state borders.[77] This book, however, focuses on the Swedish side as it hashes out how the significance of the child and the particularities of Swedish colonial histories are entangled in these cultural works of the twenty-first century.

The Not-Quite Child describes experiences of Nordic not-quiteness—of being seen and understood as almost but not quite white/Swedish/Nordic. This not-quiteness found in the materials analyzed in this book includes a trajectory, expectation, and often a desire to "become white," even when one already presents as white, since whiteness continues to be equated with Western-ness, Nordic-ness, and, in Sweden, with Swedishness.[78] This is why Nordic/Swedish not-quiteness is often explored, addressed, and elaborated on through texts that foreground the child. Throughout the twentieth century children have typically been understood as not yet there but on their way to becoming citizens.[79] The figure that I call the *not-quite child* illustrates the experiences of being understood and categorized as almost but not quite Swedish (and therefore also not quite white) as the texts pay close attention to the disruptions to the trajectory of becoming and growing that the child experiences. In my analyses of how these cultural texts that foreground Finnish, Tornedalian, and Sámi people in Sweden construct the not-quite child, I draw from both theorizations of childhood having queer and subversive potentials and scholarship on race, racialization, and postcolonial/settler colonial ideologies and practices, particularly in the Nordic region.

If a child inherits not-quiteness from their parents, passing almost completely as white Swede but not quite, the child also inherits orientation toward certain objects that are not quite within their reach: In the example of discrimination against the Sámi people, this could mean access to education or to clothing other than the traditional Sámi clothing that was deemed inappropriate by the settler colonial policies. At the same time, the child who is legible as white in the Swedish welfare state has a potential to grow up to line up and become Swedish. This ability distinguishes the experiences described in the texts I analyze in this book from experiences of other kinds of not-quiteness in the Nordic region—for example, that of the transnational adoptees of color to Sweden. The not-yet-ness of the child was significant in the rhetoric that Swedes should adopt nonwhite children because they would grow up in white Swedish families and make nonwhiteness more comfortable, a discourse that became prevalent in the 1960s, as Tobias Hübinette has demonstrated.[80] Writing about this complicated demand on becoming Swedish, Richey Wyver writes that the adoptees are "forever slipping between two poles of non-recognition, almost Swedish but not quite (/not white), almost immigrant Other, but not quite . . . desired for a difference that is unspeakable; rejected for the very difference they were desired for; hyper-visible but invisible."[81] It is a privilege to be able to grow out of not-quiteness when one is legible as white, but during the twentieth century it has also often meant erasing lines that run parallel or in different directions from the dominant one. In order to delve into how different narratives navigate this, in the following chapters I look at how the texts explicitly foreground lines of whiteness in the architecture of the Swedish welfare state or imagine lines that run parallel to the dominant heteronormative reproduction. Lining up in the classroom or while walking through a village are ordinary everyday experiences of children in the twentieth century, but in the spaces of not-quiteness, such as the colonial school system for the Sámi and Tornedalian children that we see in the films discussed in chapter 1, they obtain charged/added meaning.

Centering on how the child is spatially situated provides a reorientation in space. While I approach the figures of children in context, also paying attention to adults and other objects surrounding them, this spatial reorientation through the child goes beyond the common reading of children as figures who provide the adult authors and readers with a defamiliarizing effect.[82] The problem with the latter is that the figure of the child can be incorporated simply for the adult to convey something that might otherwise not be accepted or have quite the same impact. The implication of this can be that the child is seen as someone who is not yet aware of political circumstances or histories thus perpetuating the discourse of childhood as a time of innocence and pre-subjectivity. I am more interested in the different angles of space and time that are constructed through the child's eyes or other senses and that reorient our expectations and understandings (or the idea that adults understand these historical circumstances and narratives). In Amanda Kernell's 2016 film *Sameblod* (*Sami Blood*), for example, this includes a variety of sequences that establish the Indigenous child looking away and not giving the audience access to what she is seeing, and in Eija Hetekivi Olsson's novel *Ingenbarnsland* (No child's land), it means imagining a child figure whose failures to line up make the adults around her think of her as abject, while she chooses that failure with pleasure. Katarina Kieri's 2015 novel, *Vårt värde* (Our worth), in turn, reorients both the image of the child and the not-quite child by imagining a plural child figure.

These examples of reorientation resonate with Sara Ahmed's call to reorient ourselves from the dominant understandings of spatial situatedness. She uses the example of the kitchen table, which could function as a reorientation device for the labor of writing philosophy, particularly when engaging with texts written by male philosophers who have used the writing desk as an example to talk about phenomenology but are able to do so only because the labor of cooking and child care is done by others, around different tables. Perceiving one's surroundings at the kitchen table might provide completely different ways of thinking and understanding the world; it also makes one aware of the dynamics of privilege when it comes to having access to tables and desks that are associated with uninterrupted time. The figures of children in literary and cinematic texts that the following chapters analyze are sometimes hiding underneath the table. Not only do they hear and see the struggles of their parents there, but their perception of the space around them also reorients what and how they see and feel in the architecture of the Swedish welfare state.

Being under the table refers, on one hand, to the marginality that children (even the privileged child to a certain extent) are often vested with. When childhood is understood as a pre-subjective state, as a beginning, it is emphasized that the child is smaller than adults, has less power, and is ultimately inferior to them. This inferiority inherent in childhood intersects with other categories of marginalization. In her study on the figurations of childhood in nineteenth- and twentieth-century Western cultural sites, Claudia Castañeda asserts that for a long time it has been self-evident to assume that the child is a human in an incomplete form, a "potentiality rather than an actuality."[83] In racial and colonial practices, childhood became associated with the "Now of the primitive,"[84] and in colonial discourse of the nineteenth century, the "child-body was used to conjure other kinds of bodies in the time and space of a 'global' human history."[85] The texts of Nordic not-quiteness intersect the memories and experiences of racialization and colonization not only with social class but also with childhood as an identity category that has often had less power than adults.

However, being under the table can disrupt the thinking of normative linearity, of needing to become someone else. Anna Mae Duane uses the children's table at parties as an example of childhood studies in the humanities: a marginalized space that can be experienced as freeing and creative because "one's voice is out of earshot."[86] Being out of sight when children are hiding under the table or behind other furniture makes it possible to gain information about the lives of adults that the children might not want to reproduce. It can provide a creative and playful space where a child in Susanna Alakoski's novel *Svinalängorna*, for example, imagines that she becomes a dog together with the family dog. At the same time, the need to hide underneath something or to run in a bog outside of town is typically associated with danger, fear, or trauma in the texts of not-quiteness. Furthermore, since all the narratives analyzed and discussed in the following chapters address to greater or lesser extent the perception of being invisible in Swedish society, the spaces that signify being out of sight also make visual explorations of how children might experience invisibility as both empowering and shame-producing.

Thus, the spaces that function as a way to reorient familiar perspectives, familial and national lines, and continuities in these texts about not-quiteness and childhood are also charged with traumatic memories, shame, or fear. As we know from the extensive work from affect, phenomenology, and trauma studies, bodies are affected by the spaces they inhabit.[87] Maija Lanas and Tuija Huuki combine the theorization of trauma as intergenerationally affective with new feminist materialist theory in their analysis of a haunting affect experienced by a Sámi professor while giving a lecture to university students:

> Lecture halls, swans, girlhoods, snickering bodies, weasels, silences, atmospheres, graveyards, academics, swamps, teacher education, fishing, adulthood, and the rural all come together as an affective assemblage, all playing their role in the event in question. These forces pulse and vibrate among myriads of other elements so strongly that they seem to "leak" into the present of this lecture hall, in the form of Tuija's anxiety. Together, these forces and elements form a ferocious more-than-human apparatus (Barad 2007) that impairs Tuija's agency with the affective weight of the commodified, exploited history of the Sámi people." (149–50)[88]

Lanas and Huuki's analysis makes an argument about the coexistence of childhood and adulthood, among other entities that have traditionally been divided, such as human–nonhuman or past–present within the body of Tuija, the Sámi professor. The analyses in the following chapters will come back to how childhood and adulthood become merged in some of the narratives that go beyond the linear thinking of childhood as a "not-yet" and, with that, also provide a temporal reorientation. There is a child in *Svinalängorna* who in some ways obtains the role of an adult by taking care of her parents and siblings because the parents are descending into alcoholism while she imagines that she does not grow at all; there is a child in *Sameblod* who is expected to reproduce the image of Sámi adulthood but is not allowed to access everything needed for Swedish adulthood that the settler colonial power has prescribed. As these texts imagine the not-quite child, that figure becomes also more than child. In other words, the figure of the child who experiences not-quiteness is surrounded by forces of different spaces and temporalities that vibrate and leak into their present day, creating moments of disorientation, reorientation, or return to the demand to line up.

OUTLINE

In the following chapters, I analyze how various films and novels construct the figure of the not-quite child as a way to both address and rethink how this history of not-quiteness is remembered and remediated and to reflect in various ways on what it actually means to represent experiences of not-quiteness through the child. While not all the chapters will focus on memory, all the works analyzed in this book could be described as works of memory. Written in the twenty-first century, they articulate histories that have been relatively invisible in the grand narratives of collective memory, and though the child's focalization is a common mode in narratives of memory, these texts imagine child figures who refuse to memorialize narratives that establish rigid national or familial boundaries by way of generational transmission. Thus, in a similar vein to how forgetting functions in Jack Halberstam's theorization of queer failure, the protagonists' failure to remember tidied-up versions of disorderly histories unleashes "new forms of memory."[89] Together these chapters demonstrate how twenty-first-century cultural texts imagine the changing Swedish welfare state in the twentieth century and reimagine the implications and approaches to depicting fictional children who deviate from normative expectations.

Chapter 1 discusses two films, *Elina: som om jag inte fanns* (*Elina: As If I Wasn't There*, Klaus Härö, 2002) and *Sameblod* (*Sami Blood*, Amanda Kernell, 2016), both of which incorporate a child as a central figure to mediate the experiences of racialization and colonialism in Sweden during the 1930s and 1950s. Depicting Tornedalians and the Indigenous Sámi people (both groups located in the northern areas of Sweden have been to varying extent colonized by Sweden), both films construct a child who is at first portrayed to be growing to the side of the "Swedish child," and both of the children are expected to line up with a trajectory that either assumes a full assimilation or segregation from the settler colonial state, and in both films the child resists that trajectory. Engaging with scholarship on settler colonialism and meanings of race and whiteness in Sweden, the chapter analyzes the different modes of filmmaking and emphases on the narrative and visual level in these films that imagine the child eventually lining up with the dominant culture and with whiteness/Swedishness. However, as I argue in the chapter, while in *Elina* the ultimate goal is to make visible the unjust history of the Swedish welfare state through a defamiliarizing and inspiring perspective of the child's eyes, the child's gaze in *Sameblod* does not always provide information. Instead, in several sequences the child is looking away as the film meditates on what it actually means to visualize and see racialization, which is often experienced as invisible, and what it means to use the child's gaze to inspire the adult audiences.

Chapter 2 analyzes the construction of child figures who, a couple of decades later from what the films in the previous chapter depict, continue to problematize rigid lines and expectations in both the dominant national and diasporic communities. It focuses on two best-selling novels, *Svinalängorna* (Susanna Alakoski, 2006) and *Ingenbarnsland* (No child's land, Eija Hetekivi Olsson, 2011), that depict working-class Finnish-speaking families in Sweden during the 1960s–1980s. These texts that emphasize the role of social class in feelings of not-quiteness, as I argue, explicitly question the promise of hope and future in the figure of the child who is expected to grow up and line up with Swedishness or with Sweden Finnishness. As the child's resistance to do that is seen as unacceptable or abject by people surrounding her, the chapter argues that these narratives function as both a way to reorient the affective responses to the stories of the not-quite child and a way to imagine what it would mean to fail growing both up and sideways. In this the chapter engages with different theorizations of abjection and with what Jack Halberstam has called "queer failure"—failing the normative ideals can provide the child characters with alternative modes of being, becoming, and growing along parallel lines.

Chapter 3 discusses the novel *Populärmusik från Vittula* (*Popular Music from Vittula*, Mikael Niemi, 2000) along with its film adaptation by Reza Bagher (2004) and the novel *Vårt värde* (Katarina Kieri, 2015), which extend the figure of the not-quite child to depictions of the generation of Tornedalian-speakers in Sweden in the 1960s–1970s, who are the first generation to not experience discrimination as intense as their parents, although they observe the still-existent feelings and assumptions that they are inferior to Swedish-speakers. These novels delve into the impact of not-quiteness on children, and through formal choices, like irony, parody, magical realism, or plural voice, they further explore both the privilege of these children, who can increasingly easily pass as white Swedes, and the slippage between performing the idea of exceptional childhood and reality, as well as between the entangled colonial histories of racialization and white privilege in northern Sweden. Both the film and novel version of *Populärmusik* draw our attention to the fictional construction of the child by exaggerating the stereotypes or images associated with Tornedalians and with childhood/adolescence to the point of absurdity or parody while exploring how subculture, like playing pop/rock music in Tornedalen, provides the characters with a way to challenge heteronormative linearity of growing up. *Vårt värde*, in turn, imagines a child who is pluralized—the child narrator uses predominantly first-person plural voice but makes explicit that it does not refer to a group of people—which allows the narrative not only to destabilize boundaries and lines between different colonized and colonizer communities (as "we-narratives," according to Rebecca Fasselt, have done in postcolonial literature[90]) but also to resist the singularity present in the conceptual framework of "the child," whether or not it is the idealized Swedish child or the not-quite child.

Finally, the conclusion summarizes the main arguments this book has made and discusses how the figure of the not-quite child has transformed in the cultural texts depicting these minority groups in contemporary, twenty-first-century Swedish society.

———

Lastly, a brief comment on my own position on the material I am working with in this book. As a white European academic working in North America, I am increasingly aware of my privilege both in terms of access to scholarly work and time to write, as well as not having to face racism or generational trauma that the texts I work with depict and engage with. I also recognize that I have been trained primarily within "Western" academic discourses in and beyond the field of Scandinavian studies, which undoubtedly informs my interpretations and analyses, and I continue to unlearn frameworks of thinking that are harmful and exclusive. Growing up in post-Soviet Estonia has also given me a personal understanding and empathy of dealing with generational trauma and prejudice based on one's ethnicity. Both in my personal life and my professional life, I have witnessed people dealing with traumatic memories of the Soviet occupation and the legacies of colonization that Estonia has been subject to for centuries as well as the detrimental impact of the common rhetoric in Estonia that wants to realign Estonia with Western Europeanness and does not acknowledge the privilege of whiteness that most Estonians have. I have also personally experienced prejudice and insults when working in the Nordic spaces because of the common stereotypes regarding Eastern European women. Differently from most of the other Eastern European countries, Estonian language and people belong to the Finno-Ugric group, thus sharing some linguistic and cultural similarities with the three groups of people featured in the texts that I analyze in this book. In order to situate the cultural texts analyzed here and to ask better questions about them, I have prioritized being in conversation with Indigenous and other minority scholarship and writing from the Nordic region and beyond.

CHAPTER
ONE

IMAGINING RACIALIZATION AND WHITENESS THROUGH THE CHILD WHO LINES UP

Two films made in Sweden in the early twenty-first century, *Elina* and *Sameblod* incorporate a child as a central figure to mediate the histories of racialization and settler colonialism in Sweden. Both films received acclaim, primarily positive reviews, and were viewed by relatively large audiences both locally and internationally. Depicting Tornedalians in the 1950s (*Elina*) and the Indigenous Sámi people in the 1930s (*Sameblod*), both films construct a child who is at first portrayed to be growing to the side of the "Swedish child," the idealized image of the autonomous and moral child described in the introduction. Both children in these films are expected to line up with a trajectory that assumes either a full assimilation or segregation from the settler colonial state, and in both films the child resists that trajectory. As I argued in the introduction, however, a child who resists cultural ideals and conveys a strong sense of moral compass is often in a privileged position in the Nordic culture, creating a paradox that going against norms is normative and available only for certain children. *Elina* and *Sameblod* navigate this contradiction in different ways. Through various modes of filmmaking and different emphases on the narrative and visual level, each of these films imagines a child who eventually does line up with Swedishness, whiteness, and the dominant culture. However, while in *Elina* lining up has to do with a utopian happy ending provided by the melodramatic mode, in *Sameblod* it is a result of traumatic unresolved experiences of racialization and settler colonialism. Furthermore, while in *Elina* the ultimate goal is to make visible the unjust history of the Swedish welfare state through the different perspective of the child's eyes, the child's gaze in *Sameblod* does not always provide information. Instead the child is often looking away as the film meditates on what it actually means to represent racialization that is experienced as invisible.

In engaging with in/visibility, which manifests itself similarly to other texts of Nordic not-quiteness, these films draw from the history of Nordic settler colonialism. Discussing Lorenzo Veracini's and Patric Wolfe's elaborated studies on the specifics of settler colonialism, scholars like Rauna Kuokkanen and Åsa Össbo argue that settler colonialism is the most fitting framework to describe and understand the colonization of the Sámi land (Sápmi) and people within the Nordic region.[1] While the traditional understanding of colonialism typically refers to external domination, which exploits resources and people, the primary goal of settler colonialism is to access land and territory. Racial hierarchization is present in both kinds of colonialism, but in settler colonialism, writes Veracini, Indigenous people "disappear in a variety of ways: extermination, expulsion, incarceration, containment, and assimilation."[2] Analyzing how Swedish hydropower expanded in the northern areas, Åsa Össbo writes that it "has functioned as industrial settler colonialism with every ingredient necessary imposing a structure with laws and administration that dispossessed Sámi people of their lands and rights, altering and threatening the foundation on which the Sámi had built their society and culture."[3] While the messages of cultural inferiority and denigration were very much present in the Nordic countries, similarly to other settler colonial states, in the Nordic countries, Kuokkanen argues, colonialism "appears very benign . . . but is nevertheless very effective in appropriating the Sámi consciousness."[4]

The elimination of the Indigenous people through dispossession of their lands, assimilation into the Swedish culture, or segregation of some as if "frozen in time" has produced multilayered experiences of invisibility. On one hand, invisibility refers to the elimination of cultures and identities by the settler colonial power: The history and cultural practices of Indigenous people have been purposefully overlooked by the settler educational system, cultural memory narratives, and other avenues that seek to mediate the unified national identity of Swedishness. This includes the invisibility of the colonial violence and trauma caused by it both in the mainstream culture and, due to assimilation politics, increasingly among the colonized groups. Of course, just as in many other contexts regarding Indigenous and other minoritized groups, when necessary to assert the colonizer's power, the colonizer constructs ideologies that emphasize differences (whether visible or audible) that allow for a hierarchization. On the other hand, while the Indigenous Sámi people were historically categorized as different based on racial ideologies, they are often also legible as white and can pass as white Swedes. Invisibility thus entails both the erasure and elimination of colonized groups and a privilege to pass.

Making visible the experiences of discrimination, which have been invisible because of colonial politics and because these colonial subjects are typically white (even if racialized), is a complicated endeavor. In her contemplative autoethnographic article, Astri Dankertsen discusses the ambiguous nature that whiteness has for the Indigenous Sámi people. She writes that while the thinking that being Sámi has to do with somehow "looking" Sámi still persists in the Nordic countries, Sámi people are now primarily seen and see themselves as white Europeans. However, because "being Indigenous is so closely but, at the same time, ambiguously connected to being nonwhite both historically and as understood internationally," identifying with whiteness becomes a complicated matter for Sámi people.[5] First, the Sámi as an Indigenous group were constructed as racially inferior people in the past and therefore do not fit into the category of undisputed whiteness of Swedes or Norwegians. Second, because international Indigenous solidarity is a part of contemporary Sámi identity politics, being white also connects one to the negative implications of hegemonic whiteness. Dankertsen describes her own experiences as an Indigenous Sámi scholar from Norway who looks stereotypically Norwegian at academic conferences on Indigenous studies, where she becomes aware of her whiteness both as a privilege and as something that might make her work sound less authentic, especially if she were not wearing the Sámi traditional clothes and if she did not present herself as a Norwegian Sámi.

A somewhat similar articulation of invisibility caused by policies of elimination is present in the work of Tornedalian media, which has described the history of Tornedalians in northern Sweden as postcolonial and overlooked by the dominant culture. Tornedalians (who used to be called Tornedalian Finns) are people who inhabit a region in northern Sweden (the Tornio River valley) that was cut off from Finland during the 1809 border drawing between Sweden and the Russian empire (as the Finnish area was ceded to the Russian empire). Their language (now officially called Meänkieli) was long considered a dialect of Finnish but has now been recognized as an official minority language in Sweden. A 2021 documentary series, *Jag var en lägre ras* (I was a lower race), on S V T (Swedish national public television broadcaster), focuses on the history of Tornedalians who, similarly to the Sámi people, went through skull measuring in the early twentieth century and who were categorized as a lower race by Swedish racial biologists. Through its voice-over narrative and compilation of talking-head interviews, which feature both the older generation who went through violent assimilation and people from the younger generation who as a result do not speak Meänkieli, the show emphasizes that this history has not been talked about in Sweden. Of course, as Åsa Össbo brings out, Tornedalians living in the northern areas of Sweden and Finland were also early settlers to those areas. The 1809 border drawing that separated Finland from Sweden also split up both Sámi siida territories and the lands where Tornedalians now lived, dividing both groups as some of them were now inhabitants of Sweden and others of Finland. In the late 1800s and early 1900s, however, both Tornedalians and Indigenous Sámi people were essentially expected to be eliminated in settler colonial terms, whether through assimilation or segregation and erasure of cultural practices.

Discussing this history of erasure, Bengt Pohjanen argues that Tornedalians who have lived in northern Sweden for centuries were not represented in the Swedish cultural imagination, such as the celebrated Selma Lagerlöf's novel *Nils Holgerssons underbara resa genom Sverige* (The

Wonderful Adventures of Nils, 1906), which introduced Swedish geography to Swedish children.[6] In order to make the invisible racialization more visible and to make Sweden acknowledge its colonial history and racist ideologies, however, Pohjanen tries to establish an imagined community with the minorities of the world, and he assigns derogatory terms, such as *ragheads* or *negroes*, to that imagined community that would include Tornedalian-speakers in order to connect the experiences of Tornedalians and nonwhite minorities globally.[7] In this move, Pohjanen does not acknowledge the invisible or taken-for-granted power and privilege that whiteness has, even when it is marginalized or seen as not quite whiteness. As Anne Heith brings out, Pohjanen has also propagated the use of Meänmaa (Our land) for the Tornedalian region, which is problematic because part of that land is also located in the Sápmi area. Although different in their focuses and understandings of whiteness/privilege, both Dankertsen and Pohjanen articulate how complicated it is to navigate between using different visual markers to celebrate the minority identity or tell the history or present experiences of discrimination and avoid contributing to the arbitrary constructions of racialized hierarchies and stereotypes.

This chapter analyzes how the two films, *Elina* and *Sameblod*, navigate the question of how to represent not-quiteness through the figures of children in the racial and colonial histories of the early twentieth century in Sweden. Looking at the two works together provides comparative readings on various levels. As they take place in similar contexts of the settler colonial school system in northern Sweden, the films portray some shared experiences of erasure of culture and privilege to pass as white that the Sámi and the Tornedalian people in northern Sweden have. At the same time, while growing up in *Elina* means assimilating to the Swedish culture, in *Sameblod* the only accepted trajectory for the Sámi child is to remain in a segregated Sámi community, to not get access to the same amount of education, and therefore to not quite grow up in the eyes of the state. Although *Elina* ends with a happy, almost utopian resolution, making use of a melodramatic mode, whose happy endings can often function as a way to emphasize the impossibility of reconciliation, both *Elina* and *Sameblod* depict a child figure whose lining up with Swedishness is forced and troubling. Following a certain line (a specific way of doing things, identifying with a group, etc.), as Sara Ahmed writes, has a lot to do with the lines that one inherits and what is projected for one's future. It is also a part of the trajectory of growing up, as one is expected to line up with fixed paths when one grows up. This chapter argues that these cinematic constructions of the not-quite child in northern Sweden make visible the performative nature of lining up/growing up and its inevitable connection to normative familial and national reproduction in the Swedish welfare state.

ELINA

Klaus Härö's film *Elina: As If I Wasn't There* (the literal translation of the Finnish title *Näkymätön Elina* is "Invisible Elina") is based on the novel *Som om jag inte fanns* (*As If I Wasn't There*) (1978) by Kerstin Johansson i Backe, and it takes place in the Tornio River valley, two decades later than the novel, in the 1950s. The film opens with shots of a forest and a bog as the voice-over of Elina (Natalie Minnevik), a young girl, talks to her dead father in Finnish/Meänkieli, telling him that she knows he is somewhere in the bog where they used to spend time together. One of the shots shows Elina's foot stepping into the moss of the bog as it goes down and up again, and soon we see her mother, Marta (Marjaana Maijala), calling for her and telling her not to run in the bog alone. In the following sequence, we find out that Elina has been sick but is healthy enough to go to school now. Joining the new classroom with the teacher Tora Holm (Bibi Andersson) is at first exciting for Elina, but she soon realizes that the teacher has prejudice toward Meänkieli-speakers (she refers to their language as Finnish), thinking they are less civilized and inferior and that Holm's task at the school is, as Holm herself puts it, "to bring order to the wilderness." As Elina stands up against Holm's unjust treatment of another student, she becomes the target of the teacher's prejudice. The more Elina resists becoming and passing as a Swede, the more she is excluded from the community and seeks a sense of belonging at the nearby bog. The film includes several sequences of Elina moving confidently around the bog, helping a local farmer to save a cow from drowning, and finding consolation in the soil, water, and moss of the bog along with her memories of her father. When Elina continues to resist Holm's methods of dealing with children, Holm decides to pretend that Elina is invisible in order to discipline her. This leads Elina to run to the bog once more, except that this time she gets stuck and starts sinking into the bog pool. She is saved by another teacher, Einar, a new addition to the school, who has been more sympathetic toward Elina and who makes it to the bog just in time to help Elina's mother and sister Irma pull Elina out. After this incident, the other schoolchildren and Einar join Elina's resistance to Holm, which prompts Holm to ask for Elina's forgiveness in one of the final scenes of the film.

While *Elina* is based on a novel that focuses more on Elina's grief over her father's death, the film addresses more directly the entangled colonial histories in Norrbotten, where the film is said to take place. This large county in northern Sweden includes both the Indigenous Sápmi lands as well as Tornedalen, the Tornio River valley where Tornedalians have lived for centuries. This borderland region in *Elina* is significant as the film depicts a complicated semi-colonial history of living between cultures, countries, and languages. Along with standard Finnish and the Sámi languages, it was forbidden to speak Meänkieli in Swedish schools throughout more than half of the twentieth century. As part of the politics of Swedishization, which increased at the end of the nineteenth century, the overwhelming attitude toward the use of Finnish language on the Swedish side of the border was that of suspicion, which was explained by security issues (Finland being under czarist Russian rule and possibly producing spies, for example).[8] The government financially supported the building of new schools at the end of the nineteenth century and required the exclusive use of Swedish in school.

In telling this story about a mistreated child from the Tornedalian community in Sweden, *Elina* draws from the elements of melodramatic mode. This is a common move in Klaus Härö's films, which have often focused on difficult histories by depicting innocent victim-heroes (often children) whose stories seek to provoke pathos among the viewers and eventually provide a resolution and healing. These films, including *Elina*, could certainly be read as simplified renditions of complicated histories where the happy endings promise national or familial healing, and their recurring child figures are more aligned with a normative reproduction of the nation and of the idealized child in Nordic culture.[9] Furthermore, as Lydia Kokkola, Annbritt Palo, and Lena Manderstedt bring out, neither the author of the book that *Elina* is based on, nor Klaus Härö (a Finnish film director), nor the actors playing the main characters are Tornedalian, and the languages spoken in the film are Swedish and mostly standard Finnish, with only a few words and pronunciations in Meänkieli.[10] Thus, with these positionalities in mind, the utopian happy ending that realigns the child with normative Swedishness could be read as an attempt to show a simplified version of a complicated history that is, through the apology of Holm, resolved for the majority audiences in Sweden and Finland. However, the utopian happy endings and simple surfaces of melodramatic mode also inspire alternative readings. As Jonathan Goldberg argues in his analysis of the films and theoretical writings of Douglas Sirk, Rainer Werner Fassbinder, and Todd Haynes, melodrama can inhabit a space "in whose extraordinary negations arise further questions, inarticulate inextinguishable feelings, the possibilities of impossibility."[11] Furthermore, drawing from Haynes and from Thomas Elsaesser's influential analysis of family melodrama, Goldberg writes that invisible is "the motor of melodrama,"[12] where the emotions of the characters spill into various features of mise-en-scène like mirrors, decor, colors, and shadows, as well as camera work and music.[13] The film version of *Elina* foregrounds the impact of colonial/racial history on the child by incorporating the melodramatic mode and its emphasis of visual cues to make visible impossible situations where one is expected to grow up to become Swedish but at the same time feels like one cannot quite do so.

From the early sequences, the film establishes its portrayal of the teacher Tora Holm as an unpleasant person who represents outdated pedagogical and colonialist attitudes. When Holm walks with Elina to the classroom after their first meeting, the camera focuses on Elina reaching for the teacher's hand, but Holm pulls it away, thus implying that she is a strict and unkind person, someone whom the audience should see as a villain. In the classroom, Holm punishes another student, Anton, for asking for Elina's help with a word he does not know in Swedish. Holm forbids Anton to eat lunch that day, a common punishment in Swedish schools that was abolished in 1957. When Elina tries to explain that Anton asked her for help because he does not know the word in Swedish, Holm says he should only be asking help from the teacher and that the children are at the school to learn Swedish. When Elina sees Anton not having any food during the lunch hour, she decides to abstain from food too. This act of solidarity develops into a long-lasting conflict between Holm and Elina, and it is something the film version introduced. Namely, in the novel Elina does not eat lunch because she does not like pea soup, and when she eats meatballs the next day, Holm mocks her and says that children from such poor families should eat anything that is given to them. Härö's film version, where Elina does not eat because she supports Anton, however, emphasizes that Elina stands up for injustice caused by colonial and assimilationist pedagogy. This allows the film to imagine a not-quite child whose actions are motivated by a higher moral and, eventually, to inspire the adults to change their ways.

The figure of the child who brings about a moral redemption or healing for the grown-up is a common trope in Hollywood cinema that Härö has mentioned as inspirational for his filmmaking.[14] The child is also a recurring figure in many of these films that incorporate melodramatic mode, as Christof Decker has argued. Decker coins the term "melodramatic child" to signify a cinematic figure of the child who is "exceedingly vulnerable and thus easily victimized; . . . signifies a specific form of innocence, lacking the knowledge, prejudice and preconceptions of adults; . . . it has been regarded as the promise of a different, less painful and depressing future."[15] Decker argues that in three American films of the late 1990s, *Pay It Forward* (dir. Mimi Leder, 2000), *The Sixth Sense* (dir. M. Night Shyamalan, 1999), and *Artificial Intelligence* (dir. Steven Spielberg, 2001), the child figure is "a utopian inspiration for the adult world. Helping, communicating, initiating social change, or preserving the memory of the human race, it becomes a force of improvement."[16] In such narratives, according to Decker, the child functions as someone who saves the adults from their mistakes and ultimately serves as a healing force for the nation. While the social change inspired by the child in these films involves coming to terms with national crimes and traumas in American history, including slavery, it is important to remember that the child played by Haley Joel Osment in all of these three films featured in Decker's analysis, is a white American boy. What differentiates Elina from the children Decker writes about is that while the children in the films that he studies are all white American boys (even though one of them is robotic), Elina is positioned as someone who is not quite Swedish and not quite white. What happens when the features of the melodramatic child intersect with the not-quite child? Can a figure who is expected to become Swedish but who also experiences not quite being included in Sweden initiate social change? Does she promise a less painful and better future for Sweden or for the Finnish- or Meänkieli-speaking minorities, or does she defy national boundaries and go against the traditional image of the child as a herald for a future of a nation? Is it possible for her to inspire change if she is not seen or if her resistance to power is seen as a behavior to be suppressed? By making use of lighting, music, and elements of mise-en-scène, *Elina* visually constructs the not-quite child who draws from the aspirations of the melodramatic child but eventually demonstrates that the inspiring and healing force of the melodramatic child is possible only if the child is returned to the trajectory of lining up with the normative familial/national ideals.

Elina's challenging of Holm's authority and the resulting conflicts in the film refer, on one hand, to a common trope of power play between children and adults in various texts of children's culture. Peter Hunt, for example, brings out that this power relationship is inherently part of children's literature already on the level of authorship: Since it is rarely the children who are writing children's books, the adults who are no longer children have the power to write *about* children *to* children.[17] Moreover, Elina's standing up for justice and her independence could suggest that she is able to perform the ideal image of the Swedish child. However, the film positions Elina and Holm in some of the scenes in the classroom to visualize power structures that go beyond the child-adult hierarchy. In a sequence where Holm is alone with Elina in the classroom and tells her to apologize for her rebellious attitude, the camera positions Holm in front of the strong daylight coming from the window, brightening up Holm's head and leaving Elina in the shadow of the blackboard (fig. 1). The shot of Holm in front of the window brings to mind some of the films of Ingmar Bergman and his cinematographer Sven Nykvist, whose use of light has been an inspiration for Härö's cinematographer Jarkko T. Laine.[18] Bibi Andersson, who plays Holm in *Elina*, is also known for her roles in several of Bergman's films, and in *Elina* she bears a resemblance to the male characters who in those films often represent institutions of power, like the church, academia, or patriarchy more broadly. The shot with Holm in front of the window in *Elina* particularly resembles the shots of the protagonist pastor Tomas Ericsson (Gunnar Björnstrand) in *Nattvardsgästerna* (*Winter Light*, dir. Ingmar Bergman, 1963), one of the primary models for the use of light for Laine.[19] The intense light coming from the window in several scenes in *Winter Light* functions as a problematization of religion and the power of the church as an institution in the lives of the middle-class Swedish people. In *Elina*, in turn, the light coming from the window behind Holm illuminates the power of institutions that maintain colonialist mentality toward the minorities living in northern Sweden.

With this intertextual reference to light in Bergman's film, *Elina* emphasizes the ways in which colonial and religious discourses have been connected in racial hierarchies that separated between the colonizer as civilized and enlightened and the colonized as not civilized, inferior people who live in spiritual darkness. In the context of settler colonialism, these ideologies were similar as the assimilation of Indigenous populations to the settler colonial societies (which resulted in elimination) was often understood as a way of "civilizing" the colonized populations. In visual culture, as Richard Dyer argues, depictions of light coming from above have been explicit symbols of superiority as the light makes white bodies glow and suggests they are enlightened. The explicit juxtaposition of Holm in the strong daylight and Elina in the dark shadow of the board visualizes the construction of racialized distinction between Swedes and Tornedalians/Finns, both of whom are white. This momentary visual darkness of Elina's white body complicates Dyer's reading of white bodies in northern Europe as "the whitest whites in the white racial hierarchy."[20] Arne Lunde, among others, has challenged this description of northern Europe as homogeneous and white by pointing out that the Scandinavian actors in classical Hollywood cinema "become truly white in American terms (only after) constructed as white in assimilation process."[21] While Lunde's analysis brings out another

FIGURE 1. Holm stands in front of the window, illuminated by the light, while Elina's body is darkened in the shadow of the blackboard. Frame grab from *Elina*.

example of white bodies who were considered not-quite/not-yet white as they migrated to a different continent, and who had to "become truly white" through assimilation, *Elina* visualizes the experiences of not-yet/not-quite white people who were racialized within the Nordic region. At the same time, the brief visual darkening of Elina, which seeks to represent the constructed difference of a body that is othered, is also reminiscent of the problematic rhetoric that aligns the experiences of racialized white Tornedalians with communities of color and risks contributing to racial stereotypes that locate a raced body in darkness.

In its use of light and darkness *Elina* also emphasizes the intersection of social class and racialization of Tornedalians and Finnish-speakers in Sweden. Throughout the whole narrative, the film shows that poverty makes the not quite Swedish minority depend on the goodwill of Swedes and causes them not to fight against the discriminatory power structures. Elina's mother, Marta, does not support Elina's rebellion against Holm as she explains that Holm has helped them with shoes and other necessary items. The sequences at Elina's home show the interior almost always in darkness, with lamps or windows as limited sources of light. The dark domestic space is where Marta explains to Elina that Holm is a kind person and that they must keep in good graces with her and how Elina has been ungrateful when she has refused to eat the school lunches. The film, then, makes visible the perception that Meänkieli-/Finnish-speakers inhabit spaces that are dirtier and darker in the effort to visualize them as not quite Swedes, as well as the justification for the forced assimilation policies in Sweden.

The sequence where Marta washes the school's hallway makes explicit this contrast between light and darkness caused by race and class. The establishing shot shows us the schoolhouse from outside in full daylight. Then the camera cuts to Marta in a long shot. She is washing the floor in a dark hallway with a deep dark space behind her and very little light coming from the hallway windows. Tora Holm steps in front of the camera, stops for a moment, and then walks slowly toward Marta with shoes in her hand. When Marta notices her, she gets up, and with that her body becomes lighter in the daylight coming from the windows. In the contrast of the dark hallway, the coming of Holm with the shoes makes Marta's body lighter as she smiles and thanks Holm for her help. This use of light visualizes the belief that the Swedish welfare state, represented here by the educational institution, is enlightened and morally exceptional as it provides aid to those it considers less civilized and in poverty. Holm then proceeds to tell Marta about Elina's behavior. In the next sequence Marta comes home to Elina and her sister Irma; she looks distraught as she sits down in the dark shadow. Elina asks her what is wrong in Finnish, but Marta scolds Elina in Swedish for rebelling against Holm. She does not want Elina to resist the injustice, because of their dependence on the aid from the Swedish welfare state, and thus she accepts the assimilationist policies, which includes the requirement for the Meänkieli/ Finnish-speakers to speak Swedish. As these examples of lighting and other elements of mise-en-scène in *Elina* demonstrate, the film seeks to make visible the intensity of historical injustice experienced by people in the northern areas of Sweden. By incorporating moments where the otherwise unseen racialization is made visible through shadows, the film contributes to the problematic rhetoric that emphasizes the racialization of Tornedalians in Sweden by making use of racial stereotypes and ideologies. At the same time, the sequences where Tornedalian characters are darkened visually are brief and temporary thus maintaining that they can pass as white Swedes at any moment.

THE BOG AS A SITE OF LIMINALITY
AND NOT-QUITENESS

The nearby bog has a significant function in the film to visually explore Elina's experience of grief and not-quiteness, which is ultimately connected to the memory of her father. In several sequences throughout the film, Elina goes to the bog because she feels the presence of her dead father there—it was the place where they used to spend time together—and to escape the injustice that she experiences at school. While this film is intended for both children and adults and thus does not linger on the potential uncanny of bogs for too long, the inherent conception of bogs as dangerous, dark, mysterious places that might hide bodies functions as a reminder of Elina's father's death. She believes that her father is waiting for her in the bog, and in several sequences the use of a handheld camera creates an impression that someone is with Elina. On one hand, the bog sequences function as a didactic move to suggest that Elina avoids dealing with her grief. Instead of going to the cemetery with her mother to see her father's grave, she prefers to imagine that her father is with her in the bog. The bog, however, is significant on more levels as it accompanies Elina's frustration about the injustice she experiences because of her Tornedalian heritage. The bog embodies her not-quiteness; at first it provides a space for escape and play, but it becomes dangerous and tries to overcome Elina's body. Thus, Elina needs to be saved from the bog/not-quiteness and return to the predictable path of lining up with Swedishness.

The forest and the bog where Elina runs and plays reflect on both the space of the proximate and nearly invisible border between Finland and Sweden and the stereotypical depictions of Finns living in forest settings, "primitive," poor, and less civilized in Swedish media during the twentieth century. The bog thus refers not only to a geographical border between the two nation-states and the several cultural communities living in the northern parts of the Nordic region but also to feelings of in-betweenness. In cultural imagination, bogs, which are neither water nor land, are often seen as liminal and ambiguous spaces. According to Derek Gladwin, many Irish postcolonial Gothic texts incorporate bogs because their multidimensionality challenges the binary thinking that is typically prevalent in nationalist and imperial projects.[22] Karin Sanders describes this multidimensionality in her analysis of bog bodies as she writes that bogs are "thresholds between surfaces and depths, ambiguous sites of origin. . . . They bring about spatial and temporal disorientation."[23] Moreover, she argues that bog bodies fascinate us because they are both "'rooted' in and 'uprooted' from a sense of national identity; they are both familiar and strange."[24] *Elina* does not depict the bog as overtly dangerous throughout most of the film (until the sequence where she almost drowns there), nor does it reveal any bog bodies, but the bog is differentiated from other spaces in the film as external to life in the Swedish village, where the minorities are expected to become Swedes, even if there is no hope for them to fully do so.

Elina's movement through the bog visualizes the constancy of rooting and unrooting the Swedish and Tornedalian/Finnish identities. The camera shows us how she keeps moving through the bog as it visualizes her resistance to unrooting her Tornedalian/Finnish identity and the forced rooting of Swedish identity. She repeats several times the mantra that her father taught her to stay safe in the bog: *One must keep moving; one cannot stop.* The camera follows her movement closely. In the close-ups of her feet stepping into the moss that goes down under her weight and then immediately rises back up, the bog is depicted as the ultimate refuge from a fixed and forced rootedness in one national identity. This up-and-down movement in the bog as a site of not-quiteness could be read as a visual image of Kathryn Bond Stockton's theorization of sideways growth discussed in the introduction: growing to the side of cultural ideals that locates energy and vitality in the back-and-forth instead of the reproductive. Before Elina gets stuck, the bog sequences also provide her with more agency as the audience hears her thoughts and shares her gaze through several point-of-view (POV) shots, differently from the other sequences of the film. The bog is a space where Elina can speak Finnish freely and where she feels connected to her father, who, as we can assume from Elina's and Holm's memories of him, had also subverted the hegemony of Swedish language (he had told Elina to speak Finnish and Holm describes him as rebellious).

Running and playing in the bog also remediate common images of childhood in Western culture. Karen Lury argues that children playing with mud and water in films often functions as an ignorance of cleanliness and as a representation of the joy and autonomy of childhood.[25] As the autonomy and free roaming are even more significant in the images of the Nordic child, Elina performs this idealized child figure in many ways. However, the bog, where Elina has more agency and where she expresses her frustrations over injustice caused by the institution that wants to erase part of her identity, makes Elina's body visibly different. In some shots it makes her look dirtier and darker, and the deep dark water almost overtakes her in the sequences when she has run to the bog after Holm has called her invisible. By doing so, the film creates an explicit correlation between racialized Tornedalian bodies and their invisibility, presenting a paradox in that the feelings of difference and displacement increase as Elina becomes invisible in the spaces that represent Swedish state, education, and society.

Becoming overtaken by mud and water in *Elina* ends up with her almost drowning and thus challenges the cultural depictions of a safe, playful, and autonomous childhood in the Swedish welfare state. Instead, as a not quite Swedish child, Elina's liminality becomes visible in the bog, which eventually becomes dangerous for her. The injustice and discrimination that she experiences in the Swedish institution makes the space where she has freely roamed life-threatening since she becomes stuck right after Holm has tried to invite her away from the bog but instead leaves her there. Elina is differentiated from the other children of the village, however, who are also roaming quite freely but are afraid of the bog and do not go there. In most of the sequences, the other children do not resist the required assimilation and injustice that they experience. They are also seen as not quite Swedish; Holm says that she has to bring order to their lives and teach them Swedish, but they have accepted their situation—or at least they do not see the point in resisting. Their not-quiteness is invisible enough that it gets lost in the traditional promise of a "not-yet" in the figure of the child. In other words, they are not quite Swedish because they have not yet learned everything they need to become Swedish through the assimilationist educational policy. They suffer silently through the injustice at school, but they do not resist and therefore do not end up in dangerous situations as Elina does.

Elina thus constructs the not-quite child as a figure whose not-quite-ness is something to be overcome and resolved. The need to keep moving in the bog entails a potential danger. If one stays in one spot for too long, one might get stuck and drown in the bog water with no trace. While the bog functions as a space of refuge and agency for Elina, the film also suggests she might disappear in there. This is visible in several long shots where Elina's body blends with the forests in the background, or in the close-ups of her body and skin in the intimate contact with the moss, mud, water, and tree branches that make it look like the bog swallows her. After Holm has announced and pretended in the classroom that Elina is invisible, Elina runs to the bog. The camera shows her face in a close-up as she lies on the moss of the bog and says she will never leave her father. Now the bog seems to be overtaking her, suggesting a tragic fate of someone who resists the assimilationist policies of becoming Swedish. Elina's running to the bog prompts Holm to go after her, but when Elina does not listen to her teacher, and the other children are observing her, Holm leaves Elina in the bog. The boundary where the forest becomes bog functions as a barrier between them, as Holm is afraid to go closer to Elina, and the branches on the boundary of the forest and the bog hit her face. Elina looks at Holm as she is leaving and forgets the rule about having to keep moving in the bog. She becomes stuck and starts to slowly sink. In his study of Nordic ecocinema, Pietari Kääpä argues that as a liminal space, the bog in *Elina* "facilitates a moment of intercultural awareness, enabling understanding between the protagonists of the film."[26] However, as I have demonstrated, the bog sequences are charged with liminality, which is ultimately seen as dangerous and as something that the not-quite child needs to be saved from.

SAVING THE NOT-QUITE CHILD

Elina achieves the resolution to the child's not-quiteness by incorporating a white, grown-up Swedish savior figure, the newly arrived teacher Einar Björk, who questions Holm's actions, rescues Elina from drowning, and brings about the reconciliation between Holm and Elina. As the film introduces and establishes the savior figure, similarly to its melodramatic depiction of Elina as a not-quite child who suffers from injustice, it makes extensive use of framing, lighting, and various elements of mise-en-scène to emphasize Elina's troubling situation and to imagine a happy ending to it. In an early sequence of the film, where Einar enters the village, everything in the mise-en-scène predicts a resolution. As the camera cuts to both adults and children looking expectedly toward the road, the soundtrack changes to a cheerful melody, and the warm lighting contrasts the earlier sequences of Elina and Holm in cold, low-key lighting. Einar's car has broken down and he has had to borrow a horse from a local villager; thus his appearance on the village road, alongside a horse, slowly making his way toward the people, makes an explicit reference to a white savior figure that, as Matthew Hughey articulates it, draws from cultural imaginaries of the Christ figure and stabilizes and reduces the complexity of intercultural interactions into a digestible narrative of redemption.[27] Einar has a different attitude toward the children from the first moments of meeting them; for instance, he learns some words in their language and tries to understand the children's circumstances; thus, typically to common images of white saviors, his storyline moves the narrative toward resolution while he learns on the way about the different and difficult life of the Tornedalian minority in this Swedish village.

As he witnesses Holm's cruel and unjust behavior toward Elina, Einar tries first to convince Elina to eat and not think about what Holm has done. This is not successful because Holm overhears them and tells Einar that their job is to educate the Finnish-speakers, which she calls a "hopeless task." Einar does not confront Holm but follows her silently inside. He then tries to find other ways to help. He sees Elina in the forest and attempts to make a better connection with her, asking for her help in identifying edible mushrooms. When he proposes that they could tell the local authorities about Holm's actions, Elina says her mother would not like it and runs away. The camera contrasts this conversation, which takes place in the tighter space in the middle of the birch trees, with the open space of the bog. The sequences taking place in the forest illustrate the confinement that Elina experiences when confronted with her sister, Einar, her mother, or Holm. Following this encounter in the forest, Einar goes to talk to Elina's mother. As he steps into the barn, he is depicted as too tall and clumsy in the tight, dark space. This visual illustration of his following exclamation that he has never been in a barn before further establishes him as a well-meaning representative of the dominant culture who is unaware of the history and power structures in the village. He feels compassion for Elina in her situation but also declines to address it fully. He does not explain to Elina's mother what has happened and simply recommends that Elina might want to take a sandwich to school with her.

In these sequences, Einar is depicted as clumsy and nervous because he does not know about the experiences and history of the Tornedalians in northern Sweden. He tries to help, but his ignorance and attempts not to confront the dominant culture fully might make things worse. For example, in the sequence where Elina and her mother are carrying a heavy box of food on the side of the road, Einar stops and offers to give them a ride. This well-meaning act, however, becomes dangerous when Elina accidentally starts the car and it almost crashes into Holm, who is on her bike. Holm charges Einar by saying that this happens when there are no adults who take responsibility and that no one will want to have children in charge. Elina's mother sides with Holm, which prompts Holm to promise her that she will find winter shoes for Elina. At this point the audience might feel sorry for Einar, who in his clumsiness and unaware-ness has simply tried to help. The Swedish audience watching the film in the early 2000s might understand Einar the most because he represents a new worldview for the institution that confronts racist and discrimi-natory attitudes. The colonialist and derogatory style of teaching that Holm represents, which was still common in the 1950s, is condemned in contemporary Sweden, while the experiences and history of Tornedalians are still largely invisible.

Einar thus plays a significant role in reducing the uncomfortable narrative of Elina as a not-quite child in Sweden into a digestible narrative of redemption. He also facilitates a return to a moral certainty. As Linda Williams argues in her influential essay on the melodramatic mode, it is often melodrama's tendency to "find solutions to problems that cannot really be solved without challenging the older ideologies of moral certainty to which melodrama wishes to return."[28] When Elina has gotten stuck in the bog, it is Einar who plays the key role in saving her. Elina's mother is also helping her, but she cannot pull her out by herself. Elina is slowly sinking into the bog pool water, and her sister has to run through the forest to the school to get Einar and make it back in time to save Elina. When Einar hears about Elina, he takes Holm's board with the class plans as something sturdy to help save Elina. Here, then, he visually takes down Holm's colonialist "life work" of bringing civilization to the wilderness as he finally fulfills his role as a savior of the not-quite child.

The sequence where Einar saves Elina makes use of teasing delay, which, as Williams writes, "needs to be linked with melodrama's larger impulse to reverse time, to return to the time of origins and the space of innocence that can musically be felt in terms of patterns of anticipation and return."[29] As the camera cross-cuts to Elina in the bog pool and Irma running with Einar, the film teases with the idea that Einar might be too late to save her. This expands the time that Elina is in the bog pool and also allows for her to have a conversation with her mother before Einar gets there. Elina tells her mother that she came to the bog because she thought her father needed her there and because she is a troublemaker just like him. Elina's mother, however, explains to Elina that her father was courageous and that she would indeed like Elina to be like him. Being a "troublemaker" in this conversation is reduced to the fact that he was sick but refused to rest, even though earlier in the film it is implied that he might have resisted the assimilationist politics as it is he who told Elina to keep speaking Finnish. Elina, being like her father, changes in this sequence from resisting the assimilationist policies to being courageous; thus the film returns her to the trajectory of performing the features of the idealized Swedish child who is autonomous, competent, and moral. While her running into the bog had been a combination of the discrimination she experienced and her grief for her father, this reconciling conversation between Elina and her mother brings her father's death to the foreground and does not address Elina's resistance to Holm's injustice. The expansion of time in this sequence, along with the music that supports anticipation, sets the stage for reconciliation and melodrama's return to innocence. What this means in *Elina* is that the child who has experienced not-quiteness and discrimination because of the Swedish welfare state is rescued from her path of resistance to assimilation politics by showing explicitly that the space associated with the identity and heritage that is not Swedish is dangerous for her. The audience can sigh in relief when Einar makes it just in time to help Elina's mother pull her out of the bog.

In the final sequence, after he has saved Elina from drowning, Einar sides with the children in supporting Elina as she again walks out of the dining hall after more hurtful remarks from Holm. The sequence builds up its emotional affect as Irma, who until now has been ashamed of Elina's resistance, decides to go outside to support Elina and one by one other children and Einar follow her. When they have all gone outside, the composition of the children sitting together on the stairs in the long shot makes a powerful impression of unity and resistance. Seeing Einar join the children leads Holm to suddenly change her attitude, go outside as well, and ask Elina for forgiveness. As she makes her way down to the lowest stairs through the group of children, the power structure between her and Elina changes visually, at least for this moment. Holm cries and admits she has been unfair and behaved badly, "even though (her) intentions were good." She tells Elina to go inside with the other children and eat so that she can grow strong and do well in life. In her analysis of crying in melodrama, Linda Williams argues that tears sustain the fantasy that the demand for satisfaction that can never be satisfied will in fact be satisfied. In *Elina* the tears on Holm's face help to reconcile the image of the Swedish welfare state and its institutions as antiracist and morally exceptional, which is possible only in fictional accounts that can go back in time, bring out injustice within these institutions of the past, and at the same time fix them. In this way the film provides moral and emotional healing for the audiences who might be disturbed and perhaps even feel vague guilt or shame about the history of systemic discrimination in Sweden. There is also an invitation for emotional healing for audiences who share Finnish or Tornedalian heritage as they can, along with Elina, receive the apology from the representative of the Swedish institution. In their article on apology in *Elina* and in *Sameblod*, Kokkola, Palo, and Manderstedt write that by funding these films, "which encourage viewers to feel hurt and shame, the nation enacts an apology via substitution."[30]

It is the melodramatic mode of the film that helps to fully carry out the reconciliation and emotional healing that result in Einar's actions as a white savior and in this final sequence of Holm's apology. While exhibiting traits similar to Decker's "melodramatic child" as she inspires national and familial healing for the grown-up world in this Nordic context, the child has to be saved from the dangerous path of not-quiteness by a grown-up. As argued before, the reconciliation in the film is inspired by Elina but possible only with Einar's help, in order to restore the image of a caring welfare state. The sequence of Holm's apology to Elina provides a reconciliation from a feeling of collective shame through the listening child, who is not yet an adult and will continue on her path to become Swedish. The happy ending of Härö's film, then, aligns its depiction of childhood with the traditional and normative vision of the child as a herald of futurity, a not yet citizen whose becoming promises familial and national continuity. The film reconciles the uncomfortable image of an institution that causes trauma and displacement for the child in the welfare state. Elina's "not-quiteness" is resolved; she is again visibly similar to the other children on their way to becoming Swedes.

The sequence where Holm apologizes, however, includes a visual cue that reminds the viewer that the happy ending, just as in many other melodramas, as Jonathan Goldberg or Thomas Elsaesser have argued, is only a facade. The happy ending is utopian and impossible, thus at the same time undoing the moral certainty toward which the film has moved. As the camera focuses on Holm, who apologizes through tears, it positions Anton in the background so that whenever Holm is speaking, we can see Anton's face as well. Holm does not ask for forgiveness from Anton or from the other children who have similarly experienced her discriminatory attitude and rigid pedagogy. It was Anton, after all, whom Holm first forbid to eat lunch, which started Elina's active resistance to Holm. Anton's face in the sequence of Holm's apology, then, reminds the viewer that the reconciliation between the not-quite child and the Swedish welfare state is a fantasy. "There are no happy endings," writes Goldberg; "history is not simply moving ever forward."[31] In other words, by imagining a reconciliation that assumes that the not-quite child is taken back on track to line up with Swedishness, *Elina* includes a possibility that moving forward in the way the film imagines it is not really a happy ending.

SAMEBLOD

Sameblod, directed by Swedish-Sámi filmmaker Amanda Kernell, depicts a South Sámi girl named Elle-Marja (Lene Cecilia Sparrok) in Swedish Sápmi in the 1930s. The majority of the film is an extended flashback of Elle-Marja as a young girl, but it is framed by her as a grown-up (Maj-Doris Rimpi) in her later years of life, when she goes by the name Christina. The opening sequences show us her son and granddaughter as they are driving to Elle-Marja/Christina's sister's funeral in Sápmi and encouraging Elle-Marja/Christina to participate in the family's activities, which she rejects as she repeats the internalized stereotypes about the Sámi people and says she does not want to have anything to do with them. The extended flashback that soon follows begins with Elle-Marja and her sister Njenna (Mia Erika Sparrok) getting ready to leave for the boarding school for Sámi children. The film's portrayal of the boarding school where children of Sámi reindeer herders had to go resembles the school setting in *Elina*. The children are not allowed to speak their first language (South Sámi in this case) at school and are allowed to speak only Swedish. The derogatory attitudes and violence that the children experience because of their indigeneity, however, manifest themselves much further than only at the school. The Sámi children are mocked by the other children and youth living in the village, and Elle-Marja faces derogatory and prejudiced attitudes in almost every encounter where she is outed as a Sámi by Swedes. While her Swedish schoolteacher, Christina Lajler (Hanna Alström), seems to support Elle-Marja's interest and progress in learning Swedish language and literature, she rejects Elle-Marja's wish to continue her studies, basing her decision on the racial biology texts that she is reading as she states, "Sámi brains are not capable."

The film follows Elle-Marja's realization that no matter how well she does in school, she is expected to stay in Sápmi in order to herd her family's reindeer and to not "die out," as Lajler puts it. Along with the other children at the school, Elle-Marja goes through a humiliating experience of researchers from Uppsala measuring their skulls and taking photographs of their naked bodies. Elle-Marja eventually decides to run away from school; takes a train to Uppsala; and after failed attempts to stay for an extended period at the home of a young Swedish man, Niklas, she enrolls in the girls' school in Uppsala under the name Christina Lajler from Germany. She makes one last trip back to Sápmi to ask her mother for her father's silver belt in order to pay for the school. This request is not well received by her mother, who gives Elle-Marja the silver belt only after the daughter has killed one of their reindeer. The camera then cuts back to Elle-Marja/Christina in her later life, which was depicted in the early sequences of the film. Now she goes to the church where her sister's body is still in the coffin and asks for her forgiveness, and then she walks and climbs up the mountains to reach the area where her family used to live.

Through this journey of becoming someone else, a Swedish girl Christina, *Sameblod* visualizes the experience of not-quiteness as it relates to indigeneity and racialization in Sweden. *Sameblod* can be situated among the various cinematic depictions and reflections on Sámi history and identity that have come out during the late twentieth and early twenty-first centuries in the Nordic region. It shares characteristics with historical dramas such as *Pathfinder* (*Ofelaš*, 1987) and *Kautokeino Rebellion* (*Kautokeino-upprøret*, 2008) by Nils Gaup in mediating the traumatic memory of the Sámi people through a format that is relatively easily understandable for a wide range of audience.[32] *Sameblod*, too, incorporates experiences that have become monuments in Sámi collective memory, such as the violent visits of the researchers of race biology, discrimination at boarding schools, racist and derogatory encounters with those identified as Swedes, and leaving Sápmi. Some of the questions that *Sameblod* is asking, however, connect it to recent more experimental and self-reflexive Sámi documentaries. These films, such as *Sámi nieida jojk* (*Sámi Daughter's Jojk*, dir. Liselotte Wajstedt, 2007), *Bihttoš* (*Rebel*, dir. Elle-Máijá Tailfeathers, 2014), and *Sparrooabbán* (*Me and My Little Sister*, dir. Suvi West, 2016), ask questions like what it means to grow up to become a different person or what the impacts of internalized colonization are intergenerationally. While Wajstedt and Tailfeathers approach these questions in a more experimental way, *Sameblod* shares their focus on a self-reflexive cultural memory work that challenges cultural revivalist narratives.[33]

Answering the question of where the idea for *Sameblod* came from, Amanda Kernell says she has always wondered, "Can you really become another person, and what happened to this generation? . . . What does it do to you to grow up in a time where you were seen as an inferior race?"[34] As *Sameblod* engages with these questions, it goes beyond simply making racialization visible through problematic visual contrasts of darkness and light that we see in *Elina*, as it reflects on the meaning of seeing (who is seeing what/whom) through its emphasized incorporation of mirrors, watching, and looking away in several sequences. Furthermore, in its pursuit to depict what internalized racialization and colonization *feels* like, *Sameblod* constructs tactile images that linger on the skin of the not-quite child (both her actual skin and the fabric of her clothes). This produces a different embodied reaction for the film audience than with *Elina*; instead of pathos and strife for justice enhanced by the melodramatic mode, *Sameblod* contemplates the bodily impact of colonization and racialization on a child who is about to "grow up" and become an adult Sámi who, according to the laws in 1930s Sweden, must live in a segregated community.

THE GAZE AND TOUCH OF THE INDIGENOUS CHILD

Within the early sequences, *Sameblod* establishes its emphasis on the sensory elements, particularly sight and touch, as it contemplates the racialized not quite whiteness of the Sámi people. The first sequence of the film shows us elderly Christina in a close-up profile shot. She is lighting a cigarette and looking toward something, possibly through the window that is behind her. We hear her son calling her name in the distance as the camera lingers on her; she breathes heavily and touches her ear (which, as we later find out, is a significant bodily memory of the violence she encountered as a child). Then the camera cuts to her looking out of the car window, her gaze pointed again for several seconds at something we cannot see until she responds to her son's comment about the Sámi music playing on the CD that she has nothing to do with those people. While the early sequences depict Christina at an old age, a similar focus on her eyes and her skin as a child occur frequently throughout the rest of the film. This framing of the Indigenous child's gaze in *Sameblod* engages with and rethinks the idea that the child's eyes provide a different, easily understandable, defamiliarized perspective for the adult audiences and, further, that this perspective is often inspired by the moral compass of the child.

Instead of directly addressing the camera or always providing the viewers with POV shots (though there are several shots from behind the head and shoulders of Elle-Marja as she is looking toward the lake, forest, or people), the use of the shots that depict her in a close-up or medium shot looking away functions to visualize the experience of a not-quite child who is not able to readily assume the idealized figure of the child resisting injustice (the way that Pippi Longstocking or even Elina are imagined to do). In her analysis on Mohawk artist Shelley Niro's video constellation *The Shirt*, Monika Siebert argues that looking at the camera and then looking away in Niro's project responds to the long history of how Indigenous people have been represented in European and Anglo-American cultures. While the direct gaze in *The Shirt* secures the Indigenous subjectivity and agency, looking elsewhere functions as a "plea for disengagement from the entangled North American gaze, from its contests over agency and subjectivity and from the imperatives of resistance it imposes."[35] *Sameblod* is in many aspects a completely different project, a historical drama that primarily portrays the history of colonization and racism toward the Sámi people. However, the camera's focus on looking away, which disengages from the settler colonial gaze, is a helpful concept to analyze the emphasis on Elle-Marja's gaze in this film. This disengagement resonates with Troy Storfjell's point about *Sameblod* in his analysis on Elle-Máijá Apiniskim Tailfeathers's film—namely, that these films challenge "settler audiences with the interweaving of the personal and the political in Indigenous lives" and that they tell their stories "without the expectation that they should relate everything they write to the colonial center of the settler state."[36] Furthermore, as Harald Gaski has demonstrated, Sámi cultural

FIGURE 2. Elle-Marja looks elsewhere after the violence of the photographers and the local boys. Frame grab from *Sami Blood*.

traditions (particularly, the lyrics of *yoik*, the traditional Sámi vocal genre), often have "both the goal and intention that a Sami should be able to understand more than a non-Sami."[37]

In the sequence that follows the photographing/measuring and the attack by the local boys, Elle-Marja looks in the mirror as she washes away the blood from her ear. We see a brief glimpse of her gaze in the mirror, and then the camera cuts to a close-up of her touching her face and looking toward the mirror. The camera lingers on her look for a few seconds before cutting to a fifteen-second-long take of her in a medium close-up shot, looking away (fig. 2). This emphasis on her look constructs a gaze that disengages from the imperative of resistance that might be expected from the child figure in a Swedish film made in 2016 or, in general, from a child figure in a film that deals with historical injustice. The disengagement in Elle-Marja's gaze illustrates, on one hand, the ways in which the film narrative deals with the impossibility of the Sámi child in the 1930s to resist the settler colonial power, but it also reorients the child's gaze so that the expected/assumed new perspective is not visible or accessible. There is a similar emphasis on her looking away in the sequence where the young Swedish man Niklas, whom she visits in Uppsala, has asked her to leave his family's house because his parents do not approve of a romantic relationship between them. When he has closed the door, the camera lingers on Elle-Marja, who turns her head back toward the door (also toward the camera but never looking directly at it) and then looks slightly away. This is followed by a long shot of her sitting in the park and then a close-up high-angle shot of her face until she touches her ear.

Connecting the different acts of perceiving (gaze and touch) in the child figure is a common move in films and other cultural texts. Ingmar Bergman's *Tystnaden* (*The Silence*, 1963) is a well-known example of artistic/cinematic engagement with the child who is aimlessly wandering in a hotel and a train, in a constant state of perceiving, as Maaret Koskinen argues.[38] The camera focuses on him watching and touching the window, looking toward the camera with an empty look, not having knowledge of the whole, perceiving only fragments of the people, architecture, and paintings around him. The child in *The Silence* is, of course, a white Swedish boy, and his wandering empty look is a part of Bergman's 1960s modernist cinema. Because Elle-Marja is a Sámi girl in the 1930s, as the film made in 2016 constructs it, her gaze and its connection to the other acts of perception engage with the audience differently from those of the child who resists injustice or the child who is simply wandering. By connecting the gaze that looks away at something we cannot see with the touch of her skin, the film reflects on what it might mean for a film to visualize the experiences of racialization for the not-quite child but without creating contrasts of dark and light that would further contribute to racial stereotypes.

Sameblod thus challenges the power of seeing in making visible the effects of racialization and instead explores those through the acts of feeling and touching. It connects visibility and tactility in its incorporation of the traditional clothing, *gákti*.[39] It was a common practice to wear gákti throughout one's everyday life, and as Katariina Kyrölä and Tuija Huuki argue, "The processes of making it and wearing it are considered important and respected corporeal and affective markers of a Sámi identity" because otherwise "Sámi identity is not necessarily visually distinguishable from white non-indigenous bodies."[40] At the same time, as Kyrölä and Huuki bring out in their analysis of gákti in the documentary *Sparrooabbán*, gákti also "bears the weight of the transgenerational, affectively transmitted experiences of Sámi oppression."[41] Kyrölä and

Huuki use Valerie Walkerdine's concept "second skin" to describe how gákti functions as a psychic second skin that functions as a boundary for the collective, protecting and holding the community together.[42] In the documentary they write about, gákti is a psychic object that is both meaningful but also, in order to bring a sense of safety, can be used as a way to exclude some who do not fit in the gendered understanding (this is influenced by settler colonialism) of who gets to wear gákti and how they are allowed to or supposed to do that. In *Sameblod*, gákti also refers to its complicated history: The children in the boarding school are not allowed to wear anything else, and in several sequences of them walking through the village with the teacher, they are seen as a spectacle by the local people. Gákti functions in these moments as a second skin in that it differentiates the people who are otherwise visibly like the Swedish majority.

The sequences that feature Elle-Marja's attempts to change out of her gákti go beyond the visibility of it and focus on the materiality of the fabric as skin. Thus, not only does the film show us how gákti can be used to make invisible differences visible, but it also attempts to make the viewers physically feel it. In the moments that focus on touch and texture of the clothes, the film incorporates what Laura Marks discusses as "haptic images" in intercultural cinema. These images, according to Marks, are "often used in an explicit critique of visual mastery, in the search for ways to bring the image closer to the body and the other senses."[43] The sequence where Elle-Marja takes off her gákti to try on a dress that is hanging on the clothesline is filmed almost exclusively in close-up, drawing our attention to her touching the dress, smelling it, and then taking off her gákti and putting on the dress. The sound of the fabric as Elle-Marja touches it (fig. 3) or as it moves in the wind combines the optic image with brief haptic ones that illustrate the film's ultimate goal of representing not-quiteness and racialization as embodied and felt instead of something mastered by the gaze of the audience. Visibility is, of course, deeply connected to the felt not-quiteness, as after she has put on the dress, some Swedish young men who pass by see her and invite her to a dance party in the evening. By focusing the viewers' attention on the touch and surfaces of the gákti and the other dress as Elle-Marja gets changed, the sequence illustrates in a visual and embodied manner that the gákti functions as skin, something

FIGURE 3. Elle-Marja's hands touch the dress hanging on the clothesline. Frame grab from *Sami Blood*.

that Elle-Marja has to change into and out of in order to pass or not pass as a Swede.

Changing one's clothes is, of course, a whole lot easier than changing one's actual skin, and despite the oppression that Elle-Marja faces, the film also points to some amount of privilege that her whiteness provides for her. After changing her clothes, she passes for a Swedish girl and holds a conversation with Niklas at a dance party without him realizing that she is Sámi. She is outed by her sister and the schoolteacher who have come looking for her. As she belongs to the reindeer-herding Sámi in the 1930s, who were officially required to be segregated, Elle-Marja is forced to wear her gákti and does not own any other clothes. In order to "change her skin" she has to steal different clothing, and when she is found out at the dance party because her sister has told one of the school workers about what Elle-Marja has done, she is punished and then has to change back to her gákti. Our skin, as Jennifer Barker puts it, functions both as a covering and an uncovering, because of its "simultaneous proximity to the public world and to the secretive inner body."[44] Gákti as a second skin uncovers the Sámi identity that would otherwise be quite invisible to other people. Wearing a different dress covers the part of Elle-Marja's identity that she has been taught to feel ashamed about.

Because of the experience of the gákti as a second skin, which has become oppressive, Elle-Marja decides to destroy it on her way leaving Sápmi. While still wearing the gákti on the train to Uppsala, she notices that people are looking at her suspiciously. She steals another dress from one of the sleeping passengers, and then the camera cuts to her in that dress, looking down at a fire where she is burning the gákti as the light from the flames is flickering on her face. The next cut shows us a medium close-up of her gákti being slowly consumed by the flames. We see the fabric changing color and starting to melt. The camera lingers on the fire quite briefly but long enough to create a sense of unease as we witness the burning of something that has functioned more than just clothes, as something that is almost like skin. Discussing the function of skin as a boundary between us and the rest of the world, Maurice Merleau-Ponty famously wrote that one is always on the same side of one's body.[45] This notion of skin as a rigid boundary becomes contested in discussions about the porosity of skin that reveal that humans are enmeshed with more-than-human worlds.[46] In *Sameblod*, however, the implication of settler colonial politics on Elle-Marja's body is that the second skin is a rigid boundary indicating something about one's real skin, and one needs to destroy it in order to be able to pass as and become a Swede. As a child/teenager, she is seen as a not-yet, a not-yet citizen, and, thus, under these oppressive circumstances, she changes the direction of her not-yetness to line up with the children on their way to growing up to become Swedes.

LINING UP AND BECOMING WHITE

While the scenes at the boarding school where the students are lined up neatly by their desks as they answer the teacher's questions or sing Swedish songs resembles similar scenes in *Elina*, the visual focus on lining up is much more prevalent in *Sameblod*. Sara Ahmed writes that whiteness is a straightening device, and when bodies "line up," they disappear into the "sea of whiteness."[47] Discussing the bodily experiences of those who do not approximate "the habitus of the white bourgeois body,"[48] Ahmed emphasizes that one feels the non-alignment with the ideal white bodies spatially and bodily; one feels that standing out of line, which is uncomfortable in a world where lining up with whiteness is the expected route, and that the discomfort and inability to orient oneself toward objects in the same way that privileged bodies can is reproduced over time and passed on through generations. Both *Elina* and *Sameblod* feature a lining up that is forced and administered by institutions, represented by the school system in these two films. The children have to physically line up in order to be straightened into Swedishness and whiteness. At the same time, becoming Swedish is not fully available for either the Tornedalians or the Sámi (who experience a more regulated denial) because they were perceived to be inferior races at that time. In both films lining up is charged with fear or shame, as the teacher is walking around the classroom and punishing those who speak Sámi languages or Meänkieli/Finnish or have not finished their homework. *Sameblod* features a variety of sequences with the physical act of lining up: The children are walking in a line behind the teacher to the school building, or they are lined up to greet the visitors who are there to measure their skulls and take photographs of their bodies. The latter sequence begins with the visitors arriving in a car and then cuts to two different shots of the Sámi children standing in a line, first in a medium shot and then a long shot that accentuates the straightness of the line. The visitors then move down the line, touching some of the children's clothing or hair and making comments such as "Such fair hair. Not bristly at all." Accentuating the sound of surprise in this comment, the film stresses that looks are not always enough to be straightened into whiteness: Despite standing in a straight line and looking like white Swedes, the Sámi children are continuously reminded that they are not quite in line with whiteness. Soon after this sequence, there is another shot of lining up in one of the film's most unsettling scenes, where the visiting scientists measure the children's skulls and take naked photographs of them. After the camera has shown them measuring Elle-Marja's head and forcing her to remove her clothes for the photographs, other children stand in a line to be photographed. In these examples, lining up becomes a painful reminder of the children's difference from normative Swedishness.

Throughout the first third of the film, Elle-Marja is depicted as a child who willingly aligns herself with the expectations and norms at the school, and she expresses a desire to become a teacher, similarly to their Swedish teacher. After realizing that she does not have any other choice but to live in the segregated Sámi community, however, she rejects this expected trajectory for her growing up as a Sámi (in settler colonial terms). As brought out earlier, growing up is closely connected with becoming in the rhetoric around childhood. One is expected to inherit likeness to one's family, to reproduce certain genealogies of descent, and to become affiliated with a group, often a nation-state or a minority culture. One of the prominent examples of the implications of this expectation for Elle-Marja in *Sameblod* is the sequence where Elle-Marja is having breakfast with Niklas at his house after she has spent her first night in Uppsala there. Niklas's parents ask him to come to the other room, which we can see through the glass door between them and Elle-Marja. The camera positions Elle-Marja in a close-up shot in the foreground, and as we see that the door is not fully closed, we know she can hear what they say. Niklas's parents express their concern that Niklas has not thought through his relationship with Elle-Marja/Christina and that although it might be difficult to live in the northern areas of Sweden, there are resources for the Sámi people there. The main concern along with these points that Niklas's mother brings up is that Elle-Marja/Christina might become or already be pregnant. When Niklas negates the possibility of that, his mother says he does not know what Elle-Marja/Christina is after.

Elle-Marja/Christina is seen here through Niklas's mother's eyes as a threat to the expected trajectories of reproduction, which in the 1930s in Sweden emphasized the importance of reproducing the white Swedish nation. The implications of this are similar to how Mary Zaborskis describes the experiences of Indigenous children in North America where they function as racialized queer children and are, differently from innocent white children who are free of a past, seen as having a past and therefore "barred from the future, and this barring is enacted precisely through promising futurity."[49] Niklas's mother suggests that the only possible future for Elle-Marja/Christina is in Sápmi because, as the settler colonial state has structured it, there are resources for her there. Those resources would, of course, ensure that Elle-Marja does not fully line up with whiteness and Swedishness. This encounter with Niklas's parents shows Elle-Marja that she has not yet been successful in passing as a Swede, but because of her age she is able to enroll in the girls' school in Uppsala under the name of Christina Lajler from Germany. This means she can learn the necessary techniques and knowledge that she does not yet have in order to later successfully pass as a Swede. Passing is not becoming, Sara Ahmed argues, because assuming the image of another does not erase the history and identity that one already has. *Sameblod*, however, ponders an experience where passing is very close to becoming. In her growing up and becoming an adult, Elle-Marja/Christina performs and takes on another identity that includes a different name and a different skin. This also means she rejects the straight line of descent that she is expected to follow as a segregated Sámi in 1930s Sweden. She resists growing up in the rigid line that is defined by the colonial politics of Sweden and enforced by both the majority of Swedes and the Sámi communities at that time. The only way to do that, however, is to line up with normative Swedishness, which means an erasure of her Sámi identity and thus effectively functions as the kind of elimination by the settler colonial politics that the Sámi people who were not allowed to continue herding reindeer experienced.

While the opening sequences that show us Christina reluctantly attending her sister's funeral and sitting at a bar at the hotel, agreeing with the derogatory comments that other Swedish tourists make about the Sámi people, the closing sequence of the film imagines a possible resolution for Christina/Elle-Marja that seeks to untie the line of whiteness/Swedishness. Differently from the resolution in *Elina* that ties nicely most of the loose ends (except for the one about Anton and other children), *Sameblod* imagines Christina first going to the church and asking forgiveness from her dead sister. Then she climbs up the mountains and arrives at a site where some Sámi people have gathered to mark the reindeer calves. We see her looking around, getting closer to the site, and the closing sequence ends with Christina/Elle-Marja in a close-up profile shot with the background in shallow focus. She is again looking at something that the audience does not see in this take, which lasts for a few seconds until a cut to the credits. With this ending, the film emphasizes that although there might be a resolution for Elle-Marja/Christina, it is not made available for the audiences watching the film to consume.

Both *Elina* and *Sameblod* foreground child figures who experience racialization and oppression in the Swedish welfare state because of their not-quiteness. Both films portray these children as eventually on the trajectory to becoming Swedes. The implications and requirements for that to happen, however, are radically different. This shows us, on one hand, the significant changes in historical contexts and racial hierarchies regarding the Indigenous Sámi people in the 1930s and the Tornedalian-speakers in the 1950s. It also demonstrates the different cinematic approaches to representing and resolving experiences of not-quiteness and racialization. The child figures in these films provide in-depth engagement with what it means to line up with Swedishness. Furthermore, they trouble the construction of a fictional child who makes visible problems in the Swedish welfare state. Even though both films imagine children who do line up with Swedishness, they also suggest the impossibility of that endeavor. In the following chapter, I engage with texts that emphasize the failure to line up, exploring possible alternatives to growing/lining up that failure might provide.

CHAPTER TWO

FAILING CHILDHOOD AND RETHINKING GROWING UP SWEDISH

Susanna Alakoski's *Svinalängorna* and Eija Hetekivi Olsson's *Ingenbarnsland* are two best-selling novels from Sweden that situate their child protagonists who experience shame, prejudice, and discrimination in the center of the developing urban welfare state projects in the latter half of the twentieth century.[1] Depicting the families of Finnish-speaking labor migrants in Sweden during the 1960s through the 1980s, these two texts construct not-quite children who, as those portrayed in the films analyzed in the previous chapter, are able to pass as white Swedes but are frequently reminded that because of their ethnicity and social class, they cannot quite align themselves with Swedishness. Taking place in the midst of the urban welfare state project, these texts not only extend the child figures who problematize the rigid lines and categories of familial and national belonging further into the core of the welfare state, but they also foreground failure to perform the idealized Swedish child, who had become increasingly important in symbolizing the citizen of the Swedish welfare state. This chapter engages with Jack Halberstam's theorization of queer failure in order to show that while failure can provide some unexpected subversive potentials for these child protagonists, the wondrous anarchy of childhood that Halberstam sees in queer failure can, similarly to Kathryn Bond Stockton's "sideways growth," become privileged in the image of the Swedish child. So as to make that privilege visible, both novels portray the children and the spaces around them through different iterations of abjection. In some of the passages, the texts emphasize feelings of revulsion and the appearance of bodily fluids that could be read along the lines of Julia Kristeva's semiotic-psychoanalytic formulation of the abject, which allows the subject to negotiate boundaries between themselves and others. My analyses will show, however, that abjection in these novels is imagined as another alternative to expected lines and trajectories.

While the history of the Finnish labor migrants who came to Sweden during the second half of the twentieth century, and who are now one of the largest national minority groups in Sweden, differs from the settler colonial history of the Indigenous Sámi and Tornedalian people, the misconceptions and attitudes toward Finnish-speakers also draw from a long (semi-)colonial history between Finland and Sweden as well as the resulting racialized categorization of Finns as inferior to white Swedes.[2] Looking at these two novels together allows us to see the persistence of child figures in cultural texts that make these histories visible. This chapter discusses how the two novels establish a failure to remember important events in Finnish history that the children hear from their parents, particularly World War II, as something that contributes to the children refusing to memorialize rigid national boundaries. Since, as Halberstam writes, memorialization has a tendency to "tidy up disorderly histories," forgetting can resist grand narratives and unleash new forms of memory.[3] Though it is important for their parents to remember the impact of war in Finland, the child protagonists of *Svinalängorna* and *Ingenbarnsland* refuse to memorialize narratives that establish rigid national boundaries by way of anticipating generational transmission of memory and identity, or they fail to understand because they are never told all the details of the disorderly histories. What they observe in their everyday life instead is that the dominant ways of remembering Finland, the emotional impact of war, and its entanglement with histories of colonial ideologies and with poverty have rendered some stories invisible. This has further contributed to their parents' feelings of inferiority and exclusion. The chapter will then turn to how each novel constructs its child protagonists within the welfare state architecture and structures, which become oppressive and function as sites of not-quiteness, failure, and abjection.

Svinalängorna is a first-person narrative told from the perspective of the child Leena in a family of Finnish labor migrants in a small Swedish town, Ystad, during the 1960s and 1970s. It opens with Leena's family getting ready to move into a new apartment in Fridhem. This rental housing neighborhood was built as part of the Million Program, the Swedish welfare state's large-scale project to create affordable and functional housing for the large number of people who had moved to the urban centers that did not have enough housing. Much of the novel's narrative oscillates between the everyday rhythms of the working-class family trying to survive financially, decorating their apartment, cooking, or looking for clothes at the local charity organization and the parents' increasing drinking binges. Through Leena's eyes and ears, the narrative describes her parents' hopes for a better life in Sweden, their memories about Finland, and her parents' slow descent into alcoholism as they are confronted with prejudice and stereotypes based on their ethnicity and working-class status. While Leena suffers from the traumatic everyday that is a result of her parents' abuse of alcohol, the novel presents the impact of prejudice and stereotypes regarding Finnish-speakers through the adults' talk. The narrative suggests that the feelings of inferiority and not-quiteness that the Finnish migrants articulate are invisible in Sweden (not talked about, not understood), but the differences of these migrants are nevertheless made visible in the eyes/ears of Swedes.[4] *Svinalängorna* focuses on the traumatic impact of failure on its child protagonist, and although it temporarily blurs the boundaries between the child and the family dog as a way to imagine a parallel world, it ultimately maintains that the refusal of adulthood is not really an option. The film adaptation of the novel takes this further as it depicts childhood in the Finnish-speaking family as a repressed memory that can be healed only with the help of a Swedish savior figure, thus recalling in a completely different line of events the resolution in *Elina*, discussed in the previous chapter.

Ingenbarnsland, which situates its child protagonist, Miira, in a similar context—growing up in a Finnish working-class family in a Swedish urban area, a suburb of Gothenburg—albeit about fifteen years later, provides productive points of comparison. Namely, *Ingenbarnsland* constructs a child who reacts to the expectations and impossibilities to line up in a radically different way. Miira goes to a Finnish-language classroom, an initiative that Sweden Finnish organizations had been successful in establishing by the 1980s. Miira, however, experiences her Finnish-language education as something that is used to reinforce the stereotypes of Finns as suitable only for working-class jobs and will cause her to be a forever migrant, even though she grows up in Sweden. Similarly to *Svinalängorna*, the novel follows in many ways the conventions of coming-of-age narratives, describing the everyday life of the child as she goes through different stages of school and puberty, roaming independently on the streets of the various suburbs. Her family struggles with finances as well, but in this story the child protagonist has a more active role in resisting various kinds of stereotypes stemming from ethnicity, class, or gender and of not wanting to identify with the rigid categories of Finnishness or Swedishness. Failing to align with these categories, and with gendered expectations, results in a more subversive negotiation of boundaries and lines in *Ingenbarnsland*.

Both *Svinalängorna* and *Ingenbarnsland* make explicit references to the idyllic and unreachable image of childhood conveyed in some of the most popular texts in Swedish (children's) culture and construct stark contrasts to it in the lives of their child protagonists. One of the passages in *Svinalängorna*, for example, visualizes the impossibility of lining up with the ideal childhood in a family where the parents struggle with alcoholism and belonging in their new country. The child protagonist lists everything that is going well during a brief period when her parents are sober, but through the subtle hints of impossibility or disillusionment, the narrative suggests that the sober period does not last long or does not even truly exist. The child's list of good things features laughter, homemade food, idyllic family time, a white loaf of bread that rises in the oven and "räcker till alla världens barn" (is enough for all the world's children), and Pippi Longstocking, who has "rött hår på vår svartvita teve" (red hair on [their] black-and-white TV).[5] Seeing red color on the black-and-white TV set or baking enough bread for all the world's children makes it apparent that what the child describes seeing is illusory and, furthermore, that the kind of life that Pippi's image promises is not available for her. By connecting this Pippi reference to the hyperbolized image of having enough bread for all the world's children, the novel emphasizes its commentary on a dominant narrative of exceptionalism in the self-image and international reputation of Sweden as it constructs experiences of people who find themselves excluded from the welfare state and who observe problems within it or within its well-meaning but at times patronizing gestures.[6] Furthermore, it constructs a child figure who experiences her everyday as a continuous failure to attain the promises of the Swedish welfare state.

Ingenbarnsland, in turn, opens with a passage that similarly alludes to Pippi Longstocking, but it performs a grotesque image of the ideals that Pippi stands for. Namely, the first sentence of the novel describes the child protagonist Miira "bankade skiten ut" (beating the shit out of) her classmate Lasse, who, as we later find out, has bullied some of the other girls in Miira's class.[7] The first paragraph of the novel paints quite a graphic image of the violent outburst of the child, whose braids "flaxade vilt omkring" (fluttered wildly around) as her arms, like "små propellrar" (small propellers), whip Lasse's head so much that the "fläsket därunder korvade sig" (flesh under his skin darkened) and Miira imagines her face, like rubber, expand and tear off from the body, "spottade snorgift" (spitting out poisonous snot).[8] Throughout the novel, as Miira fights for justice and resembles Pippi in many ways, *Ingenbarnsland* depicts her behavior as grotesque and abject and maintains that she, too—also a child of the Finnish labor migrants in Sweden, about two decades later than *Svinalängorna*—fails to line up with Swedishness and Swedish childhood. However, in *Ingenbarnsland* failure becomes a way to subvert these normative categories. Through constructions of failure and abjection, then, as I will demonstrate, these two novels unsettle and reorient the image of Swedish childhood.

Writing about the queer art of failure (primarily in the cultural context of the United States), Jack Halberstam writes that since heteronormative thinking has equated success with advancement, family, capital accumulation, and hope, then counter-hegemonic, queer, and other subordinate ways of thinking might help us to associate failure with "nonconformity, anticapitalist practices, nonreproductive life styles, negativity, and critique."[9] Highlighting the impossibilities of, for example, feminine success that is measured by male standards, successful adulthood that means heterosexual parenting, or the idea that everyone can become successful in a capitalist society where success means wealth accumulation combined with reproductive maturity, Halberstam argues that not succeeding, forgetting, and unbecoming can "offer unexpected pleasures."[10] Similarly to Kathryn Bond Stockton's theorization of "sideways growth," which reads children who are in various ways queered as growing back-and-forth instead of up, with energy and pleasure and without reproductive extensions, Halberstam suggests that the unexpectedly pleasurable way to fail normative expectations would be to refuse adulthood (at least as long as it continues to be equated with heterosexual norms). Instead, writes Halberstam, failure "preserves some of the wondrous anarchy of childhood and disturbs the supposedly clean boundaries between adults and children, winners and losers."[11] The texts analyzed in this chapter imagine what it means to fail the wondrous anarchy of childhood when, similarly to the notion of sideways growth, it has become privileged and not attainable for the not-quite children. As discussed further in the introduction, Pippi Longstocking as the ideal Swedish child and citizen has often been mediated as anarchic, and her refusal of adulthood or social conventions became aligned with the idea of citizens of the welfare state as independent, taken care of, and moral. *Svinalängorna* and *Ingenbarnsland* imagine scenarios where refusing adulthood is not really possible and where failure might mean further trauma, though it might also provide alternatives to the normative.

As these novels imagine the slippage between privilege and the potentials of failure and anarchy of childhood, they engage with abjection. They visualize bodies and spaces that are made abject by normative and exclusionary discourses and, similarly to their foregrounding of failure, construct performances of self-abjection as a way to resist. My analyses think along with Maggie Hennefeld and Nicholas Sammond's rethinking of Julia Kristeva's formulation of the abject, which Kristeva argues has an integral part in subject formation where the (abstract) child negotiates boundaries between themselves and their mother or as the sovereign subject regulates itself corporeally.[12] In abjection, writes Kristeva, "there looms ... one of the violent, dark revolts of being, directed against a threat that seems to emanate from an exorbitant outside or inside, ejected beyond the scope of the possible, the tolerable, the thinkable."[13] Abjection "disturbs identity, system, order. What does not respect borders, positions, rules. The in-between, the ambiguous, the composite."[14] It is a sensation that follows when the subject becomes aware of the impossibility of excluding the antisocial or threatening elements with finality. Different kinds of bodily fluids, the body's inside (like blood, spit, urine), might then show up to "compensate for the collapse of the border between inside and outside,"[15] and, through abjection, allow the subject to formulate its own boundaries. The formation of sovereign individuality through expulsion of what is seen as a threat to boundaries, according to Hennefeld and Sammond, has also meant that privileged groups of people have expelled those who are considered Other. In order to object to the erasure of those "abjected to secure the sovereignty of the dominant minority," these bodies can perform abject objection, the coauthors argue.[16] Hennefeld explores what this means in her analysis of abject feminism, which functions similarly to Mikhail Bakhtin's understanding of grotesque realism as it responds to the "confusing separation between inherently grotesque bodies as simultaneous sites of joyful collective liberation and individualizing abject alienation."[17] As I will elaborate further in what follows, we can see the engagement with abject objection particularly in *Ingenbarnsland*, where the child figure emulates the slippage between joyful liberation and abject alienation as she performs the figure of the anarchic child of the Swedish welfare state.

Taking place in the Swedish welfare state either during the era of continued growth in the 1960s–1970s or 1980s, when the welfare state started to become increasingly more neoliberal, and addressing experiences where the characters are not successful in lining up with Swedishness nor with the ideal Swedish childhood, the child figure in *Svinalängorna* and *Ingenbarnsland* focalizes fissures in the narratives of success in the Swedish welfare state. On one hand, equating success with capital accumulation is relatively universal in the Western world, and both novels make visible stories about hope for earning more money (as the Finnish labor migrants have moved to Sweden in search for better work opportunities) and the resulting disappointment, exhaustion, or alcoholism among the labor migrants and other excluded communities in Sweden. At the same time, Halberstam's theorization of failure comments more specifically on the United States, where success is often believed to happen to good people and "failure is just a consequence of a bad attitude rather than structural conditions."[18] In the rhetoric of the Swedish welfare state, failure to provide for oneself should not be possible. As Henrik Berggren and Lars Trägårdh poignantly describe it with their term "Swedish theory of love," the welfare state is supposed to make sure there are structures in place to provide everyone with the basic necessities so that people can be independent of other people and not indebted to anyone, whether emotionally, socially, or financially.[19]

As elaborated in the introduction, Pippi Longstocking became a figure and image to exemplify and embody this idea of success as autonomy and morality, but not only that. Throughout the neoliberalization of the Nordic welfare states, as Eva Söderberg concludes, Pippi also became the front figure of the neoliberal success story of Sweden that the secretary-general of the Organization for Economic Cooperation and Development, José Ángel Gurría, in 2011 called a "Pippi Longstocking economy."[20] Failing to line up with Swedishness is, then, particularly visible through the figure of the child, and in these two texts about Finnish labor migrant families, failure looks, on one hand, like disappointment, shame, hidden memories, borrowed money, dirty rooms and hallways, sweaty and leaky bodies that are considered to be abject—sites that, according to the idea of the caring welfare state as the "People's Home," should not even exist or be seen in Sweden. These same bodies, memories, and rooms, however, can also attain the characteristics of queer failure. That is, in both novels they can function as a way to disrupt clear boundaries between lining up and not lining up, between the wondrous and the abject anarchy of childhood.

Since *Svinalängorna* and *Ingenbarnsland* foreground the lack of finances and the realities of working-class people in Sweden, some aspects about not lining up with idealized Swedishness at the center of the welfare state could certainly speak more broadly to working-class experiences and the working-class childhood in Sweden. Indeed, much of the scholarship on Alakoski's and Olsson's works emphasizes how these novels also belong to the Swedish working-class literature, some scholarship more adamantly arguing that working-class realities are the predominant light in which to read these novels and others suggesting a more intersectional reading.[21] Satu Gröndahl has argued that Sweden-Finnish literature has predominantly been defined as "social-realist literature with themes of working life and harsh conditions of immigrants, characterized by power constructions and societal practices that marginalize minority languages."[22] According to her, this has also meant the exclusion of works dealing with the middle class or with educated and well-integrated Sweden Finns, a tendency that might have contributed to or drawn from stereotypical depictions of Finnish-speakers in Swedish media during the twentieth century as poor and less civilized. *Svinalängorna* and *Ingenbarnsland* engage with these stereotypical depictions as they imagine the entangled histories of working-class identities, poverty, and Finnish ethnicity in the racialized hierarchies of whiteness in the twentieth century.

MEMORY OF FINLAND AS A SITE OF NOT-QUITENESS

Many Finnish labor migrants arrived in Sweden during the 1960s and 1970s (particularly during 1969 and 1970, which saw the migration of about forty thousand migrants from Finland to Sweden each year).[23] They often faced prejudice and stereotypes because they were seen to bring with them working-class environments and because Finnish-speakers had been depicted in Swedish culture and media as poor, less civilized, and primitive long before that.[24] Rochelle Wright, for example, has argued that such images were popular in Swedish rural melodramas of the 1940s and 1950s.[25] While the Finnish labor migrants were talked about as having problems in Swedish society, as Marja Ågren has demonstrated, Finnish-speakers were at the same time perceived as proximate and familiar, migrants who would be able to easily assimilate in Sweden with the appropriate help from the state. Ågren also points out that it was important for the Finnish migrants to be seen as a minority in Sweden rather than as labor migrants.[26] This eventually resulted in various achievements for the Sweden Finns (as the minority is officially called now): opportunities for children to learn Finnish and receive some of their education in Finnish, the official recognition of Sweden Finns as one of the national minorities, and more efforts to revitalize Sweden Finnish culture and find pride in it, as Anu Koivunen argues.[27]

In her analysis of Sweden Finnish literature during 1956–1988, Marja-Liisa Pynnönen argues that many of the 1970s novels written by Finnish-speaking authors in Sweden depicted situations where Finnish children drew attention to the Swedish schoolteachers teaching a skewed understanding of Sweden's actions during World War II and that these novels often portrayed Swedes as "hysterically afraid of Russians."[28] *Svinalängorna* and *Ingenbarnsland*, too, engage with migrant memory narratives that differ from the host culture, but in their focus on children with Finnish parents in Sweden and the experiences of not quite being part of the Swedish society, they explore memory as contested and as what Michael Rothberg would call multidirectional—negotiating, borrowing, and cross-referencing histories that are only seemingly separate.[29] References to memory in these two novels are brief and easy to gloss over, but as these memories intersect with ethnic and class identities, they do have an important role in the novels' articulations of not-quiteness, particularly as experienced by the Finnish migrants in Sweden. That is, the child focalizers understand memory as a multidirectional site of not-quiteness where recollections of poverty in Finland, Sweden's moral exceptionalism during and after World War II, and Finland's participation in that war become entangled. This contributes to their resistance to rigid categories that are often upheld by fixed narratives of national and diasporic memory.

The child focalizer has had a prominent role in narratives that address the traumatic memories of the twentieth century, such as the Holocaust or World War II in Europe. Often, the child functions in these stories as a figure of innocence and victimhood, providing adult readers with a perspective of a witness who is not yet implicated by the history and politics. Writing the child, argues Susanne Baackmann, features often in postwar German literature that seeks to come to terms with the history of complicity, claiming the innocence of the child to either recreate "unknowing" Germans as victims or as a way to confront such problematic thinking.[30] Another common use of the child is to represent the generations who come after the atrocities and navigate the memories that are not their own but are passed on to them, as Marianne Hirsch shows in her influential work on, what she calls, "postmemory."[31]

Svinalängorna constructs several scenes of memory transmission where Leena is listening to fragments of the adults' memories of Finland, including World War II. Consistent with the traditional narratives in Finnish cultural memory, Leena's father speaks proudly of the Finnish soldiers in the war, while Leena's mother, Aili, and her friend Helmi describe their feelings of fear and shame during the war and when thinking or talking about it in present-day Sweden. Aili and Helmi speak for extended periods of time almost every day. They tell Leena to go and play outside, but she hides under the table or behind the staircase until they forget about her and she can listen. They talk about various topics, such as politics, sex, pregnancy, parquet flooring, and of not having enough money. Leena notices a difference between their conversations about these topics and when they talk about Finland. Before doing the latter, they pull curtains in front of the windows and start whispering: "Det var som att de inte ville att någon skulle höra vad de sa eller som att de ville gömma sig lite."[32] (It was as if they didn't want anyone to hear or as if they wanted to hide themselves a bit.) With that the novel visualizes the feelings of inferiority and shame regarding Aili's and Helmi's Finnish background, which are articulated in spaces invisible and inaudible to other people. In order to hear about their memories of Finland, Leena has to also make herself invisible as she hides under the table and listens:

> Då fick jag höra saker om Finland. Om hur det hade varit i Finland när mamma och Helmi var små och det var krig. Kriget fanns men det fanns inte. De sa att det var omöjligt att prata om det. Ingen frågade och det var lika bra det, för det hade varit jobbigt för folk att fatta om de verkligen berättade. Och svenskarna verkade ha så svårt att både skratta och gråta åt saker som var jobbiga. Det var nästan det värsta av allt tyckte Helmi.[33]

> Then I could hear things about Finland. About how it had been in Finland when Mother and Helmi were small, and war was going on.

The war existed and also it didn't. They said that it was impossible to talk about it. No one asked and it was just as well because it would have been tough for people to understand if they had actually told the whole story. And it seemed like it was difficult for the Swedes to either laugh or cry at things that were tough. That was almost worst of all, thought Helmi.

The war that both existed and did not exist, as Helmi and Aili put it, refers to the significantly different impact and understanding of World War II in Sweden and Finland and the resulting collective memories and affects regarding the war.[34]

Svinalängorna might be gesturing toward the problematic neutrality politics (or, more accurately, the public memory of those politics) of Sweden, which, as historians now have argued, were not all that neutral and meant implicit collaboration with Nazi Germany, resulting in collective feelings of vague guilt in the decades following the 1960s.[35] What Helmi and Aili's comments emphasize, however, is a general ignorance of Finnish wars in Sweden during the 1970s, stemming from the belief that Sweden's neutrality politics as well as occasional humanitarian aid or accepting Finnish war children during the war was sufficient. Furthermore, as comes out in their later conversations about working-class life in Finland, because of these politics Sweden was typically presented and understood as a morally exceptional country that was financially thriving (partly because the neutrality politics allowed Sweden to avoid high military expenses) and whose aid was supposed to be accepted with gratitude.[36] In reality, it made Helmi and Aili feel inferior and poorer—and they have carried those feelings with them as labor migrants in Sweden, cleaning the houses of wealthy Swedes.

Several memory studies scholars have explored the challenge of migration that lacks a common or shared memory with the host nation. Discussing the Turkish diaspora in Germany, which does not share the German collective memory of national guilt regarding World War II, Andreas Huyssen asks whether it is "possible or even desirable for a diasporic community to migrate into the history of the host nation."[37] Huyssen's discussion implies a temporal and spatial distance between the migrating and host groups that makes it challenging to take on memories that are not shared. *Svinalängorna* depicts an experience of migrating into a memory of another group that has been proximate, both temporally and spatially. This proves to be challenging precisely because of so much that is shared. Based on shared time and space, the proximate Finnish migrants are almost part of the group they are migrating into but not quite. That not-quiteness manifests itself in the differing and invisible narratives of memory, which are intersected with memories and present experiences of class differences and postcolonial ideologies. With this, memory in *Svinalängorna* becomes multidirectional in a similar vein to how Michael Rothberg describes it: Instead of promoting collective memories that compete with each other (exclamations that the Holocaust was the worst collective trauma or, conversely, seeking acknowledgment of other collective traumas by comparing them to the Holocaust), he suggests that memory is always subject to "ongoing negotiation, cross-referencing, and borrowing" and that memories circulate the only "*apparently* separate histories."[38] While Rothberg's examples that excavate intersecting histories of the Holocaust or the Algerian War do not focus on class, *Svinalängorna* imagines a multidirectional memory that includes the memory of poverty, combined with conflicting narratives regarding the memories of World War II and postcolonial history in northern Europe. The proximity of Sweden and Finland (both temporally and geographically) is significant in this intersection because just as memories circulate histories that are separate, they also circulate histories that are assumed to be shared but that feature deviations from what is shared, resulting in disorderly histories that dominant monumentalizations of memory seek to tidy up.

Ingenbarnsland, too, depicts the child who is listening to the intersection of different memories of war and poverty. Miira has access to these memories primarily through listening to her mother talking on the phone with Miira's grandmother, who lives in Finland. This novel, however, adds another layer to the entangled proximate histories. Namely, the child protagonist Miira pays most attention to the fragments of memory about her mother's side of the family, particularly her grandmother, who was one of the approximately 430,000 Karelian evacuees who (according to the peace treaty of Paris during World War II) were forced to leave their home region in the Karelian district, located on the borderlands between Finland and Russia. Or, as Miira has put together from the memory fragments she has heard, her grandmother escaped from Karelia to Finland after Finnish soldiers had burned down her house. As Anna-Kaisa Kuusisto-Arponen argues, while the forced displacement deeply impacted the identity of the Karelian people, who lost social networks and faced stigmatization, their difficult experiences were at first not visible or written about in Finland.[39] This had to do with the Finnish national narrative that, as Kuusisto-Arponen points out, emphasized the adaptation of Karelian people to postwar Finland, thus identifying Karelians only with the nation-state territory and denying them the ceded area. The narrative of heroic survival that has been remediated by the Karelian community has, at the same time, transferred feelings of rootlessness and placelessness to the next generations of Karelian descent.[40] This recalls how Marianne Hirsch has theorized postmemory—the relationship that the "generation after" "bears to the personal, collective, and cultural trauma of those who came before."[41] In this relationship, the memories of the "generation before" take over the memories of the next. Hirsch's writings on postmemory, however, mostly approach the child as someone who carries on the memories of their parents or grandparents in familial and national lines within heteronormative kinship structures. Learning about her grandmother's memory of Karelia, which is outside of both the homogeneous Finnish national memory and the Swedish national memory of the war (where both Finnish and Karelian memories are invisible), contributes to Miira deciding that she does not want to line up with either Swedish or Sweden Finnish pasts or futures.

Ingenbarnsland emphasizes the fragmentary nature of memories when they are passed on to the next generations and that are, as Hirsch expresses it, often mediated by "imaginative investment, projection, and creation."[42] Miira hears only fragments of her grandmother's memories, similarly to Leena, but she imagines them as puzzle pieces, which she tries to put together into an image that is not a still nor a photograph but rather a comic strip with moving places and people. Those moving images depict her grandmother in Finland, where some men fall in love with her and others tell her to leave Finland; the horror of war where her grandmother helps to send messages but is also infuriated because her friends are dying;

and a military commander calling her grandmother a Russian sex worker. The latter is the last image on her imaginary comic strip, and though Miira wants to know more, she does not want to ask, only to listen. Miira certainly has to use imagination and creativity, and she assembles many of the multidirectional memories herself.

When the text describes Miira and her family traveling on a vacation to her grandmother's place, it sets up a visual image of the child scavenging for the lost or half-spoken memories: Miira waits for everyone to go to sleep, and then she goes looking for clues about her grandmother's and mother's histories. She discovers a folder with newspaper clippings that have photographs of her grandfather being arrested, reports of domestic abuse in her grandmother's family, and a photo and text describing the children (among whom is Miira's mother) having to work long hours under the burning sun, which has resulted in burns on their backs. The last clipping is from 1966, when the grandmother and her children had large debts and had to go to the local church for food and alms. These new puzzle pieces are difficult for Miira to untangle, and she closes the folder. This gesture of closing the folder of memories functions somewhat similarly to Leena's reaction to the conflicting narratives of memory that her parents are fighting over: The more she observes her parents' feelings and memories of inferiority and their increasing drinking binges, the more often she covers her ears and does not want to hear any more. Miira uses the fragments of memory mostly to inform her position on the impact of poverty and the oppressive (often gendered) structures of memory, and she distances herself from the dominant diasporic memory of Sweden Finns and its gendered national identity as she pronounces that she does not want to carry on her Finnish heritage.

While Leena in *Svinalängorna* observes a clearly divided way of re-membering Finland and the war based on gender, Miira encounters the expectation, voiced by Finnish men around her, that emphasizes women's responsibility in reproducing the Finnish nation. The ideologies that equate the woman's body with that of a nation and see women's value primarily in giving birth to the new generations of the nation (ideolo-gies that are widespread across many cultures) were prevalent in Finland throughout the twentieth century.[43] Furthermore, Johanna Valenius's analysis of gender and the Finnish nation has demonstrated that while the most common symbol of the Finnish nation has been the Finnish Maid, who was seen as the virginal bride with blonde hair and blue eyes and who established the whiteness of Finns, the other, more negative figure was a grotesque old woman, the "Suometar-Mamma," who often wore traditional Karelian headdress and symbolized the negative racialized Finnishness.[44] Miira sees herself as different from the white Finnish women because of her mother's Karelian heritage, and other Finnish-speaking adults and children in the novel are generally portrayed as subscribing to the traditional gender roles and stereotyped expectations about Finnish labor migrants.

An explicit example of this features in the passage where Miira's Finnish-speaking classmate Jaana's father says that her developing "bröst kunde föda hela folket i Finland" (breasts could give birth to the whole nation in Finland).[45] This comment infuriates Miira because of both the gendered and national assumptions. In an earlier passage, where Miira sees that she also has started to develop breasts, she decides that "hon skulle aldrig mer åka till Finland, för barntiden var förbi. Hon hade bröst nu" (she would never again go to Finland because the time to be a child was over. She had breasts now.)[46] Neither Miira or Leena are thus obsessed or overwhelmed by the narratives of *postmemory*. The novels deviate from the assumption that the next generation would simply take and carry on troubling collective/cultural memories as postmemories. Instead, as they construct a child who does not quite line up with the normative ideals, the novels problematize the understanding of the child as an obvious carrier of memories. Instead of lining up with one line of memory, these child figures become aware of multidirectional memory and its connection to the feelings of not-quiteness that they experience in their everyday lives.

THE WELFARE STATE SITES OF NOT-QUITENESS IN *SVINALÄNGORNA*

The early chapters of *Svinalängorna* establish the experience of disappointment resulting from hope for a better life that ends up being unattainable for the Finnish labor migrants in Sweden. Leena's family is moving into a new apartment in the rental housing area called Fridhem, in the southern Swedish town of Ystad. Fridhem was built as part of the Million Program (Miljonprogrammet), a Swedish initiative to build a million new functional and affordable apartments as a solution to the lack of housing in the expanding urban areas. The Million Program, however, was often mediated and talked about as a problem area from the very beginning, although the focuses of the "problem" shifted throughout the later decades of the twentieth century.[47] According to Irene Molina, while in the 1970s all Million Program areas were depicted as dangerous and dirty in a variety of media discourses, from the 1980s on, this description has mostly been associated with areas that have a higher concentration of immigrants (particularly people of color) and their families. As the mother character in *Svinalängorna* finds out early in the novel that Fridhem is more broadly known under the name Svinalängorna, or Swine Rows, the reader observes the first indication of the impact of stigmatization to the people living in the Million Program apartments. This contributes to the Finnish migrants' already existing feelings of inferiority and awareness of the stereotypes of being less civilized and less clean, and it functions as an underlying reminder in the novel that hope leads to disillusionment.

We can see an example of the Finnish migrant hope early in the novel when Leena recounts her father practicing Swedish. With a strong Finnish accent he says, "Att vi bodde så pra nu. Suttio vem okk en alv kvatrat meter. Vi har ree rum och sök och ett stort haav allteles runtomkring hörnet" (that we lived so well now. Seventy-five and a half square meters. We have three rooms and a kitchen and a big sea right around the corner).[48] This description of the new dwellings, which often had three bedrooms instead of the two that had been common in the 1950s, echoes the optimism and hope for the future that one could see in the ambition behind the housing program that sought "to create an exemplary welfare state."[49] Leena's emphasis on her father's recognizable Finnish accent, however, gestures toward the novel's ultimate claim that in the eyes of the housing authorities, Leena's Finnish-speaking labor migrant family is seen as a possible threat to the exemplary welfare state. In the same chapter, Leena follows her mother, who walks around the apartment and lists the qualities of the newly built apartment: "Både varmt och kallt vatten, äntligen sa hon.

Äntligen äntligen."[50] (Both warm and cold water, finally, she said. Finally finally.) Leena recounts carefully all the good qualities of the apartment that they have not had before. The passage ends with her mother saying they are lucky to get that apartment and be among the first ones to move in because not all houses are ready yet, and she asks, "Tror du att du kommer att trivas här Leena?"[51] (Do you think that you will like it here, Leena?") The passage that follows this question immediately contrasts its optimism and hope. Leena's parents come home from meeting the housing administrator, her mother angry and her father sad. Her mother explains that the administrator had asked for a sobriety vow and explained how they should take care of the apartment with specifics that made it sound like she expected them to be uncivilized and untidy (as if they were pigs). In other words, from the first days in the new apartment, the family feels they are already expected to fail some of the most important components of the dream of modernity in Sweden: cleanliness and order.

Bringing out parallels between the descriptions of working-class dwelling spaces during the turn of the century and the suburbs of the Million Program as unclean places, Irene Molina claims that it was the working class and its living spaces that were to be sanitized as part of disciplining the deviating groups of the welfare state.[52] Thus, it could be Leena's parents' working-class status rather than their ethnicity that is the basis for these expectations. For Leena's mother, however, these class stereotypes become entangled with her background in Finland, which also has historically been connected to racialized stereotypes of uncleanliness and being less civilized. Through Leena's focalization that observes her parents' shame caused by the failure to be fully included in Sweden, the drinking binges that leave their apartment disarrayed are at least partly caused by the stereotypes regarding Finnish-speakers, which draw from racial/colonial ideologies. Commenting on the novel's portrayal of frequent cleaning, Sanna Kivimäki and Eila Rantonen argue that *Svinalängorna* exemplifies the integral part that cleaning has had in representing Sweden Finnish ethnicity and that cleaning becomes a symbolic way for the Moilanen family to achieve "moral purification" because they clean particularly intensively after their drinking binges and before the visits of social workers.[53]

Through Leena's perspective, however, the novel makes explicit that even though Leena's family cleans their apartment intensively when they are sober, the truly clean homes are inhabited by Swedes. Leena's classmate Nicke, who moves into an apartment in Fridhem with his mother because his father has been abusive, has a home where "det fanns inget damm" (there is no dust).[54] One of Leena's best friends, Åse, who lives in a neighboring apartment and whose mother also has problems with alcohol, has a cleaner and nicer home, at least in Leena's eyes. While Åse's character has been read as an example of how this novel primarily focuses on the lives of working-class people in Sweden, where both Åse and Leena suffer from poverty, the text suggests that Leena notices a difference nevertheless. The first time she meets Åse in the playground, she practices asking her to play in Swedish, and when Åse has gone home for dinner, Leena looks at Åse's window. Even though their balconies look the same, Leena compares her own window with Åse's, which has flowery curtains and matching flowerpots, and concludes that Åse's is much nicer. Another passage describes in detail how Åse's sister Karin shows the girls how to vacuum and clean the windows correctly. Leena thinks to herself that "när jag blev stor skulle jag ha det lika rent och fint som Karin" (when I grow up, I want to have it as clean and nice as Karin).[55] Swedish cleanliness, which seems unattainable, finds its culmination in a passage where Leena is staying over at Åse's place and Åse's mother's boyfriend, Sten, decides that Leena and Åse should learn more about orderliness. "Vet ni att ordning och reda är det viktigaste av allt flickor? Sten drog en hand genom håret."[56] (Do you girls know that cleanliness and order is the most important thing? Sten drew his hand through hair.) Sten looks like a general in Leena's eyes as he orders the girls around in the kitchen, telling them how to correctly wash glassware and to iron shirts, which they continue to do wrong, according to Sten. As this goes on, Åse looks increasingly embarrassed and Leena feels like she has to defecate.

Svinalängorna thus draws parallels between the racialized conceptions of the Finnish working class as dirty, abject, and uncivilized and the child protagonist's bodily reaction to those conceptions. As Leena's parents start drinking more, their apartment becomes increasingly dirty, the walls and floor covered with blood, urine, and excrement. Leena tries to clean some of it up, but the drinking days that are "längre än vanliga vecko-dagar" (longer than normal weekdays) become an "oavbruten gråblodig rörelse" (uninterrupted dreary blood-stained movement).[57] During those days, Leena's father turns into a "monstergorillapappa" (monster gorilla father),[58] who tears holes in the furniture, scrubs the toilet, and airs out the cat, the dog, and the blankets. Thus, in this description, cleaning the apartment becomes exaggerated and abject as the attempts of Finnish-speakers to resist stereotypes make them look more aligned with them. As with listening to the adults' hidden memories, *Svinalängorna* imagines the child protagonist in the margins of the apartment (underneath or behind the furniture) where she can be out of the way, both safe during conflicts and able to observe the contrasts between the hope for a better life in Sweden and the reality of a deteriorating everyday. The child protagonist feels in these "below" spaces that she might explode and disappear at any moment; she has stomachaches and nightmares; and she cannot wait to grow up, promising herself that once she is an adult, her life will be nothing like what she experiences here. Childhood in *Svinalängorna* is thus constructed as increasingly traumatic because of the entangled histories and effects of not-quiteness. Lining up with the ideal Swedish childhood is not possible because the child sees herself inhabiting a parallel timeline/another world, and the only imaginable escape is to grow up. From these spaces of "below," Leena takes on a somewhat traditional role as a fictional child figure who provides readers with a different perspective on the welfare state while remaining a relatively passive observer. The novel makes explicit that Leena is an innocent child who suffers because of her parents' feelings of inferiority and disappointment as working-class Finnish-speakers who are failing what they hoped to achieve in Sweden; this in turn makes Leena fail at what looks like an idyllic and safe childhood portrayed in the Swedish children's films that she sees on television.

CROSSING CHILD–ANIMAL BORDERS IN *SVINALÄNGORNA*

While the previously mentioned presence of *Pippi Longstocking* in Leena's life via adaptations on television (first aired on SVT in 1969) functions as a reminder of the ideal Swedish childhood, which is like another parallel world for Leena, when her everyday becomes worse, she says that it "var märkligt att bo ihop med en Häxa och en Gorilla när barnen i Bullerby gick på tivoli i vår stad" (was remarkable to live together with a Witch and a Gorilla when the children of Bullerby in [her] town went to Tivoli).[59] *Alla vi barn i Bullerbyn* (*The Children of Noisy Village*), another beloved and nostalgia-filled book by Astrid Lindgren, is full of idyllic images of children in ordinary situations, contrasting the utopian elements of *Pippi Longstocking* that intersect cozy images of childhood with supernatural strength and events. Writing about Olle Helbom's film adaptation, *Alla vi barn i Bullerbyn* (1960), which was likely the version playing on television in Leena's home, Malena Janson argues that the images of happy childhood in Bullerby are created by "adults' wishful thinking and feelings of nostalgia. Accordingly, just as in a large part of popular media and advertising imagery, *The Children of Noisy Village* depicts childhood as an endless playful game."[60]

The idyllic imagery of family and domestic spaces that provide Swedes with a safe and endless playful childhood in Lindgren's children's books becomes a utopia for Leena that the reader knows to be illusory. It functions as a reminder of not only the expectation to be, remember, and feel like a Swede but also the impossibility of doing just that. Leena, who does not share the carefree and idyllic childhood, functions in some ways as a grown-up when she takes care of her parents during their drinking binges, but at the same time she feels like she is not quite growing up. Whenever her parents are able to stay sober for a longer time, Leena says that every day becomes like a normal everyday, with school and family activities and Helmi and her mother's conversations like this:

— Barnen växer, sa Helmi.
— Ja, när växer de egentligen?
— Jag vet inte, men jag märker att de växer när smulorna under bordet blir färre.
— Ja annars hade man nog inte märkt det.[61]

— The children are growing, said Helmi.
— Yes, when do they actually grow?
— I don't know, but I notice that they grow when there are fewer crumbles under the table.
— Yes, otherwise one would probably not notice it.

The endless playfulness of childhood in the town of Bullerby obtains a counter-narrative here. While Helmi and Leena's mother say they can hardly notice that the children are growing, when Leena looks in the mirror during the most difficult moments of her parents' drinking binges, it seems to her that time is no longer moving, and she cannot detect any signs of herself growing older. For Leena, these brief moments of endless childhood do not mean an alternative to becoming, a conscious refusal of adulthood as a way to resist the normative expectations. Instead, she experiences them as a traumatic experience that is a result of her tragic everyday in the sites of not-quiteness.

The most intense moments of the traumatic everyday and listening to stories of shame and disappointment in Leena's narrative feature the family dog, Terrie, prominently. Early in the novel when Leena's mother talks about their humiliating meeting with the apartment manager, who treated them like "second-class people," Leena gets scared and hides under the table, followed by Terrie. Describing how it felt to be there, Leena says, "Vi hade svansen mellan benen och öronen slokade."[62] (We both had tails between our legs and our ears drooped.) Blurring the boundaries between the child's and the dog's bodies is a recurring move in literature that depicts children who experience marginalization and trauma. One of the reasons for this, as Anna Feuerstein and Carmen Nolte-Odhiamo argue, is that the categories of childhood and pethood are co-constituted because they share positions of subjection by adults and humans.[63] The interactions of pets and children can provide both emotional support within the subjugated spaces and engagement in "unexpected forms of growth."[64] These forms become possible because dogs (and other pets) do not grow up the same way that children are expected to grow up (meaning that children grow out of childhood but pets remain pets). Thus, as Kathryn Bond Stockton asserts in her analysis of novels from the 1920s and 1930s, animals, particularly dogs, have functioned as central markers of "queer child time" and as metaphors for lateral growth.[65] As a companion beside the child who does not feel like they can grow up according to the reigning cultural expectations and grows to the side of them, the dog in these texts is a vehicle for the child's strangeness. *Svinalängorna* incorporates the blurring of the child's and dog's bodies in moments that are deeply tragic and that illustrate temporal and spatial materialization of not-quiteness.

As it builds up its construction of not-quite childhood, *Svinalängorna* incorporates different kinds of child–animal interactions. The novel begins with Leena's account of the family having too many cats, who keep procreating, and of her mother having to kill the kittens. She agrees begrudgingly to keep the dog, Terrie, and tells Leena's father that instead of bringing home more animals, he should help at home and that they will not have more children either. Childhood and pethood are paralleled in this comment, thus drawing the reader's attention to how animals and children not only share subjugated spaces but are also seen as something to tame and control. In these early passages that are still hopeful and optimistic, Leena first talks about bonding with Terrie, playing with him, dressing him up in children's clothes, and imitating Terrie's behavior. The novel constructs this playfulness as a more conventional depiction of child–animal relationships that further contribute to the images of idyllic life. When Leena dresses Terrie up as a child and rocks him like her mother rocks her little brother, the dog functions as someone that the child has control over, especially as she pretends that the dog is a baby and therefore younger than she is. Dogs have been seen as "eternal children, captive outside of narrative, without past, a future, or a culture," a "minority without end" argues Kathleen Kete in her analysis of the infantilization of dogs (which includes dressing up dogs in human clothes) in dog keepers' journals of the nineteenth century.[66] *Svinalängorna* makes use of this image of the dog as an eternal child, a minority without end, as it imagines the traumatic and troubling not-quite childhood as both endless and disrupted at the same time.

The nature of the more idyllic child–animal interactions in *Svinalängorna* changes when Leena starts to describe her life during her parents' increasingly intense drinking periods and her feelings of disappearing from herself. Now she sees herself under the table with the dog, becoming like the dog. She is trying "inte tigga, inte gny. Slicka deras tår tills tungan torkade, nosen blev het av feber. Såg mig själv äta av det de tappade på golvet, delade det med Terrie som också darrade" (not to beg, not to whimper. Just lick their toes until the tongue got dry, and the nose got hot from fever. I saw myself eat what they dropped on the floor, I shared it with Terrie, who was also shaking. At night we shared a pillow).[67] This identification with the dog as another marginalized figure in moments of trauma brings to mind several other fictional examples, such as Lasse Hallström's film adaptation of *Mitt liv som hund* (*My Life as a Dog*), which features a child embodying a dog to deal with his grief of losing his mother and his dog, or Geoff Ryman's *Was*, a novel that plays on the themes of L. Frank Baum's novel *The Wonderful Wizard of Oz* and its musical film version. Analyzing Ryman's novel, Caryn Kunz Lesuma argues that in this counter-narrative to Dorothy and Toto's acceptance of the domestic space as safe, in *Was* Dorothy follows Toto's example of wildness in order to reject the overwhelming trauma she has experienced in her home in Kansas.[68] This child–pet interaction disrupts the trauma of domestication, but it also portrays a world where being non-normative is not acceptable, thus, Lesuma argues, illustrating the "danger in narratives for children that conclude by negating imaginative diversity through a return home to the heteronormativity and anthropocentrism of domestic space."[69] *Svinalängorna*, too, uses the blurred child–animal boundaries only temporarily as the experience of growing sideways to linear expectation, time, and space of becoming Swedish.

The temporality of an eternal childhood, of an expanded, never-ending everyday during the drinking binges is not liberating in *Svinalängorna*. Instead, for Leena it means remaining or getting stuck in the space and time of marginalization and not-quiteness. The ending of the novel does not provide us with a clear trajectory of how or in what direction Leena becomes/grows. It does, however, suggest a reestablished boundary between the child and the animal. In the last chapter, as another of her parents' drinking binges has started, Leena and her friends plan to spend a night in the nearby forest. Sneaking out of her family's apartment, Leena accidentally wakes up the dog, who is almost deaf now, and tells it to go back to sleep. As she and the other girls are sitting in the woods by the fire, Leena says she would like to stay in that space forever, but since that is not possible, she wants to move out of her home in two years, as soon as she is sixteen. With this passage, the novel maintains that for the not-quite child, imagining childhood as endless is oppressive and tragic. The only way to escape it, as Leena understands it, is to grow "up," and out of not-quiteness.

Pernilla August's film adaptation of *Svinalängorna* has, in fact, imagined Leena as a grown-up. The flashbacks to her childhood in the film are framed by scenes of Leena (Noomi Rapace) and her Swedish middle-class family—husband and two daughters—incorporating a trauma narrative in melodramatic mode. Leena's idyllic Lucia Day morning with her family is interrupted by a "ghost from the past"—a phone call from her mother, who is nearing death and wishes to see her. The rest of the film narrative of Leena's visit to her mother is disrupted by her memories of childhood traumatized by her parents' alcoholism and poverty, and it emphasizes that as an adult Leena is obsessed with cleaning and order. The camera lingers on her placing all the everyday items around her in order, and when she goes back to her parents' apartment, she cleans excessively. Typical of trauma narratives where the past is haunting the present, the film portrays Leena's resistance to deal with her memories and her disassociation from her childhood self. For example, one scene imagines Leena going to the swimming pool right after the initial phone call from her mother. As she reaches the end of the swimming pool, ready to jump in, she sees herself as a child, who is looking at her. The water in the swimming pool becomes a recurring motif that triggers her memories of her childhood, when being underwater and going to swimming classes functioned as a way to cope with the traumatic scenes at home. Water also functions as a connection to her mother, who taught Leena to swim. The incorporation of water, then, not only creates a parallel between her relationship with her mother and her traumatic memories of her childhood but also illustrates the film's pursuit to reconcile the familial relationships. While the child Leena's perspective in the novel also illuminates some troubling images of Finnish collective memory about World War II manifested in her father and his friend Veikko's patriotic drinking and nostalgia and pride about the "*sisu*"—a resilient Finnish spirit that in their speech combines alcohol, war battles, and violence, Leena's father's "Finnish spirit" in the film instead emphasizes his fatherly love toward Leena. The film thus focuses on the tragedy of losing a connection with both of her parents due to their alcoholism, which, in the film, is primarily caused by class differences.

Although the novel leaves the image of a displaced and invisible childhood in the Swedish welfare state unsettled, the film incorporates Leena's husband, Johan (Ola Rapace), as a Swedish savior figure to help Leena find her reconciliation with her traumatic childhood and with her mother and to provide a cathartic healing to the audience in the final scenes. In his analysis on whiteness in Swedish film, Hynek Pallas argues that grown-up Leena is made whiter by her "white Swedish family."[70] Pallas does not delve deeper into the racial construction of "white," which is not uniform. The invisibility of the proximate Finnish migrants in both of these texts is largely due to their looking like white Swedes but perceived as not quite as Swedish. The film seems to insist that Leena needs a Swedish healing force to reconcile with her past and to become a better mother to her children. Johan is depicted as a Swedish savior figure to help her do that, similarly to the classical metaphor of a white savior, who, as Matthew Hughey maintains, reduces and stabilizes the complexity of interracial and intercultural interactions into a narrative that is digestible and promotes sacrifice and redemption.[71] Johan takes charge of planning the trip to see Leena's mother and is there in each scene of Leena's hesitation to encourage her to continue. In one of the final cathartic scenes, where Leena is crying on the floor and explaining that she had felt guilty because of her parents' drinking and her brother's death, Johan says, "It's not your fault; you were just a child." Unlike the unresolved not-quite childhood in the novel, these words said by the Swedish man restore the idea of the child who should have been taken care of by the Swedish welfare state. The future of a safe childhood and family in Sweden is further restored in the end of this sequence when Leena has stopped crying and hugs her children as this final image fades into a white screen (ending literally in whiteness).

UNSETTLING THE WELFARE STATE
IN *INGENBARNSLAND*

Ingenbarnsland, which takes place about fifteen years later than *Svinalängorna*, imagines its child protagonist, Miira, from a Finnish labor migrant family in the midst of the changing welfare state. While *Svinalängorna* foregrounds the stereotypes that Finnish-speaking migrants faced in the Miljonprogrammet apartments, *Ingenbarnsland* portrays suburbs of affordable housing in Gothenburg that are inhabited by Finnish-speakers, white working-class Swedes, and an increasing number of people of color. Taking place in the 1980s, the story focuses on the rise of neoliberalism in the Swedish welfare state through the focalization of the child, who not only observes the disappointment and shame among Finnish-speaking and other groups of people experiencing a lack of success and being excluded from the welfare state society, but who also, in the vein of Halberstam's queer failure, actively resists success if that means capital accumulation and unfair advantage over others.[72] The child protagonist returns several times to the rhetoric of winners and losers as she maintains that she does not want to be a winner if that means someone else has to be a loser. As a response to the persistence of racial/ethnic/class stereotypes suggesting that she and others around her are supposed to fail and that they are abject, she often performs abjection. *Ingenbarnsland* thus unsettles the image of the child in the Swedish welfare state further as it navigates the tension between involuntary abjection and performances of self-abjection (differently from *Svinalängorna*, where the child protagonist primarily feels that she and her surroundings are made abject in the eyes of the Swedish majority population). For example, while Miira performs many aspects associated with the idealized Swedish child, symbolized by Pippi (she is generous, brave, and independent, and she questions social conventions), the novel situates her as a child who is seen as both inferior and abject because of her heritage. In other words, the novel resists portraying Miira as an innocent victim or a heroic child who would become inspiring for the adults by standing up to injustice. It finds the alternative to such depictions in a recitation of failure, grotesque, and abject.[73]

Ingenbarnsland is divided into three parts based on school grades: first through third, fourth through fifth, and sixth through ninth grade, thus emphasizing the coming-of-age of the protagonist, who wants to grow up so that she can escape the involuntary Finnish education and the resulting stereotypes and, at the same time, resists coming of age if that means she gets "ett vuxensamete. Bli(r) pervers" (an adult conscience. Becomes perverse).[74] By involuntary Finnish education, Miira means the Finnish-language program that the Finnish-speaking minority had achieved by the 1980s, which, ironically, becomes one of the sites of not-quiteness for the child protagonist. As she goes through the three school stages, most of Miira's Finnish and Swedish teachers expect the children from Finnish-speaking families not to advance academically and instead to choose low-paying jobs like those of their parents. Starting in the first chapter, Miira separates herself from the other Finnish-speaking children, particularly girls who are, in her opinion, too timid, weak, and who follow orders and rules blindly. When the girls in her class tell their teacher that she had fought her classmate Lasse, Miira's reaction is described as grotesque anger: As she thinks her classmates are traitors, she squeezes her pupils, lets out a "zombievrål som ekade över skolgården" (zombie roar that echoes over the school yard), and imagines that she could glue their lips together.[75] The teacher does not listen to Miira's reasoning that Lasse had called her and other girls "whores" and tells her that she has to stay for detention. Miira shows no intention of giving up, and on a paper where she is supposed to write "sorry, Lasse" a hundred times, she adds, "men du är kukhuvud och jag hatar dig" (but you are a dickhead, and I hate you.)[76] As she then has to take home a weekly report about her problematic behavior, she draws a parallel between fighting for her rights and the Finnish-speakers' struggle for the right to have some school programming in Finnish for their children. Miira remembers her mother's passionate speech of having to fight for the Finnish cause "med nävar och högafflar om det så skulle behövas" (with fists and pitchforks if necessary).[77] She believes it is really her fight against people like Lasse that matters and that the Finnish cause of sorting children into two different classrooms is unjust. Thus, instead of seeing the Finnish-language programming as a victory for the minority in Sweden, Miira feels that it has resulted in her being confined in a Finnish bubble.[78]

Miira's fight against forced Finnish identity becomes entangled with fighting against gendered expectations and neoliberal ideologies that she encounters. With this, the novel constructs a tension between performing the ideals that Pippi and the ideal child represent and persistently deviating from those ideals. Throughout the novel, Miira is adamant about not being called a girl or a woman (these categories are around her based on a stereotypical understanding of gender) as well as about not behaving or presenting like someone who has accumulated wealth and therefore thinks they are better than others. When her mother's acquaintance gifts her with a Barbie doll, Miira is deeply offended and bites the doll's head off, and when her father's friend visits and lifts her up in the air, saying how beautiful a woman she has become, she bites him in the head: "Det hade hon inte tänkt på förut, att hon fortfarande fick bita andra. 'Hoi' sa han och släppte ner henne. Hon tittade mordiskt på honom."[79] (She had not thought of this before, that she could still bite others. He said, "Hoi" and let her go. She looked at him with a bloodthirsty look.) In one of the many passages that follow, Miira is independently wandering on the streets in different parts of the city, and her response to people whose stares communicate disdain about her worn-out clothes and that make her feel "som en sopa" (like trash),[80] is to focus on the fact that they are dressed like "snobs" and that she would never want to look like that. Instead, Miira shoplifts clothes that are new but that would not suggest she has a fancy job and a lot of money. Being among her classmates makes Miira feel proud because she, and not them, has been brave enough to shoplift from the Angered center, but she also feels embarrassed because she knows that now she has made them feel "trashier" compared to her. As time goes by, Miira becomes increasingly invested in not letting people know when she has helped them so that they will not feel they owe her anything or that she will not have a "moral high ground" over anyone.

As Miira resists the normative understanding of success when it comes to both the neoliberal promises of wealth or the moral exceptionalism at the core of the welfare state promises, *Ingenbarnsland* makes clear that Miira is somehow inherently different (or at least she is made to feel that way) from the Swedish children and that this difference prevents her from ever truly lining up with white Swedishness and from performing the idealized image of the child. Similarly to the attempts to visualize the often-invisible racialization of the not-quite child in films like *Elina* or *Sami Blood*, analyzed in the previous chapter, *Ingenbarnsland* constructs scenarios where Miira becomes increasingly aware of anything in her looks that might give away that she is from a Finnish-speaking family. This includes her bodily features but also her clothes and hairstyle, thus reminding the reader of the performative nature of whiteness: People can often produce their whiteness through the things they do, how they speak, dress, and move themselves through space.[81] While able to pass as a white Swede, Miira notices that both she and her mother have dark hair and that Swedes and Finns are typically lighter than they are. In one of the passages, we follow Miira on her way to shoplift a book, a behavior she justifies as her way to resist the increasingly neoliberal capitalist economy that she finds herself in where people have to take loans to afford anything beyond bare minimum and have to pay interest on the loans so that, as Miira sees it, only a few people earn much more than others. Miira is not able to commit her act of subversion, however, because the store employees observe her more attentively than anyone else. Then she sees a woman who looks at her and who says, "Jävla zigenare" (Fucking gipsy),[82] and her child, holding her hand, repeats the same phrase. Miira reacts to this by thinking, "Zigenare? Hon såg inte ut som en maräng, men hade mörkt hår, var mörkare. 'Jävla . . .' sa hon, men kunde inte komma på något att säga. Blev ilsken och irrade iväg."[83] (Gypsy? She did not look like a meringue, but had dark hair, was darker. She said, "Fucking...," but could not come up with anything to say. Got angry and wandered away.)

Even though a misunderstanding, this racist comment makes Miira think about her own body and to conclude that she is darker than Swedes, which reminds the reader of her earlier observation that both she and her mother, who is from Karelia, look darker than "riktiga finnekvinnor och finnebarn" (real Finnish women and Finnish children.)[84] Though Miira is typically legible as a white child of Finnish migrants, whose visual ability to pass as white Swedes is primarily dependent on aspects like clothing or hairstyle, the racist encounter at the store establishes for her that there is something inherently different in her body. Sara Ahmed writes that "being held up" because of skin color, a name, or other feature (often for people of color but sometimes also for those who do not pass normative whiteness) "shifts one's orientation; it turns one's attention back to oneself, as one's body that does not 'trail behind' but catches you out."[85] The shift in Miira's orientation in this passage questions the idea that all white proximate Finnish migrants and their children who are on their way to becoming citizens can easily assimilate into the "sea of Swedish whiteness" and suggests that as long as their looks resemble in any way other, more visibly racialized minorities, they can be caught out. Being caught out, in turn, also means that Miira fails at performing the ideals—autonomy and standing up against unjust norms—of white Swedish childhood.

It is equally important, however, that this awareness of difference and reorientation in this passage is a result of a misunderstanding. While articulating the experience of some inherent difference in Miira, the passage simultaneously gestures toward the racialized hierarchies of the different minorities in Sweden, where the Finnish-speakers have more privilege because they are white. The woman calls Miira the derogatory term for the Roma people, who are among the five national minorities in Sweden, and although they have lived in Sweden for centuries, they are similarly often invisible in Swedish efforts and narratives of antiracism.[86] Though there are no essential differences between white passing as white and nonwhite passing as white, writes Sara Ahmed, the differences reflect primarily on the histories of structural racism and the subject's ability to move through space. With this and other encounters that Miira has when she is caught out as not Swedish, she becomes increasingly aware of the racial ideologies and prejudice regarding how different bodies (including white, nonwhite, and not-quite white) look. For example, in her interactions with her peers and teachers, she realizes that in the society around her there is a correlation between bodily markers like cleanliness and one's ability to have a job does not fall under the stereotypical jobs for people from migrant or working-class families. Even though the novel establishes that Miira actively resists thinking she is better than others, she frequently notices and is annoyed by the greasy hair and dirty clothes of her Swedish friend Vera. While Vera is at first her only friend who is identified as Swedish, and it is only through her that she gains access to other circles of Swedish teenagers, Miira maintains that she needs to take care of how she looks because otherwise she will always remain a migrant in the eyes of white Swedes. Miira's increasing attention to her body, however, does not mean she attempts to line up with the normative image of the white Swedish children or teenagers. As the following discussion demonstrates, *Ingenbarnsland* imagines the figure of the child who performs abjection as a response to the forced abjectification and failure within the welfare state spaces as it reorients the image of the ideal Swedish child/citizen who is anarchic and growing sideways but in a clean and predictable line.

ABJECT AND FAILURE OF CHILDHOOD

One of the early examples of the slippage between the wondrous anarchy and the abject in the figure of the child features in the first third of *Ingenbarnsland* when Miira stays with two different families for four weeks during her summer break, first a Swedish and then a Finnish family. When arriving at her first summer home with a Swedish family, Miira describes the neighborhood as completely different from what she is used to: The playgrounds behind white fences and closed gates are private, and the "grusgång av släta stenar och en stubbad gräsmatta med rakskurna kanter" (gravel path with smooth stones and a meticulously cut lawn with straight cut angles) make her feel like "en grovkantig bit från granitbergen i Gårdsten. Felplacerad" (a rough-angled piece from the granite hill in Gårdsten. Misplaced).[87] The feeling of misplacement is further emphasized by the contrasts that she notices between her and the Swedish children she sees playing there; she is immediately aware of her sloppy and worn clothes as opposed to their fancy, proper, and orderly attire. While Miira finds the Swedish children's playing "store" ridiculous and thinks they are more like "finvuxenminisar"(fancy mini adults) than children,[88] she also feels out of place and increasingly clumsy, "som en elefant" (like an elephant) as she walks through the rooms of the house,[89] has more food than she is used to, and accidentally breaks a glass while drinking lemonade because the glass is too fine. She attempts to teach the Swedish children games that are more daring, like running over the railroad tracks right before a train approaches, but after getting caught, she feels like the Swedish parents—and even their dog—look at her in a criticizing silence that is not like the familiar Finnish silence but instead is full of disappointment. All of this makes Miira feel disappointed in herself, in her clumsiness, in not saying anything, and because she has "fula sandaler, en ful t-shirt med hål på höger magsida och fult hår" (ugly sandals, an ugly t-shirt with holes on the right side and ugly hair.)[90] The disappointing two weeks with the Swedish family are followed by her stay with a Finnish family, who are depicted as utterly distant, less civilized, and aggressive (in other words, as a more exaggerated representation of the abject associated with migrants in Swedish media). She is attacked by the family sons and gets a deep cut in her finger when she tries to hide from them and wash herself in a nearby lake. When she has to sleep on a dirty mattress and hears the Finnish host mother tell someone on the phone that Miira is an "äcklig unge" (disgusting brat),[91] Miira gets up at night and defecates out of the window so that the feces slowly run down the walls, coloring the windows brown.

This sequence of events, where Miira feels inferior in the Swedish-speaking family, followed by being violated and called disgusting in the Finnish-speaking family, and then defecates out of the window, constructs an image of both forced and voluntary abjection. Similarly to what Hennefeld describes as "abject objection," it functions as a response to the confusion between different mediations of grotesque bodies as sites of liberation. In *Ingenbarnsland* the confusion is between child figures whose grotesque stories/imageries of resistance and growing sideways have become sites of joyful collective liberation for either the welfare state or for feminism, and the child figures whose grotesque stories of resistance and growing sideways are seen as alienating and abject because they do not fit the image of the Swedish white, self-sustainable child that Pippi represents. It does not matter that some of Pippi's stories, too, have darker elements, as *Ingenbarnsland* is primarily critical of how the rhetoric around the child figures in Swedish children's media has become idealized and unattainable.[92] Miira makes several pointed comments about such works, in a rhetorical move similar to that in *Svinalängorna*, where the idyllic life presented in several beloved Astrid Lindgren's books stands in stark contrast to the reality of the children in working-class or migrant families. For example, when Miira looks for Vera in the apartment, which she describes as drab, empty, and dirty, and where Vera suffers from domestic abuse, she sees a dog sleeping in the hallway and thinks, "som i den svenska barnfilmen där alla är glada och lediga hela tiden, bor i flera hus nära havet och har egna båtar och bryggor" (like in the Swedish children's film where everyone is happy and free all the time, lives in several houses by the sea, and has their own boats and bridges.)[93] As a response to the completely different spaces and circumstances that both Miira and Vera find themselves in, Miira performs various acts of abject objection: In addition to defecating out of the window, she spits in staircases, farts and burps loudly, laughs wildly, shoplifts, sends a bomb threat to the school, and accidentally sets the local wooded area on fire. One of the passages describes in detail how she is on the bus with Vera, takes off the bandage on the finger she had cut during her stay with the Finnish family when hiding from the violent children of the family, and tears off the scab. The finger has been fixed in a rush and some of the skin is growing wrong. Throughout the rest of the novel, Miira calls it a Frankensteinfuckyoufinger.[94] The finger with broken skin as a temporarily broken boundary between inside and outside becomes a reminder of Miira's attempts at crossing what she calls "barriers" within herself, which are a product of racial/ethnic/class stereotypes and policies and have caused her to see herself as inferior. While this means more oppressive and troubling experiences for Miira, her finger also functions like the good scar that, contrary to what we might think, as Sara Ahmed writes, should not be invisible. Even though it does cover over the injury, a good scar nevertheless exposes the injury, "reminding us how it shapes the body" and that "recovering from injustice cannot be about covering over the injuries, which are effects of that injustice."[95] Miira's Frankensteinfuckyoufinger features throughout the rest of the novel as a reminder of how the multiple injustices that she sees shape her body.

Though the child in *Ingenbarnsland*, then, engages in abject objection as an attempt to do away with the borders and barriers that separate her from Swedish-speakers and that make her feel inferior, the novel emphasizes the persistence of the borders. We can see one example of that in the chapter that describes Miira going on an extracurricular trip to England that is advertised as a productive way to practice English and get to learn about another culture. The only way she is able to go is for her mother to take out a bank loan, and both she and her mother share a hope that the trip will help her leave behind the inferiority and expected trajectories for a Sweden Finnish working-class woman. The first evening at the English host family's home goes relatively well, and Miira feels she has gotten rid of the barriers that make her behave or speak like someone who is less civilized or inferior. Once she arrives in the school building, she feels sweat dropping down her back and her hands are cold and wet. She is impressed by the straight lines of school benches in the classrooms and the equal distance between plants in flowerpots. Being at the school, however, makes her feel like she, too, is a "Neanderthal," a word she often uses about Finnish-speakers in Sweden, except this feels more serious than being a rough-angled piece from the granite hill because if she "betedde sig som hon brukade skulle de bura in henne i en barack på ett zoo" (behaved the way she used to, they would imprison her in a barrack at the zoo.)[96] Miira's hope for a chance to become someone else dissipates as the British schoolteacher also mocks her for not knowing the rules of the classroom. Miira spits in her face and leaves the school building, which she does not return to for the remainder of the trip. After leaving the school, she feels sad and ashamed because she has let "den delen av sig själv som höll i spärrarna" (the part in herself that held on to barriers) and people "i hela jävla Sverige, vinna" (in the whole damned Sweden win),[97] and because her mother had to take out the loan, and she is now going to spend the rest of her four weeks in England not going to school and not learning anything. Through this episode, the novel demonstrates how the not-quiteness that Miira has experienced in Sweden follows her in her body to another country. Even though the circumstances there are different and Miira is seen by the British schoolteachers as a Swedish child (she is, in fact, forbidden to speak Swedish with her Swedish friend because they have to speak English now), the pressure to become someone else and the humiliation in the classroom trigger her bodily memories of inferiority and forced abjection.

Another passage that highlights the persistence of not-quiteness in her body and how she is perceived takes place toward the end of the novel when Miira's family has moved into an apartment in a different neighborhood that is also part of the affordable housing project. Soon after their move to the new apartment, Miira comes home and discovers that her father has decorated her room with used furniture, discolored carpet, and beige wallpaper. Miira tears all of it down and asks her mother to buy new furniture with a loan from IKEA, which she promises to pay back with the money she earns from the cleaning job she has agreed to take on at their new apartment building. IKEA, the low-cost furniture store from Sweden that is now globally known, was particularly successful among Swedish working-class and labor migrants living in the affordable housing areas during the 1960s and 1970s before reaching the level of its international success, writes Ursula Lindqvist.[98] At the same time, IKEA has had a significant role in constructing, reproducing, and distributing the idea of "native, essential, and fixed Swedishness."[99] The company emphasizes its ability to create affordable furnishings for everyone more responsibly than corporations like Walmart but nevertheless outsourcing much of its cheap labor from the Global South. While in recent decades IKEA has sought to advertise its products to more diverse populations, as Lindqvist argues, through the way the products and stores are organized it continues to promote fixed Swedishness that supposedly allows everyone to enjoy the functional low-cost furniture but does not include people who deviate from normative (white) Swedishness in the welfare state that is, in the common Swedish expression, furnished by IKEA's founder, Ingvar Kamprad. Miira might not be aware of all of these dynamics as she gets ready to buy the furniture for her room in her welfare state apartment, but the novel implies that just as the exclusive and normative idea of Swedishness is promoted through the low-cost furniture store that is seemingly accessible to everyone, furnishing her room with the most typical Swedish products from that store does not mean she can become Swedish. Already at the store, Miira and her mother are reminded of their visible deviation from fixed Swedishness because they read as Finnish working-class people: After hearing Miira's mother say something in Finnish, the clerk at the store calls her a "finnjävel" (Finnish bastard) and Miira is ashamed of her mother's hairdo, which, in her opinion, gives away her job as a house cleaner.[100]

Furthermore, in order to pay for the new IKEA furniture, which her mother has bought on a loan, Miira reluctantly agrees to do more cleaning jobs at the new apartment building. The cleaning job that she is offered because of her family, and that she had earlier promised herself she would never do because of ethnic stereotypes, culminates in an exaggerated abject image of the Finnish-speakers in Sweden. Not only does she find herself surrounded by staircases and empty apartments covered with dirt, dust, dog hair, and piles of feces, but she also agrees to do an additional job in an apartment that, according to the apartment building owner, has had a "liten olycka" (little accident) in it.[101] Once Miira enters the apartment, she smells "bajs, blöt hund och pappas spottkopp" (shit, wet dog, and her father's saliva cup.)[102] As she goes farther in, each room in the apartment reveals more of the abject. Someone has smeared feces on the walls, and she finds a dead cat, remains of the dead person's face, and blood on the floors. Through Miira's descriptions, this apartment of the resident—who, based on their Finnish-sounding name, Ranta (which the owner of the building mispronounces), is categorized as someone from the Sweden Finnish community—makes up an exaggerated abject and grotesque image of the Finnish and working-class bodies as revoltingly deviating from the supposedly clean and tidy people of the Swedish welfare state.

The memory of the abject Finnish apartment and other instances of the repetitive cleaning jobs she promised herself she would never do because of the stereotypes associated with them is made worse when she finds out that she has not been accepted to the science-emphasis class in high school, resulting in another form of abjection: Miira starts to vomit regularly. Feeling the overwhelming pressure in her chest and stomach, she often stops at the local hotel to throw up in its bathroom. The routine expulsion of food from her body becomes another attempt to control abjection and to choose to perform it as a way to resist normative expectations. While the narrative of *Ingenbarnsland* describes Miira's behavior as something that could easily be categorized as disordered eating, she refuses to restrict her eating too much because, as she explains, if she starved herself to death, the local authorities would win. Although this novel does not engage directly with the racialized ideologies that associate white civilized bodies with control and thinness but nonwhite or not quite white people are often represented through bulging, out-of-control bodies, Miira's controlled restriction of eating could be read as an attempt to line up with the normative "healthy" Swedish bodies, as the previous categorizations of racially inferior Finno-Ugric peoples often included descriptions of less slender, bulkier bodies.[103] At the same time, the end of the novel asserts that Miira continues to fail to line up and that this failure functions as a way to subvert the power relations around her that she experiences as oppressive.

The last chapter of the novel physically and spatially visualizes Miira's resistance to line up. Miira is encouraged to participate in a local running competition. At first she does not want to do that, because she does not want to win when her peers who are also struggling with different problems in their everyday life would then lose. The only reason to participate, in her eyes, is the possibility that her white Swedish peers who think they are better than her might lose. Standing in the starting line-up for the competition, Miira makes a clear effort not to line up her body with the other competitors who are getting ready in their starting positions, because she does not want to be like any of them. Thus, she starts running later than others, but she speeds up and wins the competition anyway. Instead of stopping to hear the onlookers' encouragement or to accept a medal, however, Miira keeps running toward the forest (where her current romantic interest, Jan, is waiting for her). Ending the novel with Miira running away makes two claims about this child protagonist: First, Miira does not care about being honored as a winner nor, by extension, as an inspiring figure for the readers. Second, unlike the child in *Sami Blood* who in a sequence toward the end of the film tries to line up with the exact moves that the other Swedish girls are making in gymnastics class, Miira resists lining up. Living in a 1980s Swedish suburb and being a child of Finnish labor migrants, she shows her ability to do that in the changing society, and it imagines possible scenarios of failing to line up that function as an alternative to the normative growing up or sideways in the Swedish welfare state.

———

Svinalängorna and *Ingenbarnsland* tell their stories of Finnish labor migrants in Sweden from the 1960s to the 1980s through the figures of not-quite children who observe and experience racialized stereotypes, prejudice, and a traumatic everyday as their parents fail to attain what they hoped for in Sweden. Both novels imagine the failures that these children experience as possibly subversive in the way Jack Halberstam describes queer failure, which deliberately chooses not to line up with heteronormative and capitalist understanding of success. At the same time, as this chapter has demonstrated, the wondrous anarchy of childhood that Halberstam uses to exemplify the idea of queer failure is not always available for these not-quite children. These two texts explore how the privileged figure of the Swedish child as autonomous and morally superior (performing the joyful anarchy of Pippi Longstocking) haunts the not-quite children, whose bodies are to a varying extent seen by the dominant gaze (which they internalize) as inherently different, leading them to feel like their failures make them abject and grotesque instead. While *Svinalängorna* emphasizes the traumatic impact of this failure and abjection on its child protagonist, *Ingenbarnsland* incorporates self-abjection as a way for the child protagonist to radically resist lining up with the normative and to choose failure with pleasure.

CHAPTER
THREE

UNSETTLING THE FIGURE OF THE NOT-QUITE CHILD

As we have seen in the previous chapters, the child is a figure that recurs in a variety of texts about not-quiteness, colonial histories, and racialization as a way to challenge the idealized image of the Swedish child and to imagine alternatives to lining up and growing up or sideways. Most of the examples I have analyzed thus far provide complex and nuanced depictions of childhood instead of simply recreating the figure of the autonomous child with high morals whose growing sideways of cultural ideals would reinforce the exceptionalism and privilege of the idealized Swedish child. Focusing on the troubling experiences of racialization and forced assimilation or segregation of the almost but not quite white/Swedish minorities in Sweden, these novels and films imagine possible and impossible alternatives to growing up and becoming on a normative trajectory. In this chapter I will read closely two texts that extend the figure of the not-quite child to depictions of the generation of Tornedalians in Sweden in the 1960s and 1970s. This is the first generation to not experience discrimination that was as intense as their parents faced, although they nevertheless observe the persistent feelings and assumptions that they are inferior to Swedish speakers. Mikael Niemi's novel, *Populärmusik från Vittula* (*Popular Music from Vittula*), and Katarina Kieri's *Vårt värde*

(Our worth, 2015) explore the legacy of not-quiteness on children, and through formal choices, such as irony, parody, magical realism, or plural voice, they further explore both the privilege of these children who can increasingly easily pass as white Swedes and the slippages within performing and representing the exceptional Swedish childhood as growing up/sideways and childhoods that are not quite able to do that.

Niemi's *Populärmusik* is one of the best-known and widely read novels by a Tornedalian author in Sweden. Indeed, it was this book that made the Swedish (and other) readers much more aware of the Torne Valley region (Tornedalen) in northern Sweden, resulting in a significant increase in tourism to the region.[1] Thomas Mohnike writes that although there had been a strong archive of Tornedalian literature before the publication of this novel, it was the timing of *Populärmusik* that made it particularly widely read. Mohnike is referring to multiculturalism, which was increasingly talked about around 2000 when the book came out: "As a frame for Swedish identity, [multiculturalism] caused readers to feel a need for a novel that showed that Sweden had been multicultural even before the arrival of immigrants."[2] *Populärmusik* takes place during the 1960s and 1970s through the experiences of two children growing up in Tornedalian families. The novel has often been read as a parodic or ironic take on the stereotypes regarding Tornedalians and peripheral identities as inferior and backward and a literary engagement of the postcolonial history of Tornedalen.[3] Using humor to address the difficult history of that peripheral region in Sweden, it not only draws attention to the literary constructions of the not-quite child but also exaggerates some of the metaphors/images of not-quiteness and growing up/lining up to the point of absurdity. This does not mean that it undermines or questions the experiences of colonial and racial histories in northern Sweden but that it resists taking for granted the figure of the child as a representation of not-quiteness and becoming. Katarina Kieri's *Vårt värde* explores the life of a child during the same time as *Populärmusik*, but the child's Finnish/Meänkieli–speaking parents have left Tornedalen and never taught her their first language.[4] *Vårt värde* incorporates largely plural first-person narrative for the child narrator, a narrative technique that, as I will demonstrate, imagines alternatives to the exclusive singularity present not only in the forceful assimilation politics that the novel addresses but also within the constructions of both the Swedish child and the not-quite child.

Both *Populärmusik* and *Vårt värde* focus on a generation of children who navigate a changing era when the educational policies toward minorities are no longer as strict as they once were but who are also aware that their parents suffered from strict assimilation policies and discrimination. This generation does not face discrimination to the same extent as their parents did, even though stereotypes, misconceptions, and perceptions about their being inferior to Swedes continue to persist. With this temporal distance, the novels investigate not-quiteness that is, on one hand, rooted deeply in the bodies of the new generation and, on the other hand, becoming even less felt and visible because the children of this generation come much closer to fully lining up with white Swedishness as they grow up. As my analyses of cultural texts in the previous chapters demonstrates, this kind of lining up had been experienced as either impossible or as a traumatic erasure of identity, while growing sideways and resisting cultural norms was also often located in a space of privilege. *Populärmusik* and *Vårt värde* imagine a generation whose closer proximity to whiteness and Swedishness also means that growing up and lining up with it is more attainable and feels less traumatic. These novels continue to imagine the child/adolescent body as a site of pause and delay on the trajectory of lining up with the Swedish.

However, as this chapter demonstrates, they engage more closely with the inevitable lining up, which is not necessarily traumatic anymore but continues to quietly erase the minority identities. This anticipates a theme in other recent cultural texts about the experiences of the Tornedalians and the Indigenous Sámi people that take place in the twenty-first century—namely, the reality where one no longer has (almost) any knowledge of one's heritage or language and is searching for answers. *Populärmusik* and *Vårt värde* are particularly interested in adolescence and the changing, growing bodies of their protagonists in the peripheral regions of Sweden, particularly in Tornedalen. In this they could be read as Nordic examples of postcolonial Bildungsroman that, as Piret Peiker puts it, address "the *particular* problematics of modernity in a colony, centrally dealing with the ambivalence that modernity is seen both as alien and imposed, and potentially still full of emancipatory promise."[5] In postcolonial coming-of-age narratives, there are often not as many opportunities for typical formation and development of the protagonist, thus causing a different kind of sideways growth that is rooted in racial/colonial ideologies that see the colonized as never fully "growing up." *Populärmusik* and *Vårt värde*, however, explore what becoming/coming-of-age means in the second half of the twentieth-century Tornedalian culture, which has been read as historically colonized by the Swedish welfare state but includes the privileged history of Tornedalians who were also settlers in the Sápmi area, and the ability of this generation of children growing up in Tornedalian families to more easily pass as white Swedes.

The colonial history of Tornedalen, as discussed in the introduction and in chapter 1, is entangled with the history of the Indigenous Sámi people. Norrbotten County in northern Sweden includes both the Indigenous Sápmi lands and Tornedalen, where Tornedalian Finnish-speakers have lived for centuries, being among the early settlers to these areas. The 1809 border drawing that separated Finland (which became part of Russian empire) from Sweden split up both Sámi siida territories and the lands where Tornedalians now live, also splitting both of the minority groups as some of them were now inhabitants of Sweden and others of Finland (at first as part of the Russian empire and later the independent Finnish nation-state). In the late 1800s and early 1900s in Sweden, both Tornedalians and Indigenous Sámi people were expected to be eliminated in the settler colonial terms, whether through assimilation or segregation and erasure of cultural practices. Recent decades have seen increasing efforts of revitalization of both cultures. The use of the pronoun "our" that we see in the title *Vårt värde* (Our worth) likely refers to the new official title of Tornedalian language as one of the five minority languages in Sweden, "Meänkieli" (our language), and to the concept of Meänmaa (our land, in Meänkieli), which was launched by Bengt Pohjanen as a new name for Tornedalen.[6] In Pohjanen's conceptualization, Meänmaa blurs geographical borders and signifies more a "common cultural region" that includes different municipalities in Sweden and in Finland and exists anywhere Meänkieli is spoken.[7] However, as Anne Heith points out, when writing about Meänmaa and its Swedish colonization, which erased much of Tornedalian culture in the educational materials, Pohjanen suggests, "Tornedalians have a temporal claim on Meänmaa because they were there first,"[8] thus calling the region "our own land." This claim does not take into account the significant Sámi presence in the region nor the "Sámi claims that it is Sámi land."[9] Furthermore, as Heith brings out, while there is a consensus about the name "Sápmi" for the transnational territory among Sámi, the concept of "Meänmaa" has been controversial among Tornedalians. Though the construction of the not-quite child in *Elina*, discussed in chapter 1, seeks to make visible the experiences of racialization and violent discrimination of Tornedalians in the middle of the twentieth century, all the while resolving the troubling depiction of a suffering child and bringing her back on the trajectory to line up with Swedishness as a form of assimilation, *Populärmusik* and *Vårt värde* construct their figures of not-quite children in a way that makes visible the slippage not only between the images of exceptional child figures and those who deviate from these images but also between the entangled colonial histories of racialization and white privilege in northern Sweden.

As they imagine these child figures and entangled histories, *Populärmusik* and *Vårt värde* make use of formal choices that lend themselves particularly well to narratives of contradictions and self-reflection. The novels incorporate irony and parody as well as magical realism (*Populärmusik*) or plural narration (*Vårt värde*), techniques commonly (but not exclusively) associated with postcolonial literature, to rethink the affect and significance of childhood and the child figure in stories about becoming, colonial histories, and not-quiteness. Like the camerawork and editing in the construction of the gaze of the Indigenous child in *Sami Blood*, these texts imagine formal alternatives to situations where growing up and sideways are located in the space of privilege as they reflect on the fictional construction of a child to represent the experiences of not-quiteness.

POPULÄRMUSIK

The majority of the narrative of *Populärmusik* is an extended flashback that takes place in the 1960s in a Tornedalian village in northern Sweden and is told from the perspective of a child named Matti. Each chapter describes one or two different episodes in the lives of Matti and his friend Niila, following loosely the conventions of a coming-of-age narrative. Many of the episodes are about regular everyday activities of children and teenagers who go to school, observe adults at weddings and birthday parties, and develop a strong predilection for pop/rock music. Some of the chapters include elements of magical realism: occurrences that are supernatural or so exaggerated that they seem unreal but are not questioned by the characters in the otherwise realistic narrative. Matti's story of his childhood is bookended with a prologue and an epilogue of him as a grown-up. In the prologue he has been climbing and finally arrives on top of the Thorong La mountain in Nepal. A snowstorm is about to start, and before descending Matti feels an impulse to bow down and kiss an iron plate with Tibetan inscriptions that he sees on the ground. His lips get stuck on it, causing him to panic and recall a memory of getting his lips stuck on a door lock when he was a five-year-old child in the winter in northern Sweden. Then, as Matti remembers it, his mother had come to save him by pouring a bucket of warm water on the lock. There is no one to help him on top of the mountain, however, and eventually Matti decides to urinate to free his lips. Once he has done that, he feels that "(ä)ntligen kan (han) börja berätta" (at last [he] can start his story).[10] The prologue is followed by his narration of growing up in Tornedalen.

This passage from the prologue of *Populärmusik* features in several different analyses of the novel. Satu Gröndahl reads it as a metaphor for the emancipation of the Meänkieli language both socioculturally and mentally for the narrator, who grew up speaking primarily Swedish during the era when Meänkieli and Tornedalian identity were associated with inferiority and racial stereotypes.[11] Marie Östling discusses it as an example of grotesque realism, which she traces overall in Niemi's oeuvre.[12] She writes that as Matti bows down to kiss the plate, his mouth is a "high" part of the body, which is denigrated by its contact with the urine as the unclean fluid, and in the Bakhtinian spirit of carnival, this denigration is positive in that it can give birth to something new and better. Östling agrees with Thomas Mohnike's claim that the passage functions primarily as a foregrounding of the ironic tone of the whole novel but maintains that alongside the humorous is the serious question of life or death, of surviving the near-death experience and being able to finally start narrating. Mohnike understands the passage and the different narrative modes in the rest of the novel as a constant reminder not to trust the narrator and argues that the content and "being true to a supposedly Tornedalian identity" is less "significant than telling a good story."[13] Juha Ridanpää, in turn, also reads the novel as producing literary irony, but for him the irony produces primarily sarcasm that critiques Tornedalian and Finnish stereotypes and the social processes of subordination.[14]

Analyzing literary irony is complex because, as Linda Hutcheon famously has argued, and as we see from the multiple interpretations of the passage above, it can have many meanings.[15] Sometimes irony is not intended by the writer, and interpreting irony requires the understanding of sociocultural contexts as well as recognizing possible intertextual cues. My analysis in this chapter does not aim to provide a definitive interpretation of irony in Niemi's novel but rather to discuss how the multiplicity and critical distance created by irony make visible a slippage in the image of the not-quite child. Hutcheon writes that irony "happens in the space *between* (and including) the said and the unsaid; it needs both to happen" and that, therefore, the "ironic" meaning is always "*other than* and more than said."[16] Because of this, irony "removes the security that words mean only what they say" and is particularly well-suited for articulating multiple voices and experiences.[17] Irony is often read as a form of humor that, much like parody, provides critical distance from and access to difficult histories. Also similar to parody is that when exaggerating a stereotype, for example, in order to problematize it, both irony and parody can be seen to contribute to the stereotype instead of subverting it. Or one might argue that the problematization is undone by laughter and that, just like when the carnival ends and everything returns to normalcy, parody and irony often only reinforce social norms.[18] *Populärmusik* also includes moments of parody, and in the film version by Reza Bagher, many of the episodes are exaggeratedly humorous. In the film version of the prologue, for example, in the opening sequence we see Matti climbing up the Thorong La mountain to the sound of "Vallmusik kring Stångtjärn," a herding call known in Scandinavian folk music. As he reaches the top of the mountain in faster-paced jump cuts and notices the Tibetan plate, he makes an exaggerated gesture and bows down to kiss it. As he is struggling with his lips stuck on the plate, Matti's voice-over tells the audience that this moment brought back memories of his childhood, and the camera cuts to the extended flashback on a sunny day in Tornedalen. Isn't it ironic, both the novel and the film seem to ask, that Matti needs to go to this geographically distant space and experience an unpleasant bodily memory in order to start telling his story? It is, of course, quite canonical for narratives that recall one's childhood to exhibit vivid memories that are caused by something that one sees, tastes, or experiences in their adult surroundings.[19] The irony in Matti's narrative is ultimately that while the story he is finally able to tell is about a childhood in a peripheral, postcolonial space, this depiction of Matti as a grown-up imagines him as a stereotypical white Western tourist trekking the Himalayan mountains and potentially desecrating a sacred space because he, first, decides to kiss it (without knowing what the plate is or what it means for the local culture) and then needs to urinate on it in order to loosen his lips.[20]

The multiplicity of irony, its edge, in this passage sets up the rest of the novel as not only a narrative of not-quite childhood that challenges stereotypes of Tornedalians in Sweden and articulates their history with racialization and colonial ideologies but also as a text that is aware of its own privilege. As it constructs figures of not-quite children and significant moments of becoming/growing/lining up through irony, it incorporates the figure of the child to tell the complex histories of colonialism and racial hierarchies in northern Sweden and creates critical distance from the child figure as a representation of that history. This distance has a twofold function: On one hand, the novel challenges the exceptionalism in the imagined figure of the child who fights injustice by constructing moments that seem to be significant starting points for the child to do that but where nothing significant happens, and, on the other hand, it further elaborates on the figure of the not-quite child seen in other cultural texts of this book who cannot grow up or sideways according to the ideals for Swedish childhood. The novel also explores alternatives to growing up/becoming as alignment with norms as it attempts to solve the feeling of lagging behind the rest of Sweden with a temporal synchronicity with global subcultures instead. It incorporates the queer potential of the Beatles for the Tornedalian children/teenagers who start imitating and performing the image of these androgynous rock stars from the British white working class who exemplified prolonged adolescence instead of performing Swedish childhood—that is, until they grow up and line up with Swedishness nevertheless.

CHILDHOOD AND COLONIAL BORDERLANDS

The opening of the first chapter of *Populärmusik* sets up Tornedalen as a colonized/peripheral region while simultaneously problematizing the common use of childhood and youth as a representation of the not quite yet modernized and developed space/time.[21] Matti describes being five years old and observing the town of Pajala's old-fashioned dirt road getting paved for the first time. He remembers playing with the gravel and asphalt on the new road and adds ironic commentary on the promises of progress and modernization in Sweden: "Sverige blomstrade, ekonomin växte, och till och med Tornedalen hade dragits med i framgångsruschen. Utvecklingen hade kommit så överraskande snabbt att man fortfarande kände sig fattig fast man blivit rik."[22] (Sweden was flourishing, the economy was expanding, and even Tornedalen in the far north was being swept along with the tide. Progress had been so astonishingly fast that people still felt poverty-stricken even though they were now rich.) As the following chapters suggest, however, living in Pajala at that time felt like one was left out of or behind the Swedish cultural history and society and that one typically had to move away from Tornedalen in order to find meaningful jobs and a life. Thinking of the newly paved road, the narrator makes an ironic gesture toward the promise for a better future in the figure of the child, as with the new road, saying, "Fattigdomen skulle kläs i en svart skinnjacka. Det var framtiden som lades, slät som en kind. Där skulle barnen cykla med sina nya cyklar mot välstånd och ingenjörsutbildning."[23] (Poverty would be clothed in a black leather jacket. What was being laid was the future, as smooth as a shaven cheek. Children would ride along it on their new bikes, heading for welfare and a degree in engineering.) This image of children riding their new bikes on the newly paved road recalls examples in Western literature of the late Victorian and modernist period where, as Jed Esty argues, modernization happened alongside the maturing youth. The figure of the youth who do not grow up in these works that are set in colonial contact zones, according to Esty, could be read as a symbol of the "dilated/stunted adolescence of a never-quite-modernized periphery."[24] *Populärmusik* engages with the implications of this kind of symbolism in multiple ways as it creates ironic distance from the symbolic connection between childhood, growing up, and modernization.

One example that overexaggerates and treats with irony the image of modernization represented by children playing on the newly paved road is a passage in the first chapter where Matti and his friend Niila accidentally leave their village. After Matti has seen the new road, he wonders where it could take him and how big the world is, to which his father replies that the world ends in China. When Matti and Niila notice a group of German tourists who have come to see the local church in Pajala, they get on the group's bus to, as they think of it, travel to China. The tourists do not stop them because they think Matti and Niila are the bus driver's children, thus Matti and Niila are able to fly along with the group to the Stockholm airport and are close to getting on the next plane to Frankfurt until they are discovered and brought back home. This episode borders on the possible and unbelievable and is among the novel's several events that could be read as elements of magical realism. Similarly to irony, incorporating magical realism in some of the key episodes about growing up and colonial histories functions in this novel to exaggerate and draw attention to the figure of the child as a representation of not-quiteness. Furthermore, as Maria Kaaren Takolander has argued, magical realist literature is a "fundamentally ironic form of writing that narrates the magical as real in order to highlight and critique obfuscation of the profound traumas of colonialism."[25] Both irony and magical realism are often described as multivocal and as not interested in presenting a singular narrative of truth. The ease with which Matti and Niila are able to travel on the plane is narrated in this episode as completely plausible as it exaggerates the newly paved road as a sign of modernization that brings international tourists to look at objects that are important for the peripheral Tornedalian culture and provides a way for the children who are meant to bring a future to Pajala to run away. Their embarking on this adventure could signal the start of an adventure where autonomous and competent children go through something that inspires the adults to stand up to injustice/norms, but nothing significant happens through Matti and Niila in this episode. They simply fly to Stockholm and are brought back because Niila has a stomachache at the airport.

Another passage that combines colonial history, surreal events, and irony is in the chapter where Matti and Niila are at Niila's family's cowshed after school. Niila shows Matti the loft of the cowshed, which unveils piles of trash and, to Matti's surprise, a gigantic bookshelf full of religious and ecclesiastical history books in both Finnish and Swedish. Matti has "aldrig sett så många böcker på en gång, utom i skolbiblioteket på Gamla Skolans vindsvåning. Det kändes onaturligt på något sätt, rent av obehagligt. Alldeles för många böcker" (never before seen so many books at the same time, apart from in the library on the top floor of the Old School. There was something unnatural about it, something decidedly unpleasant. Far too many books.).[26] In the midst of this excessive material reminder of the settler colonial history in the region, which feels unnatural and unpleasant, Niila opens a reader about Li and Lo, a popular book at the time that was used to teach children how to read in Swedish and promoted traditional gender roles as well as racist stereotypes, and he starts reading an extract for their homework.[27] This frustrates him because it takes great effort to spell out the words, and he throws the book down the stairs with a "våldsam kraft" (violent force), prompting them to start throwing down other books from the bookshelf "under stigande extas" (growing more and more ecstatic.)[28] This ends only when Niila's father, Isak, appears in the cowshed and Matti runs home (Isak's physical abuse of his children is a recurring theme throughout the novel). The children's joyful destruction of books from the gigantic "unnatural and unpleasant" bookshelf could be read as resistance to settler colonial education, familiarly mediated through figures of children who do not want to line up with white Swedishness, but it could also be read as simply a playful activity that causes euphoria because it is entertaining.

These two examples construct images of not-quite children who seem to perform the ideal autonomous and competent childhood, but they are not exceptional or inspiring as their actions lead to nothing. In Matti's descriptions of the school system and life in the Pajala village, we see familiar references to racialization and inferiority that other texts of the not-quite white minorities in Sweden also have articulated. One of the most cited passages in *Populärmusik* comes from the chapter where Matti has started school and describes the realization that as a Tornedalian he is "a bit" inferior to the rest of Sweden. Matti's description of his school experience resembles the impact of colonial education on the minds of Tornedalians, something like the other examples analyzed in this book:

Med tiden förstod vi att vår hembygd egentligen inte tillhörde Sverige. Vi hade liksom kommit med av en tillfällighet. Ett nordligt bihang, några ödsliga myrmarker där det råkade bo människor som bara delvis förmådde vara svenskar. Vi var annorlunda, en aning underlägsna, en aning obildade, en aning fattiga i anden. . . . Vi hade bara oändliga mängder med mygg, tornedalsfinska svordomar och kommunister.

Det var en uppväxt av brist. . . . Vi var inga. Våra föräldrar var inga. Våra förfäder hade betytt noll för den svenska historien. . . . Vi kunde inte konversera, inte deklamera, inte slå in presenter eller hålla tal. Vi gick med tårna utåt. Vi bröt på finska utan att vara finnar, vi bröt på svenska utan att vara svenskar.

Vi var ingenting.[29]

We gradually caught on to the fact that where we lived wasn't really a part of Sweden. We'd just been sort of tagged on by accident. A northern appendage, a few barren bogs where a few people happened to live, but could only partly be Swedes. We were different, a bit inferior, a bit uneducated, a bit simple-minded. . . . All we had was masses and masses of mosquitoes, Tornedalen-Finnish swear words, and Communists.

Ours was a childhood of deprivation. . . . We were nobody. Our parents were nobody. Our forefathers had made no mark whatsoever on Swedish history. . . . We were useless at conversation, reciting poems, wrapping presents, and giving speeches. We walked with our

toes turned out. We spoke with a Finnish accent without being Finnish, and we spoke with a Swedish accent without being Swedish.
We were nothing.

This passage certainly articulates internalized colonization experienced by Tornedalian people, and it draws explicit parallels with the common rhetoric in colonialist developmental historicism, which saw colonized peripheral spaces as less developed than areas in the center of the progress of European modernity.[30] After this description of his childhood as deprivation, Matti concludes that in order to "become human," one simply has to move away from Tornedalen. As people throughout his life empty the village like "en flyktingvåg" (a wave of refugees), they feel like it is "frivillig. Ett osynligt krig" (voluntary. A phoney war).[31] Becoming human here, of course, means becoming Swedish, and the temporal lag inherent in the idea that one is not yet but can become Swedish/white/human refers to the normative and colonialist understanding of progress and modernity.[32] The ironic tone underlying these passages articulates multiple ways of understanding this colonial erasure. On one hand, Matti's narrative describes a trauma of erasure that features in several cultural texts about Tornedalian or Sámi memories in later decades of the twentieth century, where the new generations often have no memory or knowledge of that identity because memories have been suppressed for so long.[33] On the other hand, that one can become human/Swedish simply by moving south is a poignant example of privilege of the minorities who can pass as white Swedes. At the end of this same chapter, adult Matti's bodily presence disrupts the narrative of his childhood. He describes himself sitting in a train near Stockholm, on his way to his job as a teacher, and how for a moment he lifts his eyes from writing in a notebook that he had started in Nepal. He looks out of the window and eventually "(hans) blick vänder åter till Tornedalen. Kapitel fem" ([he] switches [his] attention back to Tornedalen. Chapter five).[34] This kind of turn to the adult narrator's physical presence does not occur elsewhere in the main chapters of *Populärmusik*, and it functions here as an emphasized reminder that this story is written by adult Matti, who can easily pass as a white

Swedish man and who might be sitting next to the readers in a train in the metropolitan area of Sweden.

ACCELERATED GROWING UP

A chapter that tells the most surreal story of the novel constructs an image of an accelerated growing up that functions as an ironic take on growing up and out of not-quiteness. It is a hot summer day and Matti goes into an old shed by their school building and hides there from the school caretaker. He finds an old furnace and climbs into it. Imagining that it feels like being a fetus, as if the furnace is hatching him and he is its child, Matti tucks his chin to his knees. He feels both safe and ashamed because he is doing something that is not allowed, "förrådde någon, min mor kanske" (betraying someone, maybe [his] mother.)[35] After the caretaker has come in to look for him and has closed the furnace door, Matti realizes he is stuck and that no one can hear him. For the following couple of days, his body hurts and he is thirsty, until he starts losing the sense of time and notices that the days are getting shorter and colder. He sleeps through most of the winter, and once spring arrives, he feels that his clothes have gotten too small for him. He continues to grow as the years go by, and his body fills the furnace until there is no more space left. One night the furnace cracks open like an egg, and he pushes himself out. He looks at his body and sees that he has grown up. As he walks through the village in the winter evening, he finds four young boys sleeping at a crossroad. After seeing that one of the boys is himself, Matti lies down next to them to wait for them to wake up.

This passage, which could be read as a dream or as a surreal/magical event, creates ironic and parodic distance from different depictions of growing up. It reimagines the nostalgic longing to go back to the womb, which in psychoanalytic theories has often been described as a frequent starting point for nostalgia—a place where everyone has been but cannot return to.[36] Instead of producing nostalgia for Matti, however, the passage sees him actually reliving the growth in something similar to a womb, where he can survive without food or water, a place he can leave only after he has grown enough to make it burst open. It also reflects on Matti's desire to grow up quickly so that he can "become human" after he has left Tornedalen; indeed, this episode accelerates his growing up to the point of absurdity. Drawing parallels with hatching an egg, the passage imagines a blurring of boundaries between Matti and other materialities—the animal world and the matter of the furnace are both included in this fantasy as the environment that gives birth to him. When he is climbing into the furnace, Matti describes the smell of metal, oxide, and old fires, and he feels the soot and clumps of rust with his fingers. As he gets stuck in the furnace and his body starts filling it, his human body receives nutrition from the matter of the furnace; he does not need food or water as he is in there for several years. At the same time, once he is out of the furnace, he is not like a baby or a duckling or a machine, but instead he sees on his body signs of having grown up and of no longer being a child. Differently from the traumatic prolonged childhood imagined through the blurred boundaries between the child and the dog in *Svinalängorna*, discussed in chapter 2, then, Matti's experience of blurred boundaries between the child and the more-than-human world does not prolong his childhood but instead accelerates his growing up. In the following chapter, as he then goes back to his child body and the regular narrative of the novel continues, moving slowly toward his growing up, the expected temporality of growing up is restored. This episode, however, briefly disrupts that temporality to imagine alternatives to the privileged spaces of growing up or sideways as the Swedish child in the space that at the same time stretches out and dissolves the material boundaries of the child's body. That this alternative reads as something fantastical, surreal, or dreamlike suggests that a different kind of growing up is experienced as precisely that: impossible.

Bagher's film version of *Populärmusik* makes some significant changes when adapting this episode while it, too, emphasizes the speed of growing up in the furnace. First, instead of Matti (Niklas Ulvarson), it is Niila (Tommy Vallikari) who climbs into the furnace, and once he emerges out of it, both Matti and Niila are several-years-older teenagers, played by older actors (Max Enderfors and Andreas af Enehielm). The furnace sequence thus provides the film with a convenient transition to change the actors and accelerate the characters' growth from young children to teenagers. The sequence itself stands out as a disruption not only of the narrative but also of the largely realistic comedy of the film. The opening shot of the sequence shows Niila in the darkness of the furnace, and then the camera cuts to fast-paced shots that cross-cut Niila as a child, the Northern Lights, reindeer, the ice breaking, and the rushing waters of the Torne River, Niila as a teenager, and Matti as a teenager writing on a typewriter about the time when he kissed Niila to show him how a girl had kissed him earlier. "Smaken av en pojkes kyss" (The taste of a boy's kiss) is a line that is taken from the novel and functions in the film as a way to emphasize that these children are not only queer in the sense that they deviate from normative ideas and expectations in the Tornedalian community but potentially also referring to their sexual orientation.[37] There is no explicit commentary on that in the novel or in the film version, and while Matti has a few sexual encounters with women, neither version attempts to categorize their sexuality in any strict way.

The incorporation of snap zoom and fast-paced cuts in the furnace sequence exaggerate the speed at which Niila grows older. With this, the film both visualizes and embelllishes the image of Niila as a not-quite child who, similarly to the child figures analyzed in the other chapters of this book, realizes that while childhood might be the only time/space where one does not have to have a specific identity category, growing up also signifies a hope to escape not-quiteness, even if that means lining up with the dominant culture. Thus, while keeping its irony and parody, the film, too, refers to the serious impacts of colonial history: In one of the later sequences of the film version, when Niila impulsively leaves the group of teenagers to hitchhike to Stockholm, he says that Pajala is not even located in Sweden because anyone living north of Luleå is not really included in the Swedish society. The speed of growing up in the furnace visualizes the experience of children who feel as if they are already taking on a role of an adult because childhood as a safe or cozy space is a privileged position they do not possess; at the same time, the speed of it gestures toward an impossibility of actually growing up to line up. For Matti in the novel, the furnace provides an expanded moment that temporarily resists temporal, spatial, and biological boundaries and imagines an acceleration of growing up as something fantastical, but for Niila in the film, there is no going back to the predictable trajectory and temporality of growing up.

In addition to implying the impossibility of growing up and lining up, this fantastical/magical episode is among several passages in the novel that undo normative lines and categories, particularly when it comes to gender and sexuality. Magical realist texts, as shown by Wendy B. Faris and others, lend themselves particularly well to questioning conventional understandings of identity and spatiality, enabling contradictory forces and lines to coexist.[38] Another episode that parodies and challenges normative images related to growing up through its use of the magical in *Populärmusik* is Matti and Niila's encounter with Russi-Jussi, a peddler who was born in Finland when it was still part of czarist Russia (before 1917) and whose androgynous body is the cause of fear and disdain in the village. Matti and Niila decide to visit Russi-Jussi as the last resort to help Niila get rid of his nightmares, which feature his dead grandmother trying to kill him and which leave him with scratch marks on his throat after he wakes up. The chapter includes Russi-Jussi's origin story, which explains his androgynous body with a Sámi spell. As Matti narrates it, Russi-Jussi was taken to a Soviet labor camp after he had moved to Soviet Russia because he had believed in the promises of communism (as do several other Tornedalian characters in the book); he met other Tornedalian and Finnish communists who were all sent to a labor camp because they were considered to be foreign spies, and among them was a Sámi man. Before the latter died, he advised Russi-Jussi to freeze his body, break off his left small finger, which has all of his powers, and swallow it. Following these instructions, Russi-Jussi was able to turn himself into a woman and escape from the prison. His trip back to northern Finland and eventually Swedish Tornedalen, however, lasted a long time and, therefore, he was not able to turn himself completely back to a man's body. Instead, Russi-Jussi looks mostly like a man but often wears women's clothes and, at times, has a woman's body. Jussi's advice to Niila that he should cut off his grandmother's penis when he sees her again and the subsequent hallucination that Niila and Matti share, where Niila fights his grandmother's ghost and is eventually able to cut off her penis, create another ironic/parodic image of common understandings of childhood development during the twentieth century: Marie Östling reads this chapter as an example of the grotesque in gender and sexuality, as a depiction of Freud's *unheimlich* and penis envy, and as a reference to folktales where, in order for the hero of the tale to go through transformation and grow up, the old has to be buried.[39] In line with the rest of the novel, however, the description of Matti and Niila's encounter with Russi-Jussi is ironic as it doubles the stereotypical depictions of the Sámi as spell casters, Tornedalians and Finns as supporters of communism, and people with non-normative gender identities as "under a spell" to create critical distance from such thinking and also to draw attention to the spreading of these ideas among the minorities themselves.

Along with this construction of irony and parody, the chapter's ending, where Matti says that after their fight and victory over Niila's grandmother's ghost both of them got their first pubic hairs, further parodies the idea that in order to grow up and take on the normative features of one's assigned gender/sexuality, one needs to metaphorically castrate the phallic mother. While the novel does not make any explicit references to the popular psychoanalytic theories of the twentieth century, it complicates gendered expectations for growing up as a Tornedalian man in Sweden based on normative/linear assumptions. Instead, as I demonstrate in what follows, the novel's focus on the subversive potential of pop/rock music, particularly of the Beatles, queers those expectations on the child. It constructs a more cosmopolitan lining up that is removed from the expectation to align oneself with being Swedish or Tornedalian. As the title of the novel suggests, popular music becomes localized in Tornedalen through Matti and Niila, but the novel also plays with the idea that their growing up and lining up is a shared experience with the rest of the white Western world.

POPULAR MUSIC AND QUEER NOT-QUITENESS

In its exaggeration and exploration of alternative ways to imagining adolescence as a time and space of becoming, *Populärmusik* incorporates the history and impact of pop/rock music, particularly the subversive potential of the Beatles. Starting from the first chapter, where Matti ironizes the symbolic connection of childhood and modernity with the image of a newly paved road and accidentally leaving Pajala, he also describes going to his sister's room and playing her Elvis Presley record for the first time. Matti associates the sound on the record with the road-building machines: "Det var framtiden. Så där lät den. Musik som liknade vägmaskinernas råmande, ett slammer som inte tog slut, ett larm som ledde mot horisontens purpurröda soluppgång."[40] (This was the future. This was what it sounded like. Music like the bellowing of the road-building machines, a never-ending clatter, a commotion that roared away toward the crimson sunrise on the far horizon.) After Niila receives the Beatles record from his relatives who live in the United States and have come to Niila's grandmother's funeral, Matti and Niila become infatuated with the music, start imitating the performances of the Beatles, and later form a band playing their covers. The Beatles record gives them access to Matti's older sister's friend group and brings them fame in school and the town. The first time Matti and Niila listen to the record, Matti describes the experience as magical, as if there were no more oxygen and they were thrown into the ceiling, feeling the rhythm of music pulse through their bodies. In the same evening, they are watching the ice breakup of the Torne River, an annual sight important in Tornedalian culture. Matti describes the ice that is about to break as something that one cannot quite see but feels instead, as there is a general rhythm of the water bulging, about to break free, surrounding one like music: "Och till sist märker man hur bron börjar röra sig, den lossnar, den börjar stånga sig uppströms älven som en kolossal isbrytare, man står i fören medan den stampar sig fram genom packisen med fruktansvärd kraft i begynnelsen av en lång och äventyrlig resa.—*Rock 'n' roll music*! skriker jag till Niila. Han fattar."[41] (And then we feel the bridge getting dragged away from its foundations, it's melting away, it starts to swing around upstream like a colossal icebreaker, we stand forward as it barters its way through the pack ice, enormously powerful, at the start of a long and adventurous journey. "*Rock 'n' roll music!*" I yell to Niila. He knows what I mean.)

Connecting the experience of rock music and the ice breaking of the Torne River makes the sound of the Beatles, who have represented cultural globalization as well as subversive youth culture, feel familiar and localized, all the while parodying the localization of this music and its role in the lives of the Tornedalian children. Though they also listen to and mimic Elvis, it is the novelty and modernity associated with the Beatles that becomes important in feeling a sense of synchronicity with the "rest of the world," which had not been the case before. "Det var långt mellan Pajala och världen" (It was a long way from Pajala to the rest of the world), writes Matti when he recounts eventually watching Elvis Presley's several-years-old concert on Swedish television.[42] While the lateness of the Presley concert refers to the feeling of lagging behind, which is common for depictions of marginal, (post-)colonial spaces, the Beatles music provides a sense of shared modernity. Performing the image of the Beatles, however, makes the resistance to normative lining up more cosmopolitan; it feels like a shared and synchronous experience with global subcultures, an alternative to the understanding that the Tornedalian minority is temporally behind the progress of Swedish modernity and that only after they have grown up and left the village have they become human. In its humorous and ironic tone, the novel creates multiple episodes where the Tornedalian teenagers mimic and perform the image of the Beatles. At first it is just Matti and Niila in Matti's shed, using random items as makeshift guitars and microphones. Together with two other classmates, they form a band, mimicking the motions and sound of the Beatles. Though their first performances are not musically successful, they become popular among the local youth, receiving screams from teenage girls that mimic the famous screams that the Beatles received on the *Ed Sullivan Show* and after, and earning disdain from some in the older generations (particularly Niila's father, who does not allow him to play). Differently from a common tendency in theories about subcultures and political mobilization to remain "trapped in the oedipal framework that pits the subculture against the parent culture,"[43] as Jack Halberstam argues, however, *Populärmusik* goes beyond imagining subculture, specifically pop/rock music as the binary of adolescence and adulthood. For Matti and Niila, imitating the performances of the Beatles and learning to play rock music functions as a way to imagine alternative ways of being Tornedalian.

More specifically, their love for music prompts Matti and Niila to discuss the gendered meaning of rock music in the Tornedalian community and what playing music might say about their sexuality and gender. First, Matti describes how Tornedalian culture only values creativity that is efficient and beneficial. This includes pastimes like fishing or wood carving, which, as Matti observes, are expected from men in Tornedalen. He describes how the typical Tornedalian men need to always have more housework or renovation tasks because with too much free time they become violent and unpleasant toward their families. Doing music is not considered "useful" in Tornedalian culture, even though when the band plays at Matti's grandfather's birthday party, the guests are emotionally moved and ask them to play more. Niila's father never accepts his playing music, and Matti and Niila discuss whether playing music would be considered *knapsu*, a Tornedalian word for a "feminine man." Matti eventually concludes that while rock music is more often played by men and that it looks "aggressivt manlig" (aggressively manly),[44] it is still probably knapsu because it is not equal to a day of hard physical labor in the forest. Throughout the novel, it is older men in Matti's life who use that word to criticize the changing society, and as Matti puts it, one of the most important goals of a Tornedalian man was to prevent being called knapsu. In the end, Matti concludes that because they cannot stop playing music, they are just going to be knapsu.

Focusing on the music and image of the Beatles allows the novel to explore the possibility of growing sideways, which has nothing to do with the privileged image of the Swedish child. Being in their early twenties when they made their first appearance on the *Ed Sullivan Show* in 1964, writes Sasha Geffen, the Beatles exemplified a queer resistance to growing up that was not just a phase of adolescence but something that lasted longer.[45] The rock musical *A Hard Day's Night*, as Geffen demonstrates, focuses on the Beatles as "four men in their twenties who refused to grow up and enter the straight world."[46] The androgynous sexuality of the Beatles and Beatlemania both "posed a threat to traditional American masculinity" and challenged gendered expectations; they were "boys emulating girls who have grown tired of gender scripts."[47] Performing this image allows Matti and Niila in *Populärmusik* to imagine an alternative to growing up and out of not-quiteness, and their mimicking of the androgynous pop stars also disturbs the problematic depiction of

Russi-Jussi's androgynous body. This alternative prolonged adolescence promises an affiliation/synchronicity with something that is more cosmopolitan. Through the novel's ironic and parodic tone, however, the reader is reminded of the slippage in this alternative—namely, that lining up with this cosmopolitan identity actually just means lining up with whiteness. While significant in contributing to queer subcultures, the Beatles music did, as Geffen points out, borrow much from Black musicians, whose new forms of music were not able to reach broader audiences because of the racist structures of American society in the 1960s, and the Beatles' "gender transgressions arose not from direct innovation but from the repackaging of black musical idioms into a group of pretty white English boys."[48]

As we find out in the epilogue of the novel, most of the children from Matti's village have grown up and lined up with white Swedishness. The voice of adult Matti, who lives near Stockholm, where he is writing his story, tells the reader that he sometimes goes back to the Pajala village when homesickness gets too strong. He looks over the landscape and reminisces about the many children who at one point "shared his world" and have now become engineers, business managers, or Swedish teachers in Sundbyberg (near Stockholm) like himself, "med en saknad, ett vemod (han) aldrig helt lyckats bemästra" (with a longing, a sadness that he has never been able to overcome).[49] This ending suggests, then, that despite the alternative potential of lining up with the queer androgynous pop band, Matti has, just like his peers from Tornedalen, lined up with white Swedishness, and his longing and sadness are the results of the assimilation process that has successfully erased something in his identity.

VÅRT VÄRDE

Similarly to *Populärmusik*, through its child figure Katarina Kieri's novel *Vårt värde* explores the impact of not-quiteness on the generation that is removed from the more explicit and violent colonialist practices and ideologies of northern Sweden. The narrative is told from the perspective of a child whose parents have left the Finnish-speaking villages in Tornedalen to live in the Swedish-speaking towns but who frequently visit their Finnish-speaking relatives and villages. The narrator of *Vårt värde* describes, quite conventionally for accounts of those who have grown up between two or more cultures, how she feels foreign in both Finnish-speaking villages and in the Swedish towns where she has spent most of her life. Because of her parents' history with forced assimilation, she does not speak Finnish/Meänkieli and is not able to participate in conversations with some of her family members and friends; she also registers Swedish television and radio programs as mocking Tornedalian people, not really understanding their culture, where exactly Tornedalen is located, or anything about the colonial history in northern Sweden. The child narrator conveys several times that her parents' childhood was drastically different from hers because her parents were subject to oppression at school and had to work from an early age, thus not really having a childhood at all. With this comparison of their childhoods, the narrator—who describes being able to play instead of having to work at a young age, have money for dental work, or be able to simply walk around and pretend to be a Swedish pop singer—draws attention to the precarious childhoods of the past and how that experience has changed for many by the 1960s and 1970s. While her life differs significantly from her parents, who had "morbröder som sålts på auktion i seklets början" (uncles who were sold on the auction in the beginning of the century),[50] she is also aware that the shame and inferiority have been passed on to her body, which includes feeling that she is not quite suitable or worthy (a word that figures prominently throughout the novel) enough for either of the cultures.

Differently from the other novels and films discussed in this book, which construct the figure of the not-quite child through mostly prosaic descriptions of the struggles and everyday life of these minorities, the narrative of *Vårt värde* is more poetic. Instead of a straightforward plot, each chapter combines short episodes of the narrator going on trips with her parents, listening to music, or talking to her peers at school with more philosophical reflections on her identity, family, colonial history in Tornedalen, and more. Repetitions of sentences like "Vi visste vårt värde" (We knew our worth) and variations of it recur in multiple passages throughout the novel. Another significant formal difference of this novel is that the narrative voice of the protagonist often uses first-person plural, thus also constructing a version of a we-narrative or a we-novel. The child narrator also refers to herself as "I," but the speaking subject is often "we," including phrasing like "our mothers, our fathers, our worth, our cousins," even when there is no implication of there being more than one person whom the possessive pronoun "our" refers to.[51] The plural subject has been a recurring feature in many literary works, and it has become common in postcolonial fiction, according to Rebecca Fasselt.[52] In *Vårt värde*, as I demonstrate in the following, the construction of a plural child figure reorients the image of the heroic or suffering child to explore the histories of marginalization and settler colonial history in northern Sweden. Instead, it imagines the not-quite child as a pluralized figure who might simultaneously be growing up, sideways, and other directions. First I situate the novel's depiction of growing up as something that draws parallels to the other works discussed in previous chapters in that it aims to make visible the racialized white Tornedalian body (in this novel emphasizing that it is Finno-Ugric) while continuing to be aware of the privilege of a generation of children who can more easily pass as Swedish. Then I focus on the plural narrative and the construction of the plural child to hold the multiplicity of entangled colonial histories and multidirectional growing as alternatives to the exceptionalism that is often present in the ideal image of the Swedish child growing up and sideways.

GROWING UP FINNO-UGRIC

Vårt värde imagines a child with Tornedalian/Finnish heritage who is already passing as Swedish and that it is, in fact, growing up that makes her look visibly different. The narrator articulates a similar ironic ambivalence toward the promises of modernity that we saw in the narrative of *Populärmusik*. Going to the harbor with her parents, she observes that "det var ingenjörernas tid, det var förhoppningarnas och det oövervinnerligas tid" (it was the time of the engineers, the time of hopes and of invincibility),[53] their fathers looking over the harbor entrances and getting teary-eyed: "De såg det moderna, det stabila och oändliga, de såg att vi kunde fylla våra kundvagnar till brädden på lördagarna på Konsums storköpsbutik."[54] (They saw the modern, the stable, and the infinite, they saw that we could fill our carts to the brim at the Konsum supermarket.) At any moment, however, the narrator can feel like none of the hopes in engineering and modernity can prevent them from feeling that everything is foreign to them.[55] Instead of finding comfort in the changing era, the narrator increasingly feels that the time and materiality of growing up become entangled with the postcolonial era (she is both unsure about this term but also feels like it is unavoidable in her body). "Gruvstrejken var över för länge sedan, men inte vår egen pubertet, och hur gärna vi än ville kunde vi inte backa ur vare sig den eller den postkoloniala era som vi alla hade trätt in i."[56] (The mine strike had been over for a while, but not our own puberty, and however much we wanted to, we could not back away from that nor the postcolonial era that we all had joined.) However, while both the postcolonial era and puberty signify a temporality that includes borders and lines, of moving between different states, and of becoming someone else (no longer colonized in the same way, no longer a child in the same way), the novel depicts those lines as blurred and not always visible, even though they stick on the body of the narrator.

The entanglement of postcolonial time and puberty makes the differences that the narrator observes in her body feel more significant. She suspects that it is the Finnish in her that had already "gett oss breda höfter och en galopperande pubertet" (given [them] wide hips and a galloping puberty).[57] As she is growing up, she realizes that her "Finno-Ugric features" do not have the same "charm" for people around her that they might have had during her childhood. Without claiming a single distinct ethnic background, the narrator draws here from racialized stereotypes regarding Finno-Ugric peoples, a descriptor designating several million people who speak Finno-Ugric languages that differ significantly from Indo-European languages. In the Nordic region this includes Finnish-, Tornedalian-, and Karelian-speakers and the Indigenous Sámi people. While the connection of these diverse groups of people is linguistic and, as I have brought out earlier in this book, they have been impacted by differing levels of racialization as well as success in performing whiteness, all of these people have, as Johanna Laakso puts it, "had to cope with their otherness in relation with dominant European cultures a feeling of being different and alone."[58] They have all been, and continue to be, colonized, and in the various theories of race biology during the end of the nineteenth and early twentieth century, "Finno-Ugric" also described the people who were categorized as inferior to the Nordic race. Both the Sámi people and the Tornedalian-speakers (whose language is closely related to Finnish) were in the earlier theorizations lumped together as inferior, and both groups experienced skull measuring and other physical anthropological studies. While the official subscription to the theories of racial biology ended during World War II, the connotation of Finno-Ugric still carries a meaning of strangeness or difference, which has certainly been used as a source of pride but also continues to be seen in opposition to Europeanness; and as discussed in earlier chapters of this book, the understanding that Europeanness equals whiteness, Westernness, civilization continues to have a significant role in the postcolonial world. Even though she is white, drawing from these racial ideologies, the narrator of *Vårt värde* describes her "Finno-Ugric body structure" as different from the bodies of white Swedes: "Våra breda höfter, vad skulle vi med dem till? Våra finskugriska anletsdrag, till vilken nytta?"[59] (Our wide hips, what should we do with them? Our Finno-Ugric features, for what benefit?) She describes these features and the accompanying bodily feeling of inferiority as passed on through generations, the "böjda nackar och breda fötter var inga tillfälligheter, vi hade ärvt dem i rakt nedstigande led, liksom benstammarna" (bent necks and wide feet were no coincidences, we had inherited them in a directly descending line, just like the skeletal structure).[60]

As with the other cultural texts analyzed in this book, it is the time and space of childhood that has the capacity of holding not-quiteness as both/and, where one's differences might in some ways be valued and provide alternatives to lining up with one specific identity category. Once one notices signs of "growing up," these alternatives are no longer available, or they do not seem favorable. The narrator describes how part of their attractiveness as a child starts to disappear as soon as they get their first glasses and that even their mothers no longer point out "värdet av starka ben eller inre kvaliteter" (the value of strong legs and inner qualities) and instead seem to favor the "bleka och pinnsmala grannflickorna" (pale and skinny neighbor girls).[61] The slippage between the biological process of growing up and the inability to fully line up is thus felt bodily as their mothers' suggestions that they should perm their hair like Swedish teenagers, or their brothers' expectations that they learn Finnish result in a confusion over "alla långa och korta vokaler som rann in i oss och inte heller med allt mensblod som envisades med att rinna ut ur oss" (all the long and short vowels that ran into [them] or with all the menstrual blood that persisted to run out of [them]).[62] Thus, while the narrator is able to pass as a white Swede, as they are growing up they are expected to further line up with Swedishness, but they feel there is something in their body that hinders them from doing so. The gendered markers of puberty on their body become signs of otherness, like in *Ingenbarnsland*, where the development of breasts is, in the child's eyes, connected to stereotypes of Finnish-speaking women. Though less explicit in their commentary on gendered expectations among Tornedalian communities than the narrative in *Populärmusik*, the narrator mentions, alongside the descriptions of not fully lining up with Swedishness, that it is impossible to live up to the "manliga ideal" (male ideals) that they have always held high.[63]

While the child in *Ingenbarnsland*, as discussed in chapter 2, attempted in the novel's plentiful passages of excrement and other bodily fluids to abject the forced lines of Finnishness, the narrator in *Vårt värde* simply states that it is not really possible to discard some matter. In the last chapter of the novel, she describes the bodily experience of this inevitability: "Vi hade burit så mycket, det hade lagts så mycket på våra axlar, hela gränslinjen med Torneå och Muonio och Könkämä älvar, och vad skulle vi nu med allt det där fostervattnet till när ingen ändå ville veta av det, allra minst vi själva"[64] (We had carried so much, there was so much that had been laid on our shoulders, the whole borderline with Torneå and Muonio and Könkämä rivers, and what would we do with all that amniotic fluid now when no one wanted to know about it anyway, above all ourselves.) Even though it feels relatively easy for them to choose disengagement, because of the settler colonial history of erasure, which requires assimilation and derogates any differences from the normative, and because they can pass as white Swedes, they feel the material presence of the multiple memories and histories in their bodies and in their surroundings. While presenting their experiences and memories as heterogeneous and entangled, the narrator does frequently differentiate between the various minority communities and the majority population in Sweden. They mention several times that their peers from Falkenberg (a town in southern Sweden) do not understand them, do not know anything about Tornedalen, look at the thickness of their skeletal structure and without saying it, "kalkylerade med att vi innerst inne var barbarer" (counted on the fact that inside we were barbarians).[65] At the same time, however, the narrator articulates ambivalent feelings regarding both their privilege to pass and the impact of colonial histories: They say they can easily imitate Swedish pop singers, and they wonder whether it might be "att förhäva sig" (too conceited) to call their era postcolonial because "så jäkla mycket till koloniserande hade väl inte ägt rum vare sig där vi befann oss eller där vi kunde ha befunnit oss" (surely not that damn much colonizing had taken place where we were or where we could have been).[66]

A passage that visualizes the narrator's ambivalence about lining up and relates to how the cultural texts discussed in this book imagine lining up or not lining up comes from one of the early chapters in *Vårt värde*. After reflecting on her parents' and her different reactions to the modernizing that takes place in the northern areas of Sweden, the narrator says:

> "Det var vår tid. Det var vår smärta. Vi kunde stå framför fönstren uppe i sporthallens bordtennislokal och blicka in mot centrum. Det var en punkt varifrån vi plötsligt blev främmande för allt. . . . Vi visste inte riktigt vilka vi var, om det alls var meningen att vi skulle stå där med våra röda kortbyxor, och vilka var de egentligen, de som från första början hade lurat med oss dit?"[67]

> It was our time. It was our pain. We could stand in front of the windows up at the table tennis hall and look toward the city center. It was a point from where we suddenly felt stranger to everything. . . . We didn't really know who we were, if there was any meaning in standing there with our red shorts, and who were they really, those who from the very beginning had lured us there?

While *Sami Blood* features a sequence where the Sámi child is trying to synchronize her body with the movements of the other Swedish girls in a gymnastics class, in an attempt to fit in and be allowed to enter Swedishness, and in *Ingenbarnsland*, the Finnish-speaking child who resists forced lining up through the image of her doing everything not to synchronize her body with the other competitors in a running competition, in this passage of *Vårt värde*, the narrator expresses uncertainty about moving with other bodies and competing. They are also in a space of athletics and competition, but they are not sure what it means to be there, who their competitors are, and whether it wouldn't be better to "sluta räkna poäng, sätta oss på bänken och dingla med benen och låta motspelarnas tysta misstro med rätta hagla över våra kortklippta frisyrer" (stop counting points, sit on the bench and dangle our legs and let the opponents' quiet distrust rightfully fall over our short hairdos).[68] However, the narrator maintains that they do not give up, even when they do, because it does not really fit them to give up. Instead of resisting lining up by distorting the arrival in adulthood, or portraying an exceptional inspiring figure of the child who ends up lining up with Swedishness, the child's bodily response to the forced fusion of proximate cultures finds an outlet in a plural voice that takes over the singular.

PLURAL NARRATIVE

Vårt värde begins with a passage where the narrator describes how her family sometimes drove to the harbor to watch the icebreakers on the Torne River. The narrative voice of the first chapter moves between first-person singular and plural. Writing in singular, the child narrator sitting in the backseat of the car says her mother told her father not to drive too close to the edge of the road: "Jag går fast ut ur bilen,' sa mamma med en stämma så brusten att jag förberedde mig på att både den och äktenskapet där i framsätet skulle spricka"[69] ("I'm going out of the car,' said mother with a voice so broken that I prepared myself that both it and the marriage in the front seat would break.) This sentence is immediately followed by one in plural voice: "Men äktenskapen sprack aldrig, och våra mammor gick aldrig ut ur bilarna."[70] (But the marriages never broke, and our mothers never went out of the cars.) The first-person plural is used often throughout the novel, both in passages that describe various everyday situations and when the narrator meditates on what it means to live in a postcolonial time and space.

As one of the recurring themes in the novel is the dominant/colonial power's violence toward language, by choosing plural voice the narrator uses language to resist the singularity desired in assimilation politics, which sought to teach children of the minorities to become Swedes, based on a normative understanding of Swedishness. Describing the effects of assimilation politics on language, the narrator writes in the last chapter of the novel that as a child, "Vi hade haft så *mahoton* mycket att säga, dels på ett språk som centralmakten sett till att vi behärskade, dels på ett språk som centralmakten sett till att vi givit upp hoppet om."[71] (We had had so *mahoton* much to say, partly in the language that the central power had made sure we mastered, and partly in the language that the central power had made sure we gave up on.) Growing up is, in their conclusion, connected to lining up with Swedishness, which is, on one hand, easy because the narrator already speaks Swedish, even though it is a result of the language policies of the colonial power. Maintaining the plural voice here, however, provides the narrator with a way to keep the alternative, the plurality of experiences and identities, to line up with.

Recent narratological scholarship has paid close attention to the distinctiveness of collective narration in texts with we-narrators. Natalya Bekhta defines "we-narrative" as the narrator "speaking, acting, and thinking as a collective narrative agent and possessing a collective subjectivity, which the narrative performatively creates and maintains throughout its course."[72] Arguing for the importance of distinguishing between the indicative "we" and the performative "we," Bekhta brings out that in the first, an individual subject is present in the pronoun "we"—for example, when a couple tells a holiday story or a football fan relates how "we" won the game. In the performative "we," however, the "I" is erased through the creation of a collective voice. Bekhta's examples include texts that might include first-person singular, but as they are moving between singular and plural, in the case of a performative "we," the implication of the plural is still the collective voice. In *Vårt värde* the frequent use of plural first-person narrative can be read as representing a singular "I" of the child, who observes her parents and who reflects on her family history and the complicated position of growing up in line with the expectations and exciting parts of the dominant Swedish culture and the disappointments of her parents and other Finnish- and Meänkieli-speakers. However, it could also be read as a collective voice of children in a similar position, those whose parents had moved away from the Finnish-speaking villages in Tornedalen and who are coming to terms with their identities and the not-quite or in-between positions they inhabit. Using a plural voice to indicate the parents—the plural first-person narrator always refers to their mothers and fathers—supports this interpretation. At the same time, by also continuing to use singular voice, the novel makes explicit that the "we" does not necessarily signify a group of people, children, or parents. Instead, the "we" might be representing both a group and an individual. This differentiates *Vårt värde* from Bekhta's definition of we-narratives that always imply a collective narrator.

As the novel engages with whether or not one could call the life in Tornedalen and in Tornedalian/Finnish families postcolonial (as the narrator wonders about that explicitly), the use of the plural voice contributes to what Rebecca Fasselt has brought out in postcolonial texts that incorporate that mode to not only "forge a collective identity in contrast to imperial powers and Western individualist notions of subjectivity" but to also, differently from earlier work of postcolonial theory, highlight the "more ambiguous inscriptions of 'we'" and "bring into focus fissures in liberation narratives."[73] This means that instead of the earlier focus on the colonizer/colonized binary that tended to center on the Western/colonizer's power, later postcolonial literature and the postcolonial we-narratives have moved toward a more self-reflexive mode, looking at the different processes of colonization, decolonization, or postcolonialism in their specific contexts. Furthermore, Fasselt argues that some of the postcolonial texts deploy first-person plural to encode communities as "unstable and porous entities."[74] As the narrative of *Vårt värde* imagines a child whose life is informed by different communities—those that have been colonized, those that have not been for a while, those who represent the colonizer, and the overall complexity of "postcolonialism" as a term for Tornedalian history—its "we" does not attempt to create a unified collective narrator (who is either univocally writing back against the colonizer or simply suggesting an exclusively collective mind). Instead, it destabilizes boundaries and lines between and within these communities.

With its self-reflexive, pondering voice, *Vårt värde* describes coming to terms with a complex and entangled history of Tornedalen that could be read as colonized by the Swedish state but whose land is also part of Sápmi, and while Tornedalians were expected to assimilate to Swedish culture in the early twentieth century, the reindeer-herding Sámi were segregated from the dominant culture. While the narrator frequently uses the pronoun "we" and the possessive "our" in the novel, these words do not make claims for an exclusive collective identity that, as Fasselt writes, often "indexes collective ownership and distinctiveness and is, therefore, often associated with exclusionary and even violent assertions of group or national membership" and that could be read in the use of the term "Meänmaa" (*our* land), for Tornedalen as explained above.[75] Instead, the narrator lists their cousins, neighbors, and friends from different parts of northern Sweden and Finland (some who are Sámi and others who live in Finland) without giving them any specific ethnicity-related descriptors, and the plural voice that speaks of "our cousins, our brothers" further establishes the novel's description of the groups of people in northern Sweden and Finland as porous communities with entangled histories. For example, she says that sometimes she did not know what was what, "vad som var vår tid och vad som var någon annans, vad som var brytning och vad som var dialekt . . . vad som var vår smärta och vad som hade åsamkats av polarnätter långt innan vi och vår tid ens var påtänkta"(what was our time and what was someone else's, what was an accent and what was a dialect . . . what was our pain and what had been caused by polar nights a long time before we or our time even was born).[76] The plural narrative here blurs the boundaries between different groups, languages, and generations. With that, *Vårt värde* expands the meaning of postmemory, the term coined by Marianne Hirsch (and elaborated on in my analysis of not-quite childhood in the novels about Finnish labor migrants in chapter 2) that signifies traumatic memories passed on to the next generations that become so overwhelming that they become a person's memory even though they have never experienced them.[77]

Similarly to this understanding of how postmemory works, the narrator of *Vårt värde* maintains that the feeling of not being good enough was handed over to her like "medaljer att hänga om våra halsar" (medals to hang around our necks),[78] and that while their mothers did not say much more than that they were worth nothing, the narrator nevertheless feels "lärarinnornas dödande blickar och utedassets kyla mot den bara stjärten, vi hörde hur vinternätterna hade knäppt i brädväggarna och hur norrskenet hade sprakat över deras huvuden"(the deadly stares of the teachers and the cold of the outhouse against their bare bottoms, we heard how the winter nights had nipped in the timber walls and how the northern lights had glowed over their heads).[79] Remaining in plural voice as the memories and stories are told by mothers and fathers, however, disrupts the linear familial mediations of memory and kinship, and the generational time becomes nonlinear and existing all at once.

THE PLURAL CHILD

In its frequent use of first-person plural voice, then, *Vårt värde* constructs a not-quite child figure who is pluralized. While this child shares some experiences of not-quiteness that we have seen throughout the works analyzed in this book, providing more of a focus on the second-generation/ intergenerational not-quiteness, which continues to persist to a certain extent, the novel also resists the possible implications of constructing a figure of a child simply to represent marginalization and discrimination. All the child figures discussed in this book have in various ways challenged the meaning of the hegemonic/dominant image of the child in Swedish/Nordic culture, resisted lining up and growing up according to the expectations based on their race and ethnicity, and rethought the entangled colonial histories and hierarchies of whiteness in Sweden in the twentieth century. These figures have illustrated more nuanced and complicated ways to negotiate lining up and growing up, but they have nevertheless done so primarily through a single child figure who, differently from others around them, resists growing up and lining up with the norms assigned by the dominant power of the (previous) colonizer. The use of "we" in *Vårt värde* could be interpreted as a way to express a group experience of the generation whose parents grew up in Tornedalen but moved to other areas in Sweden. In sentences that talk about "our worth, our time" and that describe "our mothers and fathers" saying or doing something could easily illustrate this reading. However, the reader is aware from the beginning of the novel (and that awareness is confirmed throughout the novel) that the narrator is one person, having one father and mother. She simply uses the plural voice frequently. This move creates ambiguity and fluidity between "I" and "we," which is not only reflective of new directions in postcolonial literature as brought out above but also rethinks common cultural images and narratives of childhood.

This "plural child" figure reorients the expectation for a clearly identifiable child or a group of children who suffer from institutional injustice and prejudice or discrimination and prejudice in the society. It also blurs boundaries between the different generations and thus undoes the promise or expectation for a singular predictable futurity in the figure of the child. In its "we," the plural child narrator combines childhoods of potentially different lineages, temporalities, and geographies. Similarly to the focus on the bodily experience of the colonial history discussed above, the plurality is deeply rooted in the child's body. Among several references to the drawing of the border between Sweden and Finland in 1809, when many of the Finnish-speaking villages of the Torne Valley became part of Sweden, is one that establishes a bodily example of how plurality in the child's body might have been constructed: "Artonhundranio års gränsdragning gick rätt igenom våra kroppar och klöv våra tungor i två delar, en som kunde prata och en som inte kunde."[80] (The border drawing of year eighteen hundred nine went directly through our bodies and split our tongues into two parts, one that could speak and the other that couldn't.) While the general impression of the plural child in *Vårt värde* is an unidentified plurality, the creation of two halves as a consequence of the 1809 border visualizes a situation where one is forced into two distinct languages, cultures, and countries, and where the colonial and assimilation politics have resulted in feeling that only one of those two halves is seen as valuable. The narrator resists having to choose one or the other. She does not want to have "konturer som var så enkla att skära ut" (contours that are so easy to cut out).[81] Thus, she contends with the idea of a distinct image of the child who represents hybridity of cultures, hovering between the minoritized and dominant/colonizer's culture that are proximate but have been drastically differentiated. She resists being a child figure who signifies the temporal and spatial point of becoming, of transformation from what some have identified as being more primitive than the other.

Instead of aligning herself with an easily identifiable figure of the not-quite child, the narrator longs for an "islossningar som skulle spränga fram och lösa alla band och lägga både finska och svenska sidan under vatten och en gång för alla återställa ordningen" (ice-breaking that would burst out and open all bonds and place both the Finnish and the Swedish side under water and for once re-establish order).[82] Possibly referring to Antti Keksi's poem "Keksis kväde" (1677), about the ice-breaking that flooded the riverbanks and that has become the symbol of a specific Tornedalian space shaped by the river, the narrator imagines a new event of creation, one that would dissolve all lines and borders. If in *Populärmusik* the children saw a connection/similarity between the powerful sound of ice-breaking and rock music as the novel imagined alternative lining up with global subcultures, the fusion of waters in *Vårt värde* functions as another way to imagine an alternative to lining up with the expected figure of the Swedish child or the Tornedalian child. Finding order in the imagined underwater world that does not have borders and boundaries becomes a visual image of nonlinear resistance to growing up and lining up with the distinct contours of one or other group/identity. Furthermore, imagining the dissolution of borders, bonds, and boundaries does not lay claim to a specific territory. Instead, it suggests that "order" is possible only in a different underwater world without colonial politics, erasure, assimilation, and violence.

This renewed image of the northern Nordic region that aims for acceptance of plurality and heterogeneous identities in some ways resembles one of David Vikgren's adaptations of Keksi's poem in his poetry collection *Antikeksiskväde: Översättning, dikt* (2010).[83] The adaptation titled "kollektivversionen" (collective version) is a translation that was compiled by contributions of twenty-six people, all of whose names are printed on a map of a river that bifurcates the back cover of the book and alludes to a map of a literary history by Bengt Pohjanen and Kirsti Johansson, which marks the birthplaces of the authors.[84] As Heith argues, while Pohjanen and Johansson's map emphasizes the importance of roots and origins, the map on Vikgren's book cover "points to the themes of multiple interpretations, process and transformation," thus contributing to the "making of different versions of the Torne Valley."[85] Vikgren's version, of course, consists of different identifiable voices, a collective of people translating the poem, while the child in *Vårt värde* holds plurality that is not necessarily collective. With this plural child figure, who does not necessarily represent a specific collective, the novel imagines a reoriented alternative childhood that combines the expectations of and resistances to inherited lines, different temporalities and geographies. It imagines a time and space where one can grow in multiple directions at once, thus making it impossible to predict any specific future in "the child" or to hold the child figure up as an obvious inspiration for sideways growth or for lining up despite difficult circumstances.

While the novel disrupts the singularity or universality of the figure of the child—the idealized understanding of childhood in heteronormative culture and society—by oscillating between singular and plural, the narrative ends in singular voice: "Vi visste inte vad som skulle hända nu. 'Vad händer nu?' frågade jag."[86] (We did not know what would happen now. "What happens now?" I asked.). Her father responds by asking what happened with the fish they brought with them, and her mother says to the narrator that she can throw the fish out. Ending in singular voice might remind the reader that while the plural voice has provided the narrative a formal alternative to the expectations of childhood, it is possible only in the imaginary, textual level.

―――

Populärmusik and *Vårt värde* imagine the not-quite child figures exploring the experiences of the first generation of Tornedalians who did not experience racial discrimination to the same extent as generations before. Playing with this figure on a formal level, both novels not only offer moments of pause and delay on the trajectories of becoming Swedish that we saw in the other works analyzed in the previous chapters, but they also unsettle the construction of the child figure to represent the histories of not-quiteness and, by extension, the normative expectations of autonomy and morality in the imagination of the Swedish child. While, like all the films and novels discussed in this book, they seek to articulate the impact of colonial and racial ideologies on the bodies of people who are legible as white, the narratives of *Populärmusik* and *Vårt värde* convey a higher awareness of privilege and its meaning for people who inherit the histories of not-quiteness together with the lines of whiteness.

CONCLUSION

Consider this scene from *Sami Blood*: After having left her home in Sápmi, where she was forced into a life segregated from Swedish society, and trying to fulfill her dream of becoming a teacher by pretending not to be Sámi in the 1930s, Elle-Marja has been able to enroll at a girls' school in Uppsala and is entering a room to attend her first gymnastics class. The class has already started, and the girls are lined up in straight rows, the metronome is ticking, and the teacher gestures at Elle-Marja to find a spot among her peers. The camera follows her as she cautiously makes her way, and we see the teacher set the metronome to a slightly slower pace. Once the girls start moving in nearly perfect synchrony, Elle-Marja is not able to keep up with the movements. She misses most of them, and each of her motions that is off the beat or behind the rhythm emphasizes her difference from others (fig. 4). Wearing the same clothes as the girls in the class, Elle-Marja looks like them, but as the film audience knows, she has had to burn her gákti and adopt a new identity in order to be allowed to enter the classroom at all. As the scene goes on, she is able to imitate many of the movements but is still lagging a bit behind the rhythm of the metronome. In *Sami Blood* this scene visualizes the experiences of many Indigenous Sámi people in Sweden (and other Nordic countries) during the twentieth century: While able to pass as white Swedes, the only way for many of them to not be excluded from Swedish society was to erase their Indigenous heritage and line up with white Swedishness, and this alignment often happened in one's youth or childhood. It is also telling that the film uses the girls' gymnastics class to visualize Elle-Marja's failed attempts at passing and moving in synchrony—as Johannes Westberg has already demonstrated in analyzing the educationalization of gymnastics in Sweden in the nineteenth century, the purpose of gymnastics was to "foster national citizens that could support a strong Swedish nation" and women/girls were then seen as "fundamental to the nationalist project."[1] Throughout the scene, Elle-Marja is shown being unable to keep up with the movements that were so instrumental in the fostering of Swedish citizens.

This scene is emblematic of the argument I have made in *The Not-Quite Child*, that a recurring figure in several twenty-first-century cultural texts from Sweden is a child who disrupts, rethinks, and reembodies the expected trajectory of growing up as the Swedish child and in doing so makes visible the implications of historical racialization and colonial histories in Sweden. Elle-Marja navigates the position of a not-quite child. The twenty-first-century films and novels I have analyzed in this book navigate what it means to visualize historical racialization, becoming, feelings of lagging behind, passing, assimilation, and erasure of cultures. They imagine possible or impossible alternatives to growing up (and becoming) or sideways on a normative trajectory. As they do so, these texts incorporate the figure of what I have called the not-quite child: a child who is legible as a white Swede but at the same time, because of racialization and colonial histories, is made to feel they are not quite Swedish/white. My analyses have demonstrated how different films and novels use formal elements from a variety of genres and modes, such as melodrama, magical realism, or parody, to challenge the expectations for not only the idealized child figure in Swedish culture but also for its representational power in cinematic and literary works.

One of the main contributions of *The Not-Quite Child* to postcolonial and minority studies is that it has identified and analyzed such not-quite child figures in a variety of cinematic and literary narratives that articulate the experiences of three national minority groups in Sweden: the Indigenous Sámi people, Tornedalians, and Sweden Finns. *The Not-Quite Child* has been mindful of the crucial differences between these groups—for example, that the Indigenous Sámi people have and continue to be colonized by the Swedish (as well as Norwegian and Finnish) state and that the large wave of Finnish-speakers coming to Sweden in the twentieth century were labor migrants in search of better job opportunities. This book has shown, however, that as all these groups of people share a long cultural and (semi-)colonial history with Sweden and to varying extents

FIGURE 4. Elle-Marja's movements are off the beat or slightly behind the rhythm of the other girls in the gymnastics class. Frame grab from *Sami Blood*.

have historically been categorized as inferior race or as not quite white, even though they are typically legible as white, there are productive points of comparison in how films and novels imagine these histories in the changing Swedish welfare state of the twentieth century.

I have argued that it is particularly important to understand the prominence of childhood and the figure of the child in Swedish culture and society to fully comprehend how these novels and films imagine colonial histories and racialized hierarchies. Engaging with the history of how the image of the ideal child—a white, healthy, middle-class child who is autonomous, competent, and moral—came to signify the citizen of the Swedish welfare state, *The Not-Quite Child* has shown that the normative idea of the Swedish child is paradoxical. It expects the child to resist injustice and societal norms that are oppressive, just like Pippi Longstocking—the most famous iteration—but this resistance is celebrated only if the child lines up with "good Swedishness." Thus, resisting social norms has become both normative and exclusive. In hashing out the frameworks that show us child figures who do not quite move in synchrony with the ideal Swedish child (as they experience themselves always lagging a bit behind), I have paid close attention to how Pippi Longstocking, whose image some of the texts analyzed in this book directly engage with, herself a non-normative figure, has come to represent Swedish exceptionalism. While Pippi has been read as someone who crosses boundaries between categories like child and adult, human and more-than-human, masculine and feminine, she is often celebrated as a strong, independent girl, symbolizing not only the citizen of the Swedish welfare state but also becoming a role model for girls everywhere. Writing about the history of the progress in gender equality in Sweden and the Nordic region, Elina Oinas and Anna Collander argue that *pippifeminism* (realization of gender equality through the metaphorical use of Pippi Longstocking) can be understood as an emancipatory strategy that "places the responsibility on the individual girl to make sure that she becomes, effortlessly, a gender equal woman."[2] Much of this symbolism and rhetoric, however, does not pay attention to systemic reasons for why some girls and children are not able to "become like Pippi," thus also not paying attention to those who continue to lag behind the performance of the ideal Swedish child/girl.

Though I have not situated this project in the field of girlhood studies, all but one of the main characters in the films and novels analyzed in this book identify as girls, and the two male protagonists in *Popular Music from Vittula* are both depicted as resisting rigid boundaries of gender/sexuality. In my selection of texts for this book, I did not set out to look for examples that would feature only girl protagonists, but the overwhelming majority of narratives dealing with the histories that this book focuses on construct their child figures as girls. As the analyses in *The Not-Quite Child* have demonstrated, although the gender of the child protagonists is not typically a focus in these texts, gendered expectations, regarding both the need to perform the ideas associated with Pippi Longstocking and growing up, are featured in all of them. The protagonists in works as dissimilar as *Sami Blood*, *Ingenbarnsland*, and *Vårt värde* experience exclusion from Swedish society because they are expected to take on stereotypical traits associated with women from their respective minority communities when they grow up and, most importantly, to reproduce their not-quiteness in future generations.

My reading has further implications for analyzing the increasing archive of texts dealing with various kinds of not-quiteness and childhood in Sweden. While I have narrowed my analysis to texts that articulate the histories of the three minority groups in Sweden who are white but have historically been categorized as not quite as white and who share a long cultural/colonial history with Sweden, my theorization of the not-quite child figure in Sweden/the Nordic region contributes to a better understanding of and analyses of the articulations of other minoritized groups in Sweden. I have sought to open avenues for further research on the expanding archive of texts that articulate minoritized experiences in Sweden (or the Nordic region more broadly) and that incorporate a child figure to do that. This includes the transnational adoptees of color who, as Tobias Hübinette has demonstrated in his analysis of Swedish media discourse during the post–World War II era, were accepted in society more easily because they were children who would be growing up in white Swedish families, therefore becoming almost (but not quite) Swedes because they look visibly different.[3]

Another future research direction could be to look at how the child figures continue to show up in texts that describe the experiences of minorities that this book talks about but that take place in the twenty-first century. More specifically, the recent decades have seen an increase in texts, particularly in Sámi culture, that engage with childhood and growing up in contemporary Sweden. These cultural texts often depict one of the following: The protagonist has nearly no linguistic or other knowledge of their Sámi heritage because of the politics of erasure and assimilation that have fully taken effect on the new generations, and they work through their (and sometimes their parents') childhoods to understand this history.[4] Or the protagonist is a child figure who is certainly impacted by the heritage of not-quiteness but performs what Jill Locke has called "unashamed citizenship."[5] This child figure—for example, the one often recurring in Ann-Helen Laestadius's novels—already is or is learning to be completely unashamed of the history and heritage of not-quiteness.[6] *The Not-Quite Child* has provided a better understanding of how the child figure has been used to navigate the history of the twentieth century, and with that, its aim is also to help the reader understand what comes next—how the child continues to transform.

In addition, *The Not-Quite Child* has questioned what refusing or failing becoming and adulthood might mean in the contexts where the anarchy of childhood (which Halberstam proposes as a space to refuse normative adulthood) or "sideways growth" (Stockton's term for fictional child figures who do not grow "up" according to the cultural norms and expectations and instead delay or wander off the linear trajectory) are experienced as normative. This book has thus contributed to the methodologies of childhood studies by reading closely how novels and films not only construct child figures who deviate from the normative but also how they imagine moments (sometimes extended and prolonged moments) of impossibility, pause, delay, and hesitance to grow up or sideways. Imagining possible alternatives to these trajectories, these texts are not as invested in repeating well-known narratives of collective and cultural memories but rather aim to unleash new forms of memory that would encompass the fluidity and complexity of identities forced to exist within binaries and hierarchies.

Looking once more at the scene in the gymnastics class where Elle-Marja's movements are lagging behind the metronome, we might take note of the emphasis on the physical discomfort that Elle-Marja feels because her body is delayed. All she wants to do is move in complete synchrony with the white Swedish girls, and it is the settler colonial politics that have made it almost impossible to do that; most importantly, they have made lining up with white Swedishness the only possible trajectory to become a fully accepted citizen. All texts discussed in this book have imagined the not-quite child experiencing some kind of delay as something that the child tries to escape as quickly as possible or that she finds empowering, though usually only for a short time. The figure of the not-quite child expands these moments of pause in order to disrupt and reorient normative temporalities of growing up and of growing sideways. With that, the not-quite child also reorients the common ways of reading the child as a story of inspiration, overcoming injustice, and standing up against norms, and it directs our attention to the oppressive spaces, lines, and borders around her.

FILMOGRAPHY

Alla vi barn i Bullerbyn. Dir. Olle Helbom, Sweden, 1960.

Artificial Intelligence. Dir. Steven Spielberg, United States, 2001.

Bihttoš (Rebel). Dir. Elle-Máijá Tailfeathers, Canada, 2014.

Elina: som om jag inte fanns (Elina: As If I Wasn't There). Dir. Klaus Härö, Finland/ Sweden, 2002.

Ett öga rött. Dir. Daniel Wallentin, Sweden, 2007

Förortsungar (Kidz in da Hood). Dir. Ylva Gustavsson and Catti Edfeldt, Sweden, 2006.

Jag var en lägre ras. Television series, Sweden, 2021.

Jägarna 2. Dir. Kjell Sundvall, Sweden, 2011.

Kautokeino-upprøret (Kautokeino Rebellion). Dir. Nils Gaup, Norway, 2008.

Kidz in da Hood. Dir. Ylva Gustavsson and Catti Edfeldt, 2006

Lilja 4-ever. Dir. Lukas Moodysson, Sweden, 2002.

Mitt liv som hund (My Life as a Dog). Dir. Lasse Hallström, Sweden, 1985.

Nattvardsgästerna (Winter Light). Dir. Ingmar Bergman, 1963.

Ofelaš (Pathfinder). Dir. Nils Gaup, Norway, 2007.

Pay It Forward. Dir. Mimi Leder, United States, 2000.

Play. Dir. Ruben Östlund, Sweden, 2011.

Populärmusik från Vittula (Popular Music from Vittula). Dir. Reza Bagher, Sweden, 2004.

Sameblod (Sami Blood). Dir. Amanda Kernell, Sweden, 2016.

Sami nieida jojk (Sami Daughter's Jojk). Dir. Liselotte Wajstedt, Sweden, 2007.

The Shirt. Dir. Shelley Niro, Canada, 2003.

The Sixth Sense. Dir. M. Night Shyamalan, United States, 1999.

Sparrooabbán (Me and My Little Sister). Dir. Suvi West, Finland, 2016.

Svinalängorna (Beyond). Dir. Pernilla August, Sweden, 2011.

Tystnaden (The Silence). Dir. Ingmar Bergman, Sweden, 1963.

Valla Villekulla. Dir. Jimmy Olsson, Sweden, 2020.

Zozo. Dir. Josef Fares, Sweden, 2005.

NOTES

INTRODUCTION

1. Ryalls and Mazzarella, "Famous, Beloved," 444.

2. Nikolajeva, "Misunderstood Tragedy."

3. Bernstein, "Childhood as Performance."

4. Bernstein, "Childhood as Performance," 203. Examples of this tension include criticism of Philippe Ariés's argument "that there was no childhood in the medieval world," where scholars bring out that medieval children did exist, but do not take into account that Ariés is really talking about the idea of childhood (Honeyman, *Elusive Childhood*). Similarly, criticism and debates around Lee Edelman's *No Future* where people are (rightly) arguing that Edelman's Child is a very specific idea of childhood and the rhetoric around it does not apply to all children.

5. Bernstein, "Childhood as Performance," 204.

6. Bernstein, "Childhood as Performance," 205.

7. Hatch, *Shirley Temple*, 12.

8. Socialdemokraterna, "Vår historia."

9. Berggren and Trägårdh, *Swedish Theory of Love*, 166.

10. Berggren and Trägårdh, *Swedish Theory of Love*, 166.

11. Sandin, "Children and the Swedish Welfare State," 125.

12. Key, *Century of the Child* (*Barnets århundrade*).

13. See more in Karin Nykvist, "Dreaming Childhood" (unpublished chapter, March 2018).

14. Brembeck, Johansson, and Kampmann, "Introduction," 15.

15. There are, of course, examples that study Indigenous Sámi childhoods specifically, such as Rauna Kuokkanen's "'Survivance' in Sámi and First Nations Boarding School Narratives" (2003), which discusses and compares novels about Indigenous children in the colonial school systems in Canada and Finland.

16. Sandin, "Children and the Swedish Welfare State," 128.

17. Sandin, "Children and the Swedish Welfare State," 115, 129.

18. Mier-Cruz, "Swedish Racial Innocence," 12.

19. Berggren and Trägårdh, *Swedish Theory of Love*, 167.

20. Kjellman, "How to Picture Race?" 580.

21. Kjellman, "How to Picture Race?" 603.

22. Kjellman, "Whiter Shade of Pale," 190.

23. Edelman, *No Future*.

24. See, for example, Smith, "Queer Theory and Native Studies"; or Parvulescu, "Reproduction and Queer Theory."

25. Zaborskis, "Sexual Orphanings," 606.

26. See also Andrea Smith, who argues that an Indigenous critique "must question the value of 'no future' in the context of genocide, where Native peoples have already been determined by settler colonialism to have no future." Smith, "Queer Theory," 47.

27. See also Michelle M. Wright, "Queer Temporalities."

28. Smith, "Queer Theory."

29. Ahmed, *Queer Phenomenology*, 125.

30. Ahmed, *Queer Phenomenology*, 126.

31. Stockton writes that "innocent" children are strange because while seen as normative, they are at the same time not like us. In fact, "those who fetishize 'delay' for the child must believe in sideways growth." Stockton, *Queer Child*, 37.

32. Sandin, "Children and the Swedish Welfare State," 128.

33. Ommundsen, "Competent Children." See also Birgitte Furberg Moe's comparison of the different translations of what is considered the first original Norwegian children's book, by Jørgen Moe, *I Brønden og i Tjærnet. Smaahistorier for Børn* (*In the Well and in the Mere, Small Stories for Children*, translated title by Ommundsen). In both the English and American versions, the child protagonist is no longer depicted as a competent Norwegian child, in contrast to the original. B. Moe, "Barndomshistorier."

34. Lindgren, *Pippi Långstrump. Pippi Longstocking* was of course not received without criticisms. The Bonniers publishing house did not accept Lindgren's manuscript for publication in 1944, and once it had been published by Rabén and Sjögren in 1945, several critics wrote that the book, with its anti-authoritarian ideas, would have a negative influence on children.

35. Söderberg, "Pippi-Attitude."

36. Söderberg, "Pippi-Attitude"; Rudd, "Animal Figure."

37. Lindgren, *Pippi Långstrump i Söderhavet*.

38. Berggren and Trädgårdh, "Pippi Longstocking."

39. Berggren and Trädgårdh, "Pippi Longstocking," 51.

40. Witoszek and Mueller, "Ecological Ethics," 65.

41. Similarly to the universal environment around Pippi (such as a little town in Sweden or an exotic island in the Pacific Ocean), Lundqvist argues, people in the book are more concepts than individuals. Lundqvist, *Århundradets barn*.

42. Söderberg, "'Lillasyster ser dig!'" 63.

43. Another example of Pippi as an emblem of Swedish exceptionalism in the world is from the exhibit at Astrid Lindgren's childhood home, Vimmerby, where a doll that represents an African girl has a little Astrid Lindgren sitting on her knee. Söderberg, "'Lillasyster ser dig!'" 63.

44. While Pippi Longstocking is the most widely known character beyond Sweden, the other film characters include Karlsson (from Lindgren's *Karlsson on the Roof*), who has received a flight ban as a grown-up and had to give away his propeller because he was considered to be a heavy drone; and Alfons Åberg (from Gunilla Bergström's book series

of this character, published 1972–2012), who has moved up in social class and lost part of his identity.

45. Sandin, "Children and the Swedish Welfare State," 129.

46. Sandin, "Children and the Swedish Welfare State," 131.

47. As Brembeck, Johansson, and Kampmann bring out, speaking of real children, the expectation of competence leaves out children who for various reasons are not as competent ("Introduction").

48. Brembeck, Johansson and Kampmann, "Introduction," 11.

49. Söderberg, "Pippi-Attitude," 63. On the political changes within the Swedish welfare state during 1980s–1990s, see, for example, Fredrik Sunnemark, "Who Are We Now?"

50. Hübinette and Lundström, "Three Phases."

51. Hübinette and Lundström, "Three Phases," 430.

52. Hübinette and Lundström, "Three Phases," 429.

53. See more in Hübinette, *Adopterad*; and Törngren, Malm, and Hübinette, "Transracial Families."

54. Widhe, "Politics of Autobiography."

55. Stockton, *Queer Child*, 514.

56. See also, for example, Karin Nykvist, "Dreaming Childhood"; and Malena Janson, *Bio för barnets bästa*.

57. Doxtater, "From Diversity to Precarity." Examples of films that do so include *Zozo* (Josef Fares); *Ett öga rött* (Daniel Wallentin); *Förortsungar* (Ylva Gustavsson and Catti Edfeldt).

58. Åberg, "Conceptions," 105.

59. Åberg, "Conceptions," 104.

60. Doxtater, "From Diversity to Precarity," 203.

61. Nestingen, *Crime and Fantasy*.

62. Larsson, "Representing Sexual Transactions."

63. Larsson, "Representing Sexual Transactions"; Kulick, "Four Hundred Thousand."

64. I am thankful to Svea Larsson, who made this point in our discussion of this film and elaborated on it in her final seminar paper in my class on migration and media in Europe (2021).

65. Larsson, "Representing Sexual Transactions," 37.

66. Kukku Melkas, for example, has concluded her discussion of novels including Alakoski's *Svinalängorna* and Hetekivi Olsson's *Ingenbarnsland*, analyzed in chapter 3 of this book, saying they ultimately portray a child who finds a happy ending. Melkas, "Literature and Children."

67. Keskinen, "Intra-Nordic Differences."

68. Össbo, "Hydropower Company Sites," 126.

69. Braidotti, "On Becoming Europeans."

70. Lopez, "Introduction," 18.

71. See, for example, McClintock, *Imperial Leather*; and Storfjell, "Mapping the Space."

72. Ahmed, "Passing through Hybridity," 93.

73. Kuokkanen, "'Survivance.'"

74. Andersson, "En sanningskommission," https://www.samer.se/2629, accessed January 11, 2024.

75. Andersson, "En sanningskommission."

76. Fura, Foreword, 28.

77. See, for example, Gaski, "Indigenism and Cosmopolitanism."

78. Keskinen, "Intra-Nordic Differences" and "Re-Constructing the Peaceful Nation"; Lundström and Teitelbaum, "Nordic Whiteness: An Introduction"; Hübinette and Lundström, "Swedish Whiteness and White Melancholia"; Roos, "Approaching Text."

79. The child is often read as a device in films and literature to depict multicultural societies and hybrid identities. Eila Rantonen, for example, writes that Swedish author Jonas Hassen Khemiri "seems to employ the child protagonist to introduce and negotiate the tensions arising between the host and original cultures, which often culminates as generational conflict." Rantonen, "Writing Biography," 205.

80. Hübinette, *Adopterad*.

81. Wyver, "Too Brown to Be Swedish," 401.

82. See, for example, Rebecca Knight, "Representations." Susan Honeyman writes that she sees the value in investigating the attempts to represent the position of childhood in literature "despite (and in light of) this fact." Honeyman, *Elusive Childhood*, 5. Karen Lury, analyzing figurations of children in several influential films of the twentieth century, decides to use as her starting point the theoretical position that children are different and other to the adults thus providing new and productive perspectives on the adult world. Lury, *Child in Film*.

83. Castañeda, *Figurations*, 1.

84. Castañeda, *Figurations*, 13.

85. Castañeda, *Figurations*, 14.

86. Duane, "Introduction," 1.

87. Ahmed, *Cultural Politics of Emotions*.

88. Lanas and Huuki, "Thinking Beyond."

89. Halberstam, *Queer Art of Failure*, 15.

90. Fasselt, "(Post)Colonial We-Narratives."

CHAPTER ONE IMAGINING RACIALIZATION AND WHITENESS THROUGH THE CHILD WHO LINES UP

1. Kuokkanen, "Deatnu Agreement"; Össbo, "Hydropower Company Sites."

2. Veracini, *Settler Colonialism*, 16–17.

3. Össbo, "Hydropower Company Sites," 126.

4. Kuokkanen, "'Survivance,'" 708.

5. Dankertsen, "I Felt So White," 115. See also Gaski, "Voice in the Margin."

6. Pohjanen and Johansson, *Den tornedalsfinska litteraturen*. See more in the introduction to this book.

7. These terms are featured in Pohjanen's poem "Ragheads" ("Rättipäät," 1987). He also

makes a problematic neologism, "*l'ugritude*," which combines "Negritude" and "Ugric," in an attempt to show that the Finno-Ugric identity has been marginalized and to bring out categories that, as Anne Heith argues, "represented as different *and* similar at the same time." Heith, "Ethnicity, Cultural Identity, and Bordering," 96.

8. See more in Leena Huss and Erling Wande, "Emancipation i vardande?"

9. See, for example, Roos, "War Memory, Compassion."

10. Kokkola, Palo, and Manderstedt, "Protest and Apology." Because of this, I will refer to the language that Elina and the other schoolchildren speak often as Finnish.

11. Goldberg, *Melodrama*, 35.

12. Goldberg, *Melodrama*, 38.

13. See also Elsaesser, "Tales of Sound and Fury."

14. Passoja, "Klaus Härö."

15. Decker, "'Unusually Compassionate,'" 311.

16. Decker, "'Unusually Compassionate,'" 324.

17. Hunt, "Children's Literature." Scholarship that focuses on children's literature specifically (but often films are included) has repeatedly argued that children's literature is always about power in the relationship between the child and the adult.

18. Bacon, "Nordic Practices."

19. Bacon, "Nordic Practices."

20. Dyer, *White*, 118.

21. Lunde, *Nordic Exposures*, 14

22. Gladwin, *Contentious Terrains*.

23. Sanders, *Bodies in the Bog*, 7.

24. Sanders, *Bodies in the Bog*, 12.

25. Lury, *Child in Film*.

26. Kääpä, *Ecology and Contemporary Nordic Cinemas*, 150.

27. Hughey, *White Savior Film*.

28. Williams, "Melodrama Revised," 73.

29. Williams, "Melodrama Revised," 74.

30. Kokkola, Palo, and Manderstedt, "Protest and Apology," 5.

31. Goldberg, *Melodrama*, 41.

32. See more in Nestingen, *Crime and Fantasy*; Dancus, "Ghosts Haunting"; and DuBois, "Folklore, Boundaries."

33. On Wajstedt and Tailfeathers, see MacKenzie and Stenport, "Feminist Sámi Documentary."

34. Kernell in Swinson, "Nothing Fake."

35. Siebert, "Pocahontas Looks Back," 223. Paula Amad writes about how the return-of-the-gaze interpretive move in film studies regarding early films "is aimed at recovering resistance or at least a trace of agency for the nameless masses trapped like insects within modernity's visual archive. Read less sympathetically, . . . it might be argued that analyses dependent on the return of the gaze use it as leverage with which to historically unburden the medium of film of its entomologizing and zoologizing legacy regarding the visual representation of racial and colonial others." Amad, "Visual Riposte," 53.

36. Storfjell, "Elsewheres of Healing," 285.

37. Gaski, "Voice in the Margin," 211.

38. Koskinen, *Ingmar Bergman's* The Silence.

39. Kyrölä and Huuki describe *gákti* like this: "a long-sleeved, loose tunic, usually made of wool, cotton, felt, or silk; women's versions are a bit longer at the hem than men's. The *gákti* can be worn with a belt, leggings, traditional reindeer leather shoes, and a silk shawl, and it is adorned with contrast-colored bands, embroidery, plaits, and Silver or tin ornaate brooches." Kyrölä and Huuki, "Re-imagining," 85.

40. Kyrölä and Huuki, "Re-imagining," 86.

41. Kyrölä and Huuki, "Re-imagining," 87.

42. Walkerdine, "Communal Blessings," 99–116.

43. Marks, *Skin of the Film*, 151.

44. Barker, *Tactile Eye*, 28.

45. Merleau-Ponty, *Visible and the Invisible*.

46. See, for example, Stacy Alaimo, *Bodily Natures*.

47. Ahmed, "Phenomenology of Whiteness," 159.

48. Ahmed, "Phenomenology of Whiteness," 160.

49. Zaborskis, "Sexual Orphanings," 606.

CHAPTER TWO FAILING CHILDHOOD AND RETHINKING GROWING UP SWEDISH

1. The translations of the titles and quotes from these novels are my own.

2. Keskinen, "Intra-Nordic Differences"; Laskar, "Den finska rasen."

3. Halberstam, *Queer Art of Failure*, 15.

4. This theme of invisibility of migrants who are white and proximate features in some of Alakoski's nonfictional writing often functions as a way to claim more visibility while not fully acknowledging the privilege in these claims. See also Tuire Liimatainen, "From In-Betweenness to Invisibility"; and Weckström, *Representations of Finnishness in Sweden*.

5. Alakoski, *Svinalängorna*, 229; my translation. All the translations in this chapter are my own unless noted otherwise.

6. On Swedish exceptionalism and racial innocence, see Mier-Cruz, "Swedish Racial Innocence"; Hübinette, "Good Sweden"; Hübinette and Lundström, "Three Phases."

7. Olsson, *Ingenbarnsland*, 7.

8. Olsson, *Ingenbarnsland*, 7.

9. Halberstam, *Queer Art of Failure*, 80.

10. Halberstam, *Queer Art of Failure*, 4.

11. Halberstam, *Queer Art of Failure*, 3.

12. Hennefeld and Sammond, *Abjection Incorporated*.

13. Kristeva, *Powers of Horror*, 1.

14. Kristeva, *Powers of Horror*, 4.

15. Kristeva, *Powers of Horror*, 53.

16. Hennefeld and Sammond, *Abjection Incorporated*, 18.

17. Hennefeld, "Abject Feminism," 111.

18. Halberstam, *Queer Art of Failure*, 3.

19. Berggren and Trägårdh, *Swedish Theory of Love*.

20. Söderberg, "Pippi-Attitude."

21. See, for example, Nilsson, *Den föreställda mångkulturen*; Arping, "Att göra skillnad."

22. Gröndahl, "Sweden-Finnish Literature," 52.

23. Koivunen, "Economies of Pride and Shame." Koivunen writes further that between "1945 and 1994, 700,000–800,000 Finns moved to Sweden for shorter or longer periods, with some moving back and forth several times and many returning to Finland" (51).

24. Ågren, *Är du finsk, eller?*

25. Wright, *Visible Wall*.

26. Ågren, "'Är du finsk, eller ... ?'"

27. Koivunen, "Economies of Pride and Shame."

28. Pynnönen, *Siirtolaisuuden vanavedessä*, 202.

29. Rothberg, *Multidirectional Memory*.

30. Baackmann, *Writing the Child*.

31. Hirsch, *Generation of Postmemory*.

32. Alakoski, *Svinalängorna*, 31.

33. Alakoski, *Svinalängorna*, 31.

34. I use the word "affect" to refer to both collective emotions and things felt that are not even always articulated as specific emotions.

35. Conny Mithander argues that "Sweden officially exaggerated the Swedish guilt after the fall of the Berlin Wall due to a strong wish to adapt to that culture of guilt and repentance that permeates the European integration" Mithander, "Holocaust to the Gulag," 182.

36. Kavén, "Humanitaarisuuden varjossa"; Anna-Kaisa Kuusisto-Arponen, "Transnational Sense of Place."

37. Huyssen, "Diaspora and Nation," 154.

38. Rothberg, *Multidirectional Memory*, 3, 272; my emphasis.

39. Kuusisto-Arponen, "Mobilities of Forced Displacement."

40. Kuusisto-Arponen, "Mobilities of Forced Displacement," 552.

41. Hirsch, *Generation of Postmemory*, 5.

42. Hirsch, *Generation of Postmemory*, 5.

43. See, for example, Tervo, "Nationalism, Sports and Gender."

44. Valenius, "Undressing the Maid."

45. Olsson, *Ingenbarnsland*, 147.

46. Olsson, *Ingenbarnsland*, 103.

47. Molina, "Planning for Patriarchy."

48. Alakoski, *Svinalängorna*, 14.

49. Hall and Vidén, "Million Homes Programme," 301.

50. Alakoski, *Svinalängorna*, 13.

51. Alakoski, *Svinalängorna*, 15.

52. Molina, "Planning for Patriarchy," 47.

53. Kivimäki and Rantonen, "Koti ja yhteisöt," 154.

54. Alakoski, *Svinalängorna*, 91.

55. Alakoski, *Svinalängorna*, 56.

56. Alakoski, *Svinalängorna*, 114.

57. Alakoski, *Svinalängorna,* 186.

58. Alakoski, *Svinalängorna*, 225.

59. Alakoski, *Svinalängorna*, 223.

60. Janson, *Bio för barnens bästa?* 162. Lindgren's *Alla vi barn i Bullerbyn* has inspired Berthold Franke (director of Goethe-Institute Sweden) to coin the term "Bullerby syndrome," particularly among people in Germany who are deeply attached to Sweden because of the idealized image of the Swedish countryside and domestic spaces as they are described in the *Bullerby* books. However, according to Franke, this is not only a love for Swedish culture but also a nostalgic and utopian look toward German history as a common narrative among the people with the "Bullerby syndrome" who believe that if only World War II had not happened, Germany would have had their own Bullerby. " Die Unschuld Schwedens: Das Bullerbü-Syndrom," http://www.norrmagazin.de/kultur -lebensstil/unschuld-schwedens/.

61. Alakoski, *Svinalängorna*, 244.

62. Alakoski, *Svinalängorna*, 15.

63. Feuerstein and Nolte-Odhiamo, "Introduction."

64. Feuerstein and Nolte-Odhiamo, "Introduction," 2.

65. Stockton, *Queer Child*, 91.

66. Kete, *Beast in the Boudoir*, 82. (Kete quotes from one of the nineteenth-century authors.)

67. Alakoski, *Svinalängorna*, 219.

68. Lesuma, "Domesticating Dorothy."

69. Lesuma, "Domesticating Dorothy," 135.

70. Pallas, *Vithet i svensk spelfilm.*

71. Hughey, *White Savior Film.*

72. Karin Grundström and Irene Molina write, "The year 1974 can be considered the beginning of a process of neo-liberalisation of Swedish housing policy. It marks not only the end of massive housing production with the termination of the Million Programme, but also the elimination of existing legislation regulating tenant rent levels." Grundström and Irene Molina, "From Folkhem," 324.

73. While several stories of Pippi also feature a variety of grotesque images, they are not usually included in the promotion of the welfare state and the can-do attitudes that Pippi represents.

74. Olsson, *Ingenbarnsland*, 287.

75. Olsson, *Ingenbarnsland*, 8.

76. Olsson, *Ingenbarnsland*, 11.

77. Olsson, *Ingenbarnsland*, 11.

78. Olsson, *Ingenbarnsland*, 12.

79. Olsson, *Ingenbarnsland*, 255.

80. Olsson, *Ingenbarnsland*, 125.

81. See, for example, Ahmed, "Phenomenology of Whiteness"; Ahmed, "Passing Through Hybridity"; Lönn, *Bruten vithet*; Mullen, "Optic White."

82. The word "*zigenare*" used in Swedish carries a similarly derogative meaning.

83. Olsson, *Ingenbarnsland*, 185.

84. Olsson, *Ingenbarnsland*, 47.

85. Ahmed, *Queer Phenomenology*, 141.

86. On the history and contemporary discrimination of Roma and "antiziganism" in Sweden, see, for example, Kott, "It Is in Their DNA"; and Kotljarchuk, "State, Experts, and Roma." Kristian Borg writes in his essay "Den finska erfarenheten" on the challenges of Finnish-speakers in Sweden about the frustration among the Sweden Finnish community when Kjell Sundvall's film *Jägarna 2* featured its violent villain Jari Lipponen with a Finnish accent and long, greasy hair. Sundvall's problematic comment (which included a derogatory term for the Roma people) was that he had actually meant to have a Roma person be the villain but that doing so would have been racist.

87. Olsson, *Ingenbarnsland*, 58.

88. Olsson, *Ingenbarnsland*, 59.

89. Olsson, *Ingenbarnsland*, 60.

90. Olsson, *Ingenbarnsland*, 63.

91. Olsson, *Ingenbarnsland*, 66.

92. For example, in a chapter where Pippi has saved two children from a burning house, she is dancing wildly in the light of the flames on a board above the street, or when Pippi gives Tommy and Annika pills that would make them not grow up.

93. Olsson, *Ingenbarnsland*, 186.

94. Olsson, *Ingenbarnsland*, 73.

95. Ahmed, *Cultural Politics of Emotions*, 202.

96. Olsson, *Ingenbarnsland*, 237.

97. Olsson, *Ingenbarnsland*, 239.

98. Lindqvist, "Cultural Archive."

99. Lindqvist, "Cultural Archive," 59.

100. *Finnjävel* is a common derogatory term used for Finnish-speakers in the twentieth century.

101. Olsson, *Ingenbarnsland*, 303.

102. Olsson, *Ingenbarnsland*, 304.

103. Furthermore, as Sabrina Strings brings out in *Fearing the Black Body*, in the United States the Nordic race/northern European whiteness was seen as an ideal and was associated with tall, slim bodies. See also Eve-Riina Hyrkäs and Mikko Myllykangas, "War on Fat in Postwar Finland."

CHAPTER THREE UNSETTLING THE FIGURE OF THE NOT-QUITE CHILD

1. Ridanpää, "Pajala as a Literary Place."

2. Mohnike, "Joy of Narration," 172.

3. Ridanpää, "Politics of Literary Humour"; Heith, "Minorities and Migrants."

4. As mentioned elsewhere in this book, Meänkieli is the official name of the language spoken by Tornedalians; in the twentieth century it was often referred to as Tornedalian Finnish. I will refer to it as Meänkieli when appropriate, but the cultural texts taking place in the twentieth century often refer to it as Finnish.

5. Peiker, "Entangled Discourses," 394. See also Wangari wa Nyatetū-Waigwa, *Liminal Novel*.

6. Heith, *Experienced Geographies*.

7. Heith, *Experienced Geographies*.

8. Heith, *Experienced Geographies*, 97.

9. Heith, *Experienced Geographies*, 97.

10. Niemi, *Populärmusik*, 9; Niemi, *Popular Music*, 10.

11. Gröndahl, "Att bryta på svenska."

12. Östling, "Äta djävlar, föda ord."

13. Mohnike, "Joy of Narration," 174.

14. Ridanpää, "Politics of Literary Humour."

15. Hutcheon, *Irony's Edge*.

16. Hutcheon, *Irony's Edge*, 12, emphasis in the original.

17. Hutcheon, *Irony's Edge*, 14.

18. Hutcheon, *Theory of Parody*.

19. The most famous early example of this is Proust's "involuntary memories" in *Remembrance of Things Past*.

20. See more on the realities of tourism in the Himalayans in Yang Mu, Sanjay K. Nepal, and Po-Hsin Lai, "Tourism and Sacred Landscape."

21. Esty, *Unseasonable Youth*.

22. Niemi, *Populärmusik*, 12; Niemi, *Popular Music*, 12 (all translations of quotes from this novel are from Laurie Thompson's translation).

23. Niemi, *Populärmusik*, 12, Niemi, *Popular Music*, 12.

24. Esty, *Unseasonable Youth*, 7.

25. Takolander, "Theorizing Irony and Trauma," 112. Recent scholarship on the magical realist mode has shown that magical realist texts do not authenticate fantasy as evidence of pathology or cultural difference.

26. Niemi, *Populärmusik*, 51; Niemi, *Popular Music*, 51.

27. As Lena Keil ("Li och Lo och läroplanerna," 2008) has brought out in her comparative analysis of both the original version (1958) and the revised one (1968), the reader featured two families and promoted traditional gender roles as well as (particularly in the first edition) included racist stereotypes.

28. Niemi, *Populärmusik*, 52; Niemi, *Popular Music*, 51.

29. Niemi, *Populärmusik*, 49–50, Niemi, *Popular Music*, 48–49.

30. Esty, *Unseasonable Youth*; Mignolo, *Darker Side*.

31. Niemi, *Populärmusik*, 50, Niemi, *Popular Music*, 49.

32. Bhabha, *Location of Culture*.

33. Dancus, "Sámi Identity across Generations"; Mecsei, "Hybrid First-Person Sámi Documentaries."

34. Niemi, *Populärmusik*, 52, Niemi, *Popular Music*, 52.

35. Niemi, *Populärmusik*, 41, Niemi, *Popular Music*, 41.

36. Leunissen, "Diamonds and Rust."

37. Niemi, *Populärmusik*, 238, 237.

38. Faris, *Ordinary Enchantments*.

39. Östling, "Äta djävlar, föda ord."

40. Niemi, *Populärmusik*, 14; Niemi, *Popular Music*, 14.

41. Niemi, *Populärmusik*, 74; Niemi, *Popular Music*, 74.

42. Niemi, *Populärmusik*, 77; Niemi, *Popular Music*, 78.

43. Halberstam, *Queer Time and Place*, 160.

44. Niemi, *Populärmusik*, 204; Niemi, *Popular Music*, 204.

45. Geffen, *Glitter Up the Dark*.

46. Geffen, *Glitter Up the Dark*, 18.

47. Geffen, *Glitter Up the Dark*, 19, 23.

48. Geffen, *Glitter Up the Dark*, 26.

49. Niemi, *Populärmusik*, 237; Niemi, *Popular Music*, 237.

50. Kieri, *Vårt värde*, 26.

51. In my writing about the narrator, I will use either "she" or "they" pronoun, depending on whether the passage I'm discussing uses singular "I" or plural "we."

52. Fasselt, "(Post)Colonial We-Narratives."

53. Kieri, *Vårt värde*, 8.

54. Kieri, *Vårt värde*, 9.

55. Kieri, *Vårt värde*, 11.

56. Kieri, *Vårt värde*, 49. The mine strike likely refers to the Great Miners' Strike (Stora Gruvstrejken) of 1969–1970 in Sweden, which included miners from Kiruna, Luleå, Malmberget, and Svappavaara.

57. Kieri, *Vårt värde*, 27.

58. Laakso, *Our Otherness*, 98.

59. Kieri, *Vårt värde*, 119.

60. Kieri, *Vårt värde*, 72.

61. Kieri, *Vårt värde*, 119.

62. Kieri, *Vårt värde*, 121.

63. Kieri, *Vårt värde*, 121.

64. Kieri, *Vårt värde*, 147.

65. Kieri, *Vårt värde*, 103.

66. Kieri, *Vårt värde*, 63.

67. Kieri, *Vårt värde*, 11.

68. Kieri, *Vårt värde*, 11.

69. Kieri, *Vårt värde*, 8.

70. Kieri, *Vårt värde*, 8.

71. Kieri, *Vårt värde*, 148. "Mahoton" means "tremendously" in Finnish; it is not translated within the novel's text, but it is included in a list of words in Meänkieli and their Swedish translations.

72. Bekhta, *We-Narratives*, 11.

73. Fasselt, "(Post)Colonial We-Narratives," 156.

74. Fasselt, "(Post)Colonial We-Narratives," 164.

75. Fasselt, "(Post)Colonial We-Narratives," 163.

76. Kieri, *Vårt värde*, 137.

77. Hirsch, *Generation of Postmemory*.

78. Kieri, *Vårt värde*, 29.

79. Kieri, *Vårt värde*, 73.

80. Kieri, *Vårt värde*, 56.

81. Kieri, *Vårt värde*, 56.

82. Kieri, *Vårt värde*, 56.

83. Vikgren, *Antikeksiskväde*.

84. Heith, *Experienced Geographies*, 138.

85. Heith, *Experienced Geographies*, 139.

86. Kieri, *Vårt värde*, 149.

CONCLUSION

1. Westberg, "Girls' Gymnastics," 62–63.

2. Formark and Bränström Öhman, "Situating Nordic Girls' Studies," 5. Formark and Öhman paraphrase Elina Oinas and Anna Collander, "Tjejgrupper: rosa rum, pippifeminism, hälsofrämjande?" in *Kvinnor, kropp och hälsa*, ed. Elina Oinas and Jutta Ahlbeck-Rehn, 275–99 (Lund: Studentlitteratur, 2007).

3. Hübinette, "Good Sweden."

4. For example, Annica Wennström's novel *Lappskatteland* or Liselotte Wajstedt's documentary road film *Sami nieida jojk*. See also Satu Gröndahl's discussion of contemporary Sámi literature in Gröndahl, "Att komma hem."

5. Locke, *Democracy and the Death of Shame*.

6. For example, Laestadius's young adult novels, like *SMS från Soppero* or novels like *Stöld* and *Straff*.

BIBLIOGRAPHY

Åberg, Anders Wilhelm. "Conceptions of Nation and Ethnicity in Swedish Children's Films: The Case of *Kidz in da Hood* (*Förortsungar*, 2006)." *Journal of Educational Media, Memory & Society* 5, no. 2 (2013): 92–107.

Ågren, Marja. "'Är du finsk, eller . . . ?' En etnologisk studie om att växa upp och leva med finsk bakgrund i Sverige." PhD diss. Gothenburg: University of Gothenburg, 2006.

Ahmed, Sara. *The Cultural Politics of Emotions*. 2nd ed. Edinburgh: Edinburgh University Press, 2014.

Ahmed, Sara. "A Phenomenology of Whiteness." *Feminist Theory* 8, no. 2 (2007): 149–68.

Ahmed, Sara. *Queer Phenomenology: Orientations, Objects, Others*. Durham: Duke University Press, 2006.

Ahmed, Sara. "'She'll Wake up One of These Days and Find She's Turned into a Nigger': Passing through Hybridity." *Theory, Culture & Society* 16, no. 2 (1999): 87–106.

Alaimo, Stacy. *Bodily Natures: Science, Environment, and the Material Self*. Bloomington: Indiana University Press, 2010.

Alakoski, Susanna. *Svinalängorna* (Swine rows). Pocket ed. Stockholm: Bonnier Pocket, 2007.

Amad, Paula. "Visual Riposte: Looking Back at the Return of the Gaze as Postcolonial Theory's Gift to Film Studies." *Cinema Journal* 52, no. 3 (2013): 49–74. DOI: 10.1353/cj.2013.0015.

Andersson, Camilla. "En sanningskommission gör synligt det som varit undertryckt och förtryckt." Accessed January 11, 2024. https://www.samer.se/2629.

Arping, Åsa. "Att göra skillnad: Klass, kön och etnicitet i några av det nya seklets svenska uppväxtskildringar." In *Från Nexø till Alakoski: Aspekter på nordisk arbetarlitteratur*, edited by Birthe Sjöberg, Bibi Jonsson, Jimmy Vulovic, and Magnus Nilsson, 189–98. Lund: Lund University. 2011.

Baackmann, Susanne. *Writing the Child: Fictions of Memory in German Postwar Literature*. Oxford: Peter Lang, 2022.

Bacon, Henry. "Nordic Practices and Nordic Sensibilities in Finnish-Swedish Co-Productions: The Case of Klaus Härö and Jarkko T. Laine." *Journal of Scandinavian Cinema* 4, no. 2 (2014): 99–115.

Barker, Jennifer M. *The Tactile Eye: Touch and the Cinematic Experience*. Berkeley: University of California Press, 2009.

Bekhta, Natalya. *We-Narratives: Collective Storytelling in Contemporary Fiction*. Columbus: Ohio State University Press, 2020.

Berggren, Henrik, and Lars Trägårdh. "Pippi Longstocking: The Autonomous Child and the Moral Logic of the Welfare State." In *Swedish Modernism: Architecture, Consumption, and the Welfare State*, edited by Helena Matsson and Sven-Olov Wallenstein, 10–23. London: Black Dog, 2010.

Berggren, Henrik, and Lars Trägårdh. *The Swedish Theory of Love: Individualism and Social Trust in Modern Sweden*. Seattle: University of Washington Press, 2022.

Bernstein, Robin. "Childhood as Performance." In *The Children's Table: Childhood Studies and the Humanities*, edited by Anna Mae Duane, 203–12. Athens: University of Georgia Press, 2013.

Bhabha, Homi. *The Location of Culture*. 2nd ed. London: Routledge, 2004.

Borg, Kristian. "Förord: Den finska erfarenheten värker." In *Finnjävlar*, edited by Kristian Borg, 14–25. Stockholm: Verbal förlag, 2016.

Braidotti, Rosi. "On Becoming Europeans." In *Women Migrants from East to West: Gender, Mobility and Belonging in Contemporary Europe*, edited by Luisa Passerini, Dawn Lyon, Enriza Capussotti, and Ioanna Laliotou, 23–44. New York: Berghahn Books, 2010.

Brembeck, Helene, Barbro Johansson, and Jan Kampmann. "Introduction." In *Beyond the Competent Child: Exploring Contemporary Childhoods in the Nordic Welfare Societies*, edited by Helene Brembeck, Barbro Johansson, and Jan Kampmann, 7–29. Frederiksberg, Denmark: Roskilde Universitetsforlag, 2008.

Castañeda, Claudia. *Figurations: Child, Bodies Worlds*. Durham: Duke University Press, 2002.

Dancus, Adriana Margareta. "Ghosts Haunting the Norwegian House: Racialization in Norway and *The Kautokeino Rebellion*." *Framework* 55, no. 1 (2014): 121–39.

Dancus, Margareta. "Sámi Identity across Generations: From Passing for Nordics to Sami Self-Exposure." *Journal of Critical Mixed Race Studies* 1, no. 2 (2022): 262–76.

Dankertsen, Astri. "I Felt So White: Sámi Racialization, Indigeneity, and Shades of Whiteness." *Native American and Indigenous Studies* 6, no. 2 (2019): 110–37.

Decker, Christof. "'Unusually Compassionate': Melodrama, Film, and the Figure of the Child." In *Melodrama! The Mode of Excess from Early America to Hollywood*, edited by Frank Kelleter and Barbara Kahn, 305–28. Heidelberg: Universitätsverlag Winter, 2007.

Doxtater, Amanda. "From Diversity to Precarity: Reading Childhood in Ruben Östlund's Film *Play* (2011)." In *New Dimensions of Diversity in Nordic Culture and Society*, edited by Jenny Björklund and Ursula Lindqvist, 192–211. Newcastle upon Tyne: Cambridge Scholars Publishing, 2016.

Duane, Anna Mae. "Introduction." In *The Children's Table: Childhood Studies and the Humanities*, edited by Anna Mae Duane, 1–14. Athens: University of Georgia Press, 2013.

DuBois, Thomas A. "Folklore, Boundaries and Audience in *The Pathfinder*." In *Sami Folkloristics*, edited by Juha Pentikäinen, 255–74. Turku: Abo Akademi University, 2000.

Dyer, Richard. *White*. 20th anniversary ed. London: Routledge, 2017.

Edelman, Lee. *No Future: Queer Theory and the Death Drive*. Durham: Duke University Press, 2004.

Esty, Jed. *Unseasonable Youth: Modernism, Colonialism, and the Fiction of Development.* New York: Oxford University Press, 2012.

Elsaesser, Thomas. "Tales of Sound and Fury: The Family Melodrama." *Monogram* 4 (1972): 2–15.

Faris, Wendy B. *Ordinary Enchantments: Magical Realism and the Remystification of Narrative.* Nashville: Vanderbilt University Press, 2004.

Fasselt, Rebecca. "(Post)Colonial We-Narratives and the 'Writing Back' Paradigm: Joseph Conrad's *The Nigger of the 'Narcissus' and* Ngũgĩ wa Thiong'o's *A Grain of Wheat.*" *Poetics Today* 37, no. 1 (2016): 155–79.

Feuerstein Anna, and Carmen Nolte-Odhiamo. "Introduction: The Cultural Politics on Childhood and Pethood." In *Childhood and Pethood in Literature and Culture: New Perspectives in Childhood Studies and Animal Studies,* edited by Anna Feuerstein and Carmen Nolte-Odhiamo, 1–18. New York: Routledge, 2017.

Formark, Bodil, and Annelie Bränström Öhman. "Situating Nordic Girls' Studies." *Girlhood Studies* 6, no. 2 (2013): 3–10.

Fura, Elisabet. Foreword to *Slutbetänkande av Sannings-och försoningskommissionen för tornedalingar, kväner och lantalaiset.* Stockholm: Statens offentliga utredningar, 2023.

Gaski, Harald. "Indigenism and Cosmopolitanism: A Pan-Sami View of the Indigenous Perspective in Sami Culture and Research." *AlterNative: An International Journal of Indigenous Peoples* 9, no. 2 (2013): 113–24.

Gaski, Harald. "Voice in the Margin: A Suitable Place for a Minority Literature?" In *Sami Culture in a New Era: The Norwegian Sami Experience,* edited by Harald Gaski, 199–220. Kárášjohka: Davvi Girji, 1997.

Geffen, Sasha. *Glitter Up the Dark: How Pop Music Broke the Binary.* Austin: University of Texas Press, 2020.

Gladwin, Derek. *Contentious Terrains: Boglands, Ireland, Postcolonial Gothic.* Cork, Ireland: Cork University Press, 2016.

Goldberg, Jonathan. *Melodrama: An Aesthetics of Impossibility.* Durham: Duke University Press, 2016.

Gröndahl, Satu. "Att bryta på svenska utan att vara svensk: Språket och den interkulturella litteraturen." In *Revitalisera mera!: En artikelsamling om den språkliga mångfalden i Norden tillägnad Leena Huss,* edited by Ulla Börestam, Satu Gröndahl, and Boglárka Straszer, 56–69. Uppsala: Centrum för multietnisk forskning, 2008.

Gröndahl, Satu. "Att komma hem: Identitetsskapande i modern samisk litteratur." *Tidskrift för genusvetenskap* 42, no. 4 (2021): 101–21.

Gröndahl, Satu. "Sweden-Finnish Literature: Generational and Cultural Changes." In *Migrants and Literature in Finland and Sweden,* edited by Satu Gröndahl and Eila Rantonen, 37–56. Helsinki: Finnish Literature Society, 2018.

Grundström, Karin, and Irene Molina. "From Folkhem to Lifestyle Housing in Sweden: Segregation and Urban Form, 1930s–2010s." *European Journal of Housing Policy* 16, no. 3 (2016): 316–36.

Halberstam, Jack. *In a Queer Time and Place: Transgender Bodies, Subcultural Lives.* New York: NYU Press, 2005.

Halberstam, Jack. *The Queer Art of Failure.* Durham: Duke University Press, 2011.

Hall, Thomas, and Sonja Vidén. "The Million Homes Programme: A Review of the Great Swedish Planning Project." *Planning Perspectives* 20 (2005): 301–28.

Hatch, Kirsten. *Shirley Temple and the Performance of Girlhood.* New Brunswick, NJ: Rutgers University Press, 2014.

Heith, Anne. "Ethnicity, Cultural Identity, and Bordering: A Tornedalian Negro." *Folklore* 52 (2012): 85–108.

Heith, Anne. *Experienced Geographies and Alternative Realities: Representing Sápmi and Meänmaa.* Göteborg: Makadam, 2020.

Heith, Anne. "Minorities and Migrants: Transforming the Swedish Literary Field." In *The Novel and Europe: Imagining the Continent in Post-1945 Fiction*, edited by Andrew Hammond, 211–65. London: Palgrave Macmillan, 2016.

Hennefeld, Maggie. "Abject Feminism, Grotesque Comedy, and Apocalyptic Laughter on *Inside Amy Schumer*." In *Abjection Incorporated: Mediating the Politics of Pleasure and Violence*, edited by Maggie Hennefeld and Nicholas Sammond, 86–111. Durham: Duke University Press, 2020.

Hennefeld, Maggie, and Nicholas Sammond, eds. *Abjection Incorporated: Mediating the Politics of Pleasure and Violence.* Durham: Duke University Press, 2020.

Hirsch, Marianne. *The Generation of Postmemory: Writing and Visual Culture after the Holocaust.* New York: Columbia University Press, 2012.

Honeyman, Susan. *Elusive Childhood: Impossible Representation in Modern Literature.* Columbus: Ohio State University Press, 2005.

Hübinette, Tobias. *Adopterad. En bok om Sveriges sista rasdebatt.* Stockholm: Verbal förlag, 2020.

Hübinette, Tobias. "'Good Sweden': Transracial Adoption and the Construction of Swedish Whiteness and White Antiracism." In *Routledge Handbook of Critical Studies in Whiteness*, edited by Shona Hunter and Christi van der Westhuizen, 150–59. London: Routledge, 2021.

Hübinette, Tobias, and Catrin Lundström. "Sweden after the Recent Election: The Double Binding Power of Swedish Whiteness through the Mourning of the Loss of 'Old Sweden' and the Passing of 'Good Sweden.'" *NORA-Nordic Journal of Feminist and Gender Research* 19, no. 1 (2011): 42–52.

Hübinette, Tobias, and Catrin Lundström. "Swedish Whiteness and White Melancholia." In *Unveiling Whiteness in the Twenty-First Century: Global Manifestations, Transdisciplinary Interventions*, edited by Veronica Watson, Deirdre Howard-Wagner and Lisa Spanierman, 49–74. Lanham, MD: Lexington Books, 2014.

Hübinette, Tobias, and Catrin Lundström. "Three Phases of Hegemonic Whiteness: Understanding Racial Temporalities in Sweden." *Social Identities* 20, no. 6 (2014): 423–37. http://dx.doi.org/10.1080/13504630.2015.1004827.

Hughey, Matthew W. *The White Savior Film: Content, Critics, and Consumption.* Philadelphia: Temple University Press, 2014.

Hunt, Peter. "Children's Literature." In *Keywords for Children's Literature*, edited by Philip Nel and Lissa Paul, 42–47. New York: NYU Press, 2007.

Huss, Leena, and Erling Wande. "Emancipation i vardande?: Drag i tornedalingarnas och sverigefinnarnas språkpolitiska utveckling." In *Mellan majoriteter och minoriteter: om migration, makt och mening*, edited by Marianne Junila and Charles Westin. Helsingfors: Svenska litteratursällskapet i Finland, 2006.

Hutcheon, Linda. *Irony's Edge: The Theory and Politics of Irony*. London: Routledge, 1994.

Hutcheon, Linda. *A Theory of Parody: The Teachings of Twentieth-Century Art Forms*. New York: Methuen, 1985.

Huyssen, Andreas. "Diaspora and Nation: Migration into Other Pasts." *New German Critique*, 88 (2003): 147–64.

Hyrkäs, Eve-Riina, and Mikko Myllykangas. "War on Fat in Postwar Finland: A History of Fat-Shaming." *Fat Studies* 13, no. 1 (2024): 36–48.

Janson, Malena. *Bio för barnets bästa? Svensk barnfilm som fostran och fritidsnöje under 60 år*. Stockholm: Acta Universitatis Stockholmiensis, 2007.

Johansson i Backe, Kerstin. *Som om jag inte fanns* (*As If I Wasn't There*). Helsinki: Kustannusosakeyhtiö Otava, 1978.

Kääpä, Pietari. *Ecology and Contemporary Nordic Cinemas: From Nation-Building to Ecocosmopolitanism*. New York: Bloomsbury, 2014.

Kavén, Pertti. "Humantaarisuuden varjossa: Poliittiset tekijät lastensiirroissa Ruotsiin sotiemme aikana ja niiden jälkeen." PhD diss. Helsinki: University of Helsinki, 2010.

Keil, Lena. "Li och Lo och läroplanerna: En jämförande analys av två versioner av läsläran 'Första boken' i 1950-och 1960s-talets Sverige." BA thesis. Linköping, Sweden: Linköping University, 2008.

Keskinen, Suvi. "Intra-Nordic Differences, Colonial/Racial Histories, and National Narratives: Rewriting Finnish History." *Scandinavian Studies* 91, no. 1–2 (2019): 163–81.

Keskinen, Suvi. "Re-Constructing the Peaceful Nation: Negotiating Meanings of Whiteness, Immigration and Islam after Shopping Mall Shooting." *Social Identities* 20, no. 6 (2014): 471–85.

Kete, Kathleen. *The Beast in the Boudoir: Petkeeping in Nineteenth-Century Paris*. Berkeley: University of California Press, 1994.

Key, Ellen. *The Century of the Child* (*Barnets århundrade*). 1900. New York: G. P. Putnam's Sons, 1909.

Kieri, Katarina. *Vårt värde* (Our worth). Stockholm: Norstedts, 2015.

Kivimäki, Sanna, and Eila Rantonen. "Koti ja yhteisöt ruotsinsuomalaisten Susanna Alakosken *Sikaloissa* ja Arja Uusitalo *Meren sylissä*." In *Vähemmistöt ja monikulttuurisuus kirjallisuudessa*, edited by Eila Rantonen, 231–40. Tampere, Finland: Tampere University Press, 2010.

Kjellman, Ulrika. "How to Picture Race? The Use of Photography in the Scientific Practice of the Swedish State Institute for Race Biology." *Scandinavian Journal of History* 39, no. 5 (2014): 580–611. http://dx.doi.org/10.1080/03468755.2014.948054.

Kjellman, Ulrika. "A Whiter Shade of Pale: Visuality and Race in the Work of the Swedish State Institute for Race Biology." *Scandinavian Journal of History* 38, no. 2 (2013): 180–201. http://dx.doi.org/10.1080/03468755.2013.769458.

Knight, Rebecca. "Representations of Soviet Childhood in Soviet Texts by Liudmila Ulitskaia and Nina Gabrielian." *Modern Language Review* 104, no. 3 (2009): 790–808.

Koivunen, Anu. "Economies of Pride and Shame: Politics of Affect in New Narratives about Sweden Finns." *Collegium: Studies across Disciplines in the Humanities and Social Sciences* 23 (2017): 50–66.

Kokkola, Lydia, Annbritt Palo, and Lena Manderstedt. "Protest and Apology in the Arctic: Enacting Citizenship in Two Recent Swedish Films." *Humanities* 8, no. 49 (2019): 1–12.

Koskinen, Maaret. *Ingmar Bergman's* The Silence: *Pictures in the Typewriter, Writings on the Screen*. Seattle: University of Washington Press, 2010.

Kotljarchuk, Andrej. "State, Experts, and Roma: Historian Allan Etzler and Pseudo-Scientific Racism in Sweden." *Scandinavian Journal of History* 45, no. 5 (2020): 615–39.

Kott, Matthew. "It Is in Their DNA: Swedish Police, Structural Antiziganism and the Registration of Romanis." In *When Stereotype Meets Prejudice: Antiziganism in European Societies*, edited by Timofey Agarin, 45–75. Stuttgart: Ibidem-Verlag, 2014.

Kristeva, Julia. *Powers of Horror: An Essay on Abjection*. New York: Columbia University Press, 1982.

Kulick, Don. "Four Hundred Thousand Swedish Perverts." *GLQ* 11, no. 2 (2005): 205–35.

Kuokkanen, Rauna. "The Deatnu Agreement: A Contemporary Wall of Settler Colonialism." *Settler Colonial Studies* 10, no. 4 (2020): 508–28. https://doi.org/10.1080/2201473X.2020.1794211.

Kuokkanen, Rauna. "'Survivance' in Sami and First Nations Boarding School Narratives: Reading Novels by Kerttu Vuolab and Shirley Sterling." *American Indian Quarterly* 27, nos. 3/4 (2003): 697–726.

Kuusisto-Arponen, Anna-Kaisa. "The Mobilities of Forced Displacement: Commemorating Karelian Evacuation in Finland." *Social & Cultural Geography* 10, no. 5 (2009): 545–63.

Kuusisto-Arponen, Anna-Kaisa. "Transnational Sense of Place: Cinematic Scenes of Finnish War Child Memories." *Journal of Aesthetics and Culture* 3, no. 1 (2011). doi:10.3402/jac.v3i0.7178.

Kyrölä, Katariina, and Tuija Huuki. "Re-imagining a Queer Indigenous Past: Affective Archives and Minor Gestures in the Sámi Documentary *Sparrooabbán*." *Journal of Cinema and Media Studies* 60, no. 5 (2021): 75–98.

Laakso, Johanna. *Our Otherness: Finno-Ugric Approaches to Women's Studies or Vice Versa*. Wien: LIT Verlag, 2005.

Laestadius, Ann-Helén. *SMS från Soppero*. Pocket ed. Stockholm: Rabén & Sjögren, 2013.

Laestadius, Ann-Helén. *Stöld*. Stockholm: Romanus & Selling, 2021.

Laestadius, Ann-Helén. *Straff*. Stockholm: Romanus & Selling, 2023.

Lagerlöf, Selma. *Nils Holgerssons underbara resa genom Sverige*. Stockholm: Albert Bonnier, 1906–1907.

Lanas, Maija, and Tuija Huuki. "Thinking Beyond Student Resistance: A Difficult Assemblage in Teacher Education." *European Journal of Teacher Education* 40, no. 4 (2017): 436–46.

Larsson, Mariah. "Representing Sexual Transactions: A National Perspective on a Changing Region in Three Swedish Films." In *Regional Aesthetics: Locating Swedish*

Media, edited by Erik Hedling, Olof Hedling, and Mats Jönsson, 21–41. Stockholm: Kungliga biblioteket.

Laskar, Pia. "Den finska rasen och görandet av svenskar." In *Ras och vithet: Svenska rasrelationer i går och i dag*, edited by Tobias Hübinette, 71–95. Lund: Studentlitteratur, 2017.

Lesuma, Caryn Kunz. "Domesticating Dorothy: Toto's Role in Reconstructing Childhood in *The Wizard of Oz* and Its Retellings." In *Childhood and Pethood in Literature and Culture: New Perspectives in Childhood Studies and Animal Studies*, edited by Anna Feuerstein and Carmen Nolte-Odhiamo, 124–37. New York: Routledge, 2017.

Leunissen, Joost M. "Diamonds and Rust: The Affective Ambivalence of Nostalgia." *Current Opinion in Psychology* 49 (February 2023). https://doi.org/10.1016/j.copsyc.2022.101541.

Liimatainen, Tuire. "From In-Betweenness to Invisibility: Changing Representations of Sweden Finnish Authors." *Journal of Finnish Studies* 23, no. 1 (2019): 41–66.

Lindgren, Astrid. *Alla vi barn i Bullerbyn*. 16th ed. Stockholm: Rabén och Sjögren, 1967.

Lindgren, Astrid. *Karlson on the Roof*. Translated by Patricia Crampton. London: Methuen, 1971.

Lindgren, Astrid. *Lillebror och Karlsson på taket*. 4th ed. Stockholm: Rabén och Sjögren, 1955.

Lindgren, Astrid. *Pippi in the South Seas*. Translated by Susan Beard. Oxford: Oxford University Press, 2020.

Lindgren, Astrid. *Pippi Långstrump*. 1945. Stockholm: Rabén och Sjögren, 1969.

Lindgren, Astrid. *Pippi Långstrump i Söderhavet*. 14th ed. Stockholm: Rabén och Sjögren, 1969.

Lindgren, Astrid. *Pippi Longstocking*. Translated by Florence Lamborn. New York: Puffin Books, 2005.

Lindgren, Astrid. *The Children of Noisy Village*. Translated by Susan Beard. Oxford: Oxford University Press, 2021.

Lindqvist, Ursula. "The Cultural Archive of the IKEA Store." *Space and Culture* 12, no. 1 (2009): 43–62.

Locke, Jill. *Democracy and the Death of Shame: Political Equality and Social Disturbance*. New York: Cambridge University Press, 2016.

Lönn, Maria. *Bruten vithet: om den ryska femininitetens sinnliga och temporala villkor*. Stockholm: Leopard förlag, 2018.

Lopez, Alfred J. "Introduction: Whiteness after Empire." In *Postcolonial Whiteness: A Critical Reader on Race and Empire*, edited by Alfred J. Lopez, 1–30. Albany: State University of New York Press, 2005.

Lunde, Arne Olav. *Nordic Exposures: Scandinavian Identities in Classical Hollywood Cinema*. Seattle: University of Washington Press, 2010.

Lundqvist, Ulla. *Århundradets barn: fenomenet Pippi Långstrump och dess förutsättningar*. Stockholm: Rabén & Sjögren, 1979.

Lundström, Catrin, and Benjamin R. Teitelbaum. "Nordic Whiteness: An Introduction." *Scandinavian Studies* 89, no. 2 (2017): 151–58.

Lury, Karen. *The Child in Film: Tears, Fears, and Fairytales*. New Brunswick, NJ: Rutgers University Press, 2010.

Mackenzie, Scott, and Anna Westerståhl Stenport. "Contemporary Experimental Feminist Sámi Documentary: The First-Person Politics of Liselotte Wajstedt and Elle-Máijá Tailfeathers." *Journal of Scandinavian Cinema* 6, no. 2 (2016): 169–82.

Marks, Laura U. *The Skin of the Film: Intercultural Cinema, Embodiment, and the Senses*. Durham: Duke University Press, 2000.

McClintock, Anne. *Imperial Leather: Race, Gender, and Sexuality in the Colonial Contest*. New York: Routledge, 1995.

Mecsei, Monica. "Hybrid First-Person Sámi Documentaries: Identity Construction and Contact Zones in the Twenty-First Century." In *Arctic Cinemas and the Documentary Ethos*, edited by Anna Westerstahl Stenport, Scott MacKenzie, and Lilya Kaganovsky, 302–21. Bloomington: Indiana University Press, 2019.

Melkas, Kukku. "Literature and Children In-Between: The Entangled History of Finland and Sweden in *Svinalängorna, Mother of Mine* and *Ingenbarnsland*." In *Migrants and Literature in Finland and Sweden*, edited by Satu Gröndahl and Eila Rantonen, 83–96. Helsinki: Finnish Literature Society, 2018.

Merleau-Ponty, Maurice. *The Visible and the Invisible. Followed by Working Notes*. Evanston, IL: Northwestern University Press, 1968.

Mier-Cruz, Benjamin. "Swedish Racial Innocence on Film: To Be Young, Queer, and Black in Swedish Documentary Filmmaking." *Journal of Scandinavian Cinema* 12, no. 1 (2022): 11–27.

Mignolo, Walter D. *The Darker Side of Western Modernity: Global Futures, Decolonial Options*. Durham: Duke University Press, 2011.

Mithander, Conny. "From the Holocaust to the Gulag: The Crimes of Nazism and Communism in Swedish Post-89 Memory Politics." In *European Cultural Memory Post-89*, edited by Conny Mithander, John Sundholm, and Adrian Velicu, 177–208. Amsterdam: Rodopi, 2013.

Moe, Birgitte Furberg. "Barndomshistorier i tre århundrer: en bokhistorisk analyse av I brønnen og i tjernet." Master's thesis. University of Oslo, 2009.

Moe, Jørgen. *I Brønden og i Tjærnet: Smaahistorier for Børn*. Christiania: Feilberg & Landmark, 1851.

Mohnike, Thomas. "The Joy of Narration. Mikael Niemi's *Popular Music from Vittula*." *Journal of Northern Studies* 8, no. 1 (2014): 169–86.

Molina, Irene. "Planning for Patriarchy? Gender Equality in the Swedish Modern Built Environment." In *The Routledge Companion to Modernity, Space and Gender*, edited by Alexandra Staub, 26–40. New York: Routledge, 2018.

Mu, Yang, Sanjay K. Nepal, and Po-Hsin Lai. "Tourism and Sacred Landscape in Sagarmatha (Mt. Everest) National Park, Nepal." *Tourism Geographies* 21, no. 3 (2019): 442–59.

Mullen, Harryette. "Optic White: Blackness and the Production of Whiteness." *diacritics* 24, nos. 2–3 (1994): 71–89.

Nestingen, Andrew K. *Crime and Fantasy in Scandinavia: Fiction, Film, and Social Change*. Seattle: University of Washington Press, 2008.

Niemi, Mikael. *Popular Music from Vittula*. Translated by Laurie Thompson. New York: Sweden Stories Press, 2003.

Niemi, Mikael. *Populärmusik från Vittula*. Stockholm: Norstedts Förlag, 2000.

Nikolajeva, Maria. "A Misunderstood Tragedy: Astrid Lindgren's *Pippi Longstocking* Books." In *Beyond Babar: The European Tradition in Children's Literature*, edited by Sandra L. Beckett, Maria Nikolajeva, 49–74. Lanham, MD: Children's Literature Association and the Scarecrow Press, 2006.

Nilsson, Magnus. *Den föreställda mångkulturen: Klass och etnicitet i svensk samtidsprosa.* Hedemora, Sweden: Gidlund, 2010.

Nyatetū-Waigwa, Wangari wa. *The Liminal Novel: Studies in the Francophone-African Novel as* Bildungsroman. New York: Peter Lang, 1996.

Nykvist, Karin. "Dreaming Childhood, Dreaming Society, Dreaming Sweden: The Autonomous Child in the Welfare State." Unpublished manuscript, March 2018.

Oinas, Elina, and Anna Collander. "Tjejgrupper: rosa rum, pippifeminism, hälsofrämjande?" In *Kvinnor, kropp och hälsa*, edited by Elina Oinas and Jutta Ahlbeck-Rehn, 275–99. Lund: Studentlitteratur, 2007.

Olsson, Eija Hetekivi. *Ingenbarnsland* (No child's land). Stockholm: Norstedts, 2011.

Ommundsen, Åse Marie. "Competent Children: Childhood in Nordic Children's Literature from 1850 to 1960." In *Nordic Childhoods 1700–1960: From Folk Beliefs to Pippi Longstocking*, edited by Reidar Aasgaard, Marcia Bunge, and Merethe Roos, 283–302. New York: Routledge, 2018.

Össbo, Åsa. "Hydropower Company Sites: A Study of Swedish Settler Colonialism." *Settler Colonial Studies* 13, no. 1 (2023): 115–32.

Östling, Marie. "Äta djävlar, föda ord: Om återkommande groteska motiv i Mikael Niemis romaner *Kyrkdjävulen, Populärmusik från Vittula, Fallvatten* och *Koka Björn*." Master's thesis. Umeå, Sweden: Umeå Universitet, 2022.

Pallas, Hynek. *Vithet i svensk spelfilm 1989–2010*. Göteborg: Filmkonst, 2011.

Parvulescu, Anca. "Reproduction and Queer Theory: Between Lee Edelman's 'No Future' and J. M. Coetzee's 'Slow Man.'" *PMLA* 132, no. 1 (2017): 86–100.

Passoja, Teemu. "Klaus Härö ja *Äideistä parhain*." *Film-O-Holic.* September 29, 2005. https://www.film-o-holic.com/haastattelut/klaus-haro-aideista-parhain/.

Peiker, Piret. "Entangled Discourses in a *Bildungsroman* of Soviet Estonian Modernity: From an Ugly Duckling to Gagarin's Space Princess?" *Journal of Baltic Studies* 51, no. 3 (2020): 389–405. https://doi.org/10.1080/01629778.2020.1779095.

Pohjanen, Bengt, and Kirsti Johansson, eds. *Den tornedalsfinska litteraturen: Från Kexi till Liksom*. Överkalix, Sweden: Barents, 2007.

Proust, Marcel. *Remembrance of Things Past*. Translated by C. K. Scott Moncrieff and Terence Kilmartin. London: Chatto & Windus, 1981.

Pynnönen, Marja-Liisa. *Siirtolaisuuden vanavedessä: tutkimus ruotsinsuomalaisen kirjallisuuden kentästä vuosina 1956–1988*. Helsinki: Suomalaisen Kirjallisuuden Seura, 1991.

Rantonen, Eila. "Writing Biography by E-Mail—Postcolonial and Postmodern Rewriting of Biographical and Epistolary Modes in Jonas Hassen Khemiri's *Montecore*. In *Migrants and Literature in Finland and Sweden*, edited by Satu Gröndahl and Eila Rantonen, 204–24. Helsinki: Finnish Literature Society, 2018.

Ridanpää, Juha. "Pajala as a Literary Place: In the Readings and Footsteps of Mikael Niemi." *Journal of Tourism and Cultural Change* 9, no. 2 (2011): 103–17. DOI:10.1080/14766825.2011.562979.

Ridanpää, Juha. "Politics of Literary Humour and Contested Narrative Identity (of a Region with No Identity)." *Cultural Geographies* 21, no. 4 (2014): 711–26.

Roos, Liina-Ly. "Approaching Texts of Not-Quiteness: Reading Race, Whiteness, and In/Visibility in Nordic Culture." *Scandinavian Studies* 93, no. 3 (2023): 318–44.

——. "War Memory, Compassion, and the Finnish Child: Klaus Härö's *Mother of Mine*." In *Nordic War Stories: World War II as History, Fiction, Media, and Memory*, edited by Marianne Stecher-Hansen, 269–81. New York: Berghahn Books, 2021.

Rothberg, Michael. *Multidirectional Memory: Remembering the Holocaust in the Age of Decolonization*. Stanford: Stanford University Press, 2009.

Rudd, David. "The Animal Figure in Astrid Lindgren's Work." *Barnboken* 30, no. 1–2 (2007): 38–47.

Ryalls, D. Emily, and Sharon R. Mazzarella. "Famous, Beloved, Reviled, Respected, Feared, Celebrated. Media Construction of Greta Thunberg." *Communication, Culture & Critique* 14, no. 3 (2021): 438–53.

Ryman, Geoff. *Was*. New York: HarperCollins, 1992.

Sanders, Karin. *Bodies in the Bog and the Archaeological Imagination*. Chicago: University of Chicago Press, 2009.

Sandin, Bengt. "Children and the Swedish Welfare State: From Different to Similar." In *Reinventing Childhood after World War II*, edited by Paula Fass and Michael Grossberg, 110–38. Philadelphia: University of Pennsylvania Press, 2011.

Siebert, Monika. "Pocahontas Looks Back and Then Looks Elsewhere: The Entangled Gaze in Contemporary Indigenous Art." *Ab-original* 2, no. 2 (2018): 207–26.

Smith, Andrea. "Queer Theory and Native Studies: The Heteronormativity of Settler Colonialism." *GLQ* 16, nos. 1–2 (2010): 42–48.

Socialdemokraterna. "Vår historia." Accessed June 6, 2023. https://www.socialdemokraterna.se/vart-parti/om-partiet/var-historia.

Söderberg, Eva. "'Lillasyster ser dig!' Pippi Långstrump, Lisbeth Salander och andra Pippi-karaktärer." In *Millennium: Åtta genusvetenskapliga läsningar av den svenska välfärdsstaten genom Stieg Larssons Millennium-trilogi*, edited by Siv Fahlgren, Anders Johansson, and Eva Söderberg, 51–66. Sundsvall, Sweden: Mittuniversitetet, 2013.

Söderberg, Eva. "The Pippi-Attitude as a Critique of Norms and as a Means of Normalization: From Modernist Negativity to Neoliberal Individualism." In *Normalization and "outsiderhood": Feminist Readings of a Neoliberal Welfare State*, 91–104. Bentham eBooks, 2011.

Stockton, Kathryn Bond. *The Queer Child, or Growing Sideways in the Twentieth Century*. Durham: Duke University Press, 2009.

Storfjell, Troy. "Elsewheres of Healing: Transindigenous Spaces in Elle-Máijá Apiniskim Tailfeathers' Bihttoš." In *Nordic Film Cultures and Cinemas of Elsewhere*, edited by Anna Westerstahl Stenport and Arne Lunde, 279–86. Edinburgh: Edinburgh University Press, 2019.

Storfjell, Troy. "Mapping a Space for Sámi Studies North America." *Scandinavian Studies* 75, no. 2 (2003): 153–64.

Strings, Sabrina. *Fearing the Black Body: The Racial Origins of Fat Phobia*. New York: NYU Press, 2019.

Sunnemark, Fredrik. "Who Are We Now Then? The Swedish Welfare State in Political Memory and Identity." In *Kultura* 4, no. 5 (2014): 7–16.

Swinson, Brock. "Nothing Fake: Amanda Kernell on *Sami Blood*." *Creative Screenwriting*, June 20, 2017. https://www.creativescreenwriting.com/sami-blood/.

Takolander, Maria Kaaren. "Theorizing Irony and Trauma in Magical Realism: Junot Díaz's *The Brief Wondrous Life of Oscar Wao* and Alexis Wright's *The Swan Book*." *ariel: A Review of International English Literature* 47, no. 3 (2016): 95–122.

Tervo, Mervi. "Nationalism, Sports and Gender in Finnish Sports Journalism in the Early Twentieth Century." *Gender, Place and Culture: A Journal of Feminist Geography* 8, no. 4 (2001): 357–73. DOI:10.1080/09663690120111609.

Törngren, Sayaka Osanami, Carolina Jonsson Malm, and Tobias Hübinette. "Transracial Families, Race, and Whiteness in Sweden." *Genealogy* 2, no. 54 (2018): 1–16. DOI:10.3390/genealogy2040054.

Valenius, Johanna. *Undressing the Maid: Gender, Sexuality, and the Body in the Construction of the Finnish Nation*. Helsinki: Suomalaisen Kirjallisuuden Seura, 2004.

Veracini, Lorenzo. *Settler Colonialism. A Theoretical Overview*. New York: Palgrave Macmillan, 2010.

Vikgren, David. *Antikeksiskväde: Översättning, dikt*. Luleå, Sweden: Black Island Books, 2010.

Walkerdine, Valerie. "Communal Beingness and Affect: An Exploration of Trauma in an Ex-industrial Community." *Body & Society* 16, no. 1 (2010): 99–116.

Weckström, Lotta. *Representations of Finnishness in Sweden*. Helsinki: Finnish Literature Society, 2011.

Wennström, Annica. *Lappskatteland. En familjesaga*. Stockholm: Wahlström & Widstrand, 2007.

Westberg, Johannes. "Girls' Gymnastics in the Service of the Nation: Educationalisation, Gender and Swedish Gymnastics in the Mid-Nineteenth Century." *Nordic Journal of Educational History* 4, no. 2 (2017): 47–69.

Widhe, Olle. "The Politics of Autobiography in Katarina Taikon's *Katitzi* Series." *Children's Literature* 49 (2021): 59–73.

Williams, Linda. "Melodrama Revised." In *Refiguring American Film Genres*, edited by Linda Williams and Nick Browne, 42–88. Berkeley: University of California Press, 1998.

Witoszek, Nina, and Martin Lee Mueller. "The Ecological Ethics of Nordic Children's Tales: From Pippi Longstocking to Greta Thunberg." *Environmental Ethics* 43, no. 1 (2021): 61–78. DOI:10.5840/enviroethics20215725.

Wolfe, Patric. *Settler Colonialism and the Transformation of Anthropology. The Politics and Poetics of an Ethnographic Event*. New York: Cassell, 1999.

Wright, Michelle M. "Queer Temporalities: Space-ing Time and the Subject." In *Time and Literature*, edited by Thomas M. Allen, 288–304. Cambridge: Cambridge University Press, 2018.

Wright, Rochelle. *The Visible Wall: Jews and Other Ethnic Outsiders in Swedish Film.* Carbondale: Southern Illinois University Press, 1998.

Wyver, Richey. "'Too Brown to Be Swedish, Too Swedish to Be Anything Else': Mimicry and Menace in Swedish Transracial Adoption Narratives." *Social Identities* 27, no. 3 (2021): 394–409.

Zaborskis, Mary. "Sexual Orphanings." *GLQ* 22, no. 4 (2016): 605–28.

INDEX

Page numbers in *italics* refer to illustrations.

Åberg, Anders Wilhelm, 18
abjection, 68, 71–73; exaggerated, 103;
    forced and voluntary, 99; as response to
    stigmatization, 98
adulthood: with childhood, 27; Sámi, 28;
    Swedish, 28
Ågren, Marja, 75
Ahmed, Sara, 22, 25, 65; and lining up, 10,
    37, 62–63, 96–97, 100
Alakoski, Susanna, 3, 27, 29, 74–75, 156n4
Alla vi barn i Bullerbyn (film, dir. Hel-
    bom), 87
Alla vi barn i Bullerbyn (novel, Lindgren):
    and cozy idyllic childhood, 87
apology: as resolution for complex histo-
    ries, 23, 39, 52–53
August, Pernilla, 91

Baackmann, Susanne, 76
Bagher, Reza, 30, 112, 120
Barker, Jennifer, 61
Beatles, the, 114, 123; as a queer resistance
    to growing up, 126
Bekhta, Natalya, 135
Berggren, Henrik, 6, 12–13, 74
Bergman, Ingmar, 41–42, 59
Bernstein, Robin, 4–5. *See also* childhood:
    studies of
Bhabha, Homi: and mimicry, 21
Bihttoš (dir. Tailfeathers), 55
Bildungsroman: postcolonial, 108–9

Castañeda, Claudia, 26
child: autonomous, 3, 7, 9, 15, 17–18, 20,
    106; competent, 3, 7, 12, 15, 51, 116,
    152n33; as construction, 16; as figure
    of innocence and victimhood, 76, 86;
    Finnish, 134; gaining civil rights, 15;
    Indigenous, 25, 110; melodramatic,
    40–41; moral, 3, 7, 15, 51, 57, 145; myth
    of the Swedish, 3; Nordic, 3, 7, 13, 16, 39,
    47; paradoxes in the figure of a, 145; in
    postwar German literature, 76; queer,
    11; as representation of not-quiteness,
    115; Romani, 17; Sámi, 137; and state
    individualism, 8; as symbol of citizens,
    3, 5; Shirley Temple, 5; Tornedalian, 114,
    125, 129; as unexceptional, 18. *See also*
    not-quite child, the
childhood: abstract idea of, 5; anarchy of,
    67, 72–74; autonomous, 47; as being
    and becoming, 15, 23; deviating, 19–20;
    effigy of, 5; endless, 86–87, 90; excep-
    tional, 107; idealized and unreachable,
    15, 17, 70, 86; Indigenous, 7; innocence,
    25; and marginality, 25; Nordic, 7; nor-
    mative, 53; as not-yet, 28; and perfor-
    mance, 5, 18; and pethood, 88–89; priv-
    ileged, 17; as reorientation, 25; Sámi,
    151n15; studies of, 3–5, 26, 148; Swedish,
    2–3, 7, 12–13, 15, 17–19, 71, 73, 86, 97,
    107, 113–14; traumatic, 86, 91; unsettled,
    92–93, 141–42; working-class, 74

children's literature, 11
cleanliness: exaggerated and abject, 86; failure to perform white/Swedish, 97; and order, 85
colonization, 20, 68; bodily impact of, 56; internalized, 118; progress and modernity in the rhetoric of, 118
colonial histories, 22–23, 30, 36, 38, 115, 133; entangled, 110, 129, 138; shared, 144–45

Dankertsen, Astri, 34–36
Decker, Christof: and the melodramatic child, 40
defamiliarization, 25, 57
Doxtater, Amanda, 18–19
Duane, Anna Mae, 26. *See also* childhood: studies of

Eastern Europe: and sex trafficking, 19; as temporally othered, 21; as a threat, 20
Edelman, Lee: reproductive futurism, 9
Elina: som om jag inte fanns (dir. Härö), 29, 32–33, 36–37; bog as embodiment of not-quiteness in, 45–48; camera placement in, 41; the child aligned with normative linearity in, 53; colonialist attitudes in, 39, 49–50; dangerous liminality in, 48; emotional healing for audiences in, 52; inspiring adult audiences in, 40; lighting in, 42–44, *43*, 49; melodramatic mode in, 38–39, 49, 51; not-quite child resisting injustice in, 40; performing Nordic child, 47; plot of, 37–38; power structures in, 41; reconciliation as fantasy in, 54; and return to moral certainty, 51; rooting and unrooting identity in, 46; and semi-colonial history, 38; Swedish savior figure in, 49–52; visualizing racialization in, 44
Elsaesser, Thomas, 39, 53
Esty, Jed, 115
European Charter for Regional or Minority Languages, 22

failure, 25, 84; of childhood, 98; to perform idealized childhood, 67, 98, 104; queer, 28, 30, 66–67, 71, 74, 105; to remember, 68; as traumatic, 72. *See also* Halberstam, Jack
Faris, Wendy B., 122. *See also* magical realism
Fasselt, Rebecca, 30, 129, 136–37
Finnish labor migrants, 21, 68, 75; misconceptions toward, 68; and stereotypes, 84; as threat, 83
Finnish language, 63; in Sweden, 70, 94
Finnish-speakers, 21. *See also* Sweden Finns
Finno-Ugric identity, 22, 103; and inferiority, 131; and racial hierarchies, 131; in *Vårt värde*, 130
Framework Convention for the Protection of National Minorities, 22

gákti, 59; as second skin in *Sameblod*, 60–61
Gaski, Harald, 23, 57
Gaup, Nils, 55
Geffen, Sasha, 126
gender: equality, 1, 12, 14, 19–20, 146; expectations, 60, 70, 95, 116, 123, 126, 132; and nation, 81–82
Goldberg, Jonathan, 39, 53–54
Gröndahl, Satu, 75, 111

Halberstam, Jack, 28, 67–68, 71–72, 93, 105, 125, 148. *See also* failure
Hansson, Per Albin, 5–6
Härö, Klaus, 38, 40
Heith, Anne, 36, 109–10, 141. *See also* Tornedalian culture
Hennefeld, Maggie, 72–73, 99
Hirsch, Marianne, 76, 80, 137. *See also* postmemory
Hübinette, Tobias, 16–17, 24, 147. *See also* whiteness
Hughey, Matthew, 49
Hunt, Peter, 41

Hutcheon, Linda, 112
Huuki, Tuija, 27, 59
Huyssen, Andreas, 78–79

IKEA: as essentialized Swedishness, 101–3
Indigenous studies, 10, 22, 33–34, 57, 59, 152n26
Ingenbarnsland (Olsson), 25, 29, 67; abject objection in, 73, 99–100; bodily memories of inferiority in, 101; in comparison to *Svinalängorna*, 70, 99; defecation in, 99–100; disappointment in, 98; embodiment in, 97; exaggerated abject image in, 102–3; failure as subversive in, 93, 104–5; forced Finnish identity in, 94; a good scar in, 100; grotesque in, 71, 93–94; memory in, 79, 80–81; normative "healthy" Swedish bodies in, 103; performing abjection in, 93; performing the anarchic child in, 73; persistence of borders in, 100; plot of, 69–70; racist encounter in, 96–97; references to Pippi Longstocking in, 71, 93, 99; refurnishing the room with IKEA products in, 102; restricted eating in, 103; slippage between anarchy and abject in, 98; trip to England in, 100
innocence, 5, 76. *See also* childhood
invisibility, 33–34, 156n4; erasure, 2, 34–35; in melodrama, 39; of memories, 79–80; passing and assimilation, 2; as powerful and shame-producing, 26; as privilege, 34, 36; and racialization, 24, 33, 36, 47, 95; of Sámi people, 60–61; of Sweden Finns, 68–69, 77, 92; of Tornedalians, 47–48, 50
irony, 30, 107, 112–13

Jag var en lägre ras (SVT), 35
Janson, Malena, 87
Johansson, Kirsti, 140–41
Johansson i Backe, Kerstin, 37

Karelian people, 79–80
Kautokeino Rebellion (dir. Gaup), 55
Keksi, Antti, 140
Kernell, Amanda, 29, 54, 56
Key, Ellen: *The Century of the Child*, 6–7
Kidz in da Hood (dir. Gustavsson and Edfelt), 18
Kieri, Katarina, 25, 30, 106–7, 127
Kristeva, Julia, 68, 72–73
Kuokkanen, Rauna, 22, 33. *See also* Indigenous studies

Laestadius, Ann-Helen, 147
Lagerlöf, Selma, 35
Lilja 4-ever (dir. Moodysson), 19
Lindgren, Astrid, 87, 99. *See also* Longstocking, Pippi
lining up: charged with fear or shame, 63; in colonial spaces, 25; cosmopolitan, 123–27; to escape not-quiteness, 121; failure in, 66, 70, 86, 95, 104, 122; growing up and, 24, 37, 108, 135; hesitance in, 20; performative nature of, 37; rejecting, 65, 104–5, 134, 138, 140; with Swedishness, 36, 45, 73–74, 108, 132, 134–35; with whiteness, 10, 24, 29, 62–63, 127, 148. *See also* Ahmed, Sara: and lining up
Longstocking, Pippi, 1, 70–72, 145–46; as autonomous child, 11–14; economy, 74; as emblem of Swedish exceptionalism, 14, 154n43; as feminist icon, 12–14; growing sideways, 14; and individualism, 16; and neoliberal success, 74; as normative and subversive, 12; performing Swedish childhood, 12, 18; as "sovereign man," 13; and Swedishness, 14; triumphant, 18; vs. Tommy and Annika, 13. *See also* child; childhood
Lopez, Alfred J., 21
Lundborg, Herman, 8–9

177

Index

Lundström, Catrin, 16
Lury, Karen, 47

magical realism, 30, 107, 115
Marks, Laura, 60
Meänkieli, 35, 37, 63, 109, 160n4. *See also* minority culture; Tornedalians
Meänmaa, 36, 109–10, 137. *See also* Tornedalians
memory: as contested, 76; cultural, 77; entangled, 132; fixed narratives of, 76; fragments of, 80–81; migrant, 76; as multidirectional site of not-quiteness, 76, 79; new forms of, 68, 148; works of, 28
Merleau-Ponty, Maurice, 62
Mier-Cruz, Benjamin, 8
migration: labor, 78; proximate, 79; to Sweden, 16
Million Program, 83; as problem area, 84; as unclean, 84
minority culture, 22, 31, 64, 108–9, 133, 144; Sámi, 55, 57–59, 61, 63, 65, 108, 110, 115, 118, 130, 137, 147, 162n4; Sweden Finnish, 68, 70, 75–76, 80, 84, 91, 94, 159n86; Tornedalian, 23, 35–36, 43, 49, 107–10, 118, 124–26, 130, 140
Mohnike, Thomas, 107, 111–12
Molina, Irene, 83–84
Moodysson, Lukas, 19
My Life as a Dog (dir. Hallström), 90
Myrdal, Alva and Gunnar, 8

Nattvardsgästerna (dir. Bergman), 42
Niemi, Mikael, 30, 106–7, 111–12
Nikolajeva, Maria, 3
Nils Holgerssons underbara resa genom Sverige (Lagerlöf), 35–36
not-quite child, the, 3, 23–24, 28, 67; cinematic constructions of, 37, 56–60; melodramatic child and, 41; in northern Sweden, 37; pluralized, 129, 138; racialization

of, 95; as recurring figure, 106, 113, 144; as reorienting the child figure, 148; singularity in, 107–8; slippage in the image of, 112; as unexceptional, 116–17. *See also* sideways growth
not-quiteness, 20–21; child as a representation of, 28, 115; dangers of, 48, 53; entangled histories of, 86, 141–42; exaggeration of, 107; growing out of, 90–91, 119, 126; and indigeneity, 55; intergenerational, 138; invisible, 47, 69; legacy of, 107; and memory, 76–82; Nordic, 23–26, 33, 154n78; persistence of, 101; queer, 123; resolution to, 49, 53–54; sites of, 25, 82, 88, 94; temporal and spatial materialization of, 89. *See also* racialization

Olsson, Eija Hetekivi, 25, 29, 67, 74
Olsson, Jimmy, 14
Ommundsen, Åse Marie, 11
Össbo, Åsa, 21, 33, 35
Östling, Marie, 111, 123
Östlund, Ruben, 18–19

parody, 30, 107
Pathfinder (dir. Gaup), 55
Peiker, Piret, 108–9
phenomenology, 24, 27
pippifeminism, 146
Play (dir. Östlund), 18–19
plural voice, 30, 107
Pohjanen, Bengt, 35–36, 109–10, 140–41. *See also* minority culture
Populärmusik från Vittula (film, dir. Bagher), 112; adaptation of prologue in, 112–13; the furnace sequence in, 120–22
Populärmusik från Vittula (novel, Niemi), 30, 106–7; absurdity in, 107; accelerated growing up in, 119–20; adult narrator's presence in, 118–19; the Beatles in, 123–25; becoming human in,

117; closer proximity to Swedishness in, 108; colonial education in, 117; critical distance from the child figure in, 113–14, 116; humor in, 107, 125; irony in, 112–14, 118, 123; lining up with cosmopolitan whiteness in, 127; magical realism in, 115–16, 122–23; plot of, 111; prologue of, 111; subversive potential of pop/rock music in, 123–25; temporal synchronicity with global subcultures in, 113–14, 125

postmemory, 77, 80, 82, 137–38

privilege, 68, 106–7; awareness of, 26, 31, 113, 142; to be autonomous, 17; to be protected, 17; to pass, 2, 21, 31, 118, 129, 133; space of, 15, 108, 110; to subvert norms, 17; of white minorities, 30, 34, 36, 61, 97, 118. *See also* whiteness

Pynnönen, Marja-Liisa, 76. *See also* minority culture

racial hierarchies, 2–3, 9, 21, 33, 42, 66, 96–97, 117. *See also* not-quiteness

racialization, 20; bodily impact of, 56, 60; histories of, 20–21, 30, 110; indigeneity and, 55; internalized, 11, 56; invisible, 2, 35–36, 95; and social class, 43; visualizing, 29, 33, 44, 59. *See also* not-quiteness

Rantonen, Eila, 84, 145

reorientation, 24–25; of the child, 129, 141, 148; of the child's gaze, 58; temporal, 28

reproduction: of family and nation, 8; as meaningful, 10; as oppressive, 10

Ridanpää, Juha, 112

Roma people, 97

Rothberg, Michael, 76, 79. *See also* memory

Russian empire: border drawing between Sweden and, 35

Sameblod/Sami Blood (dir. Kernell), 25, 28–29, 32–33, 36; burning the gákti

in, 62; camera movement/framing in, 57–58; gákti as second skin in, 60–61; looking elsewhere in, 57, *58*, 65; monuments of Sámi collective memory in, 55; not-quiteness as embodied and felt in, 60; passing for a white Swede in, 61, 64–65; plot of, 54–55; and reproduction, 64; resolution in, 65; scene of gymnastics class in, 143, *145*, 148; scenes of lining up in, 62–65; tactile images in, 56, 60–61, *61*; visibility and tactility in, 59

Sámi nieida jojk (dir. Wajstedt), 55

Sámi people, 34–35; and boarding schools, 22; and colonial politics, 24–25, 35, 65, 109; and history in film, 55; and languages, 63; racialization of, 9, 20–21, 34, 57; and reindeer-herding, 61; whiteness as ambiguous for, 34, 143. *See also* minority culture

Sammond, Nicholas, 72–73

Sanders, Karin, 46

Sandin, Bengt, 6–8, 11, 15

Sápmi, 38; and Torne River Valley, 137

segregation, 35, 63–64

settler colonialism, 10, 16, 116, 152n26; and assimilation, 42; benign, 22, 33; and boarding schools, 22; and erasure, 65, 118, 132; Nordic, 33; and Swedish hydropower, 33; and violence, 21. *See also* colonial histories

sexuality: bad, 19; good and moral, 19

sideways growth, 11, 46, 68, 71; as joyful liberation and alienation, 99; as privileged, 12, 15. *See also* not-quite child, the; Stockton, Kathryn Bond

Smith, Andrea, 10, 152n26

Social Democratic Party, Sweden, 5–6

Söderberg, Eva, 12–14, 16

Sparrooabbán (dir. Suvi West), 55

State Institute for Race Biology (SIRB), 8

Stockton, Kathryn Bond, 11, 46, 68, 71, 88, 89, 148. *See also* sideways growth

Storfjell, Troy, 57

Svinalängorna (film, dir. August), 78, 91; cathartic healing in, 92; compared to the novel, 92; Swedish savior figure in, 92; trauma narrative in melodramatic mode in, 91

Svinalängorna (novel, Alakoski), 26, 28–29, 67; blurred child-animal boundaries in, 88–90; child's bodily reactions in, 85; cleaning as exaggerated and abject in, 86; cleanliness associated with Swedish homes in, 85; contrasting figure to Pippi Longstocking in, 70–71; counter-narrative to endless playful childhood in, 88; deteriorating every day in, 86; disillusionment in, 70, 82–83; family dog in, 88; gender and nation in, 81; inferiority and shame in, 77; memories of Finland in, 77; migrant hope in, 82–83; multidirectional memory in, 79; plot of, 69; prejudice in, 84; references to idealized child in, 70; Swedish exceptionalism in, 71

Sweden Finns: culture of, 75–76; diasporic memory of, 81; minority vs. migrant status, 75; recognition as national minority, 75–76; well-integrated, 75. *See also* minority culture

Swedish childhood. *See* childhood

Swedish exceptionalism, 1, 19, 44; exception to, 18; moral, 78, 95; in Nordic cinema, 18; in self-image of Sweden, 71. *See also* Longstocking, Pippi

Swedish film, 17–19, 41–42, 53, 59, 86–87, 90, 92

Swedish literature, 11, 14, 17, 74–75

"Swedish theory of love," 74. *See also* Swedish welfare state

Swedish welfare state, 74; architecture of, 24–25; as caring, 53, 74; critique of, 19; as crumbling, 17; developing urban projects of, 67; failure in, 74; as a good home, 6; as neoliberal, 73; rise of neoliberalism in, 93; unsettling, 92

Taikon, Katarina, 17

Takolander, Maria Kaaren, 115. *See also* magical realism

Temple Black, Shirley, 5

Thunberg, Greta, 1

Tornedalians, 20–22, 30, 107–9, 113, 137, 160n4; history of, 35–38; racialization of, 43–44

Tornio River valley, 35, 38, 107, 140–41; as colonial borderland, 114. *See also* minority culture

Trägårdh, Lars, 5–6, 12–13, 74

transnational adoption, 17, 24. *See also* not-quite child, the

trauma, 27, 53; in *Svinalängorna*, 88

Truth and Reconciliation Commission on Tornedalians, Kvens, and Lantalaiset, 22

Truth Commission on the Indigenous Sámi people, 23

Tystnaden (dir. Bergman), 59

Valla Villekulla (dir. Olsson), 14

Vårt värde (Kieri), 25, 106–7; ambivalence about colonial histories in, 133; ambivalence toward modernity in, 129; blurred lines of puberty and postcolonial time in, 130; entangled memories in, 132–33; Finno-Ugric identity in, 130–32; and first-person plural narrator, 107, 128–29, 134–36; the fusion of waters in, 140; gendered expectations in, 132; multidirectional growing in, 129; nonlinear resistance to growing up in, 140; plot of, 127–28; plural child figure in, 129, 138–41; uncertainty about synchronizing movement in, 134

Veracini, Lorenzo, 33

Vikgren, David, 140–41

we-narrative, 30, 129, 135

Westberg, Johannes, 143–44

whiteness: ambiguous identification with, 34–35; hierarchies of, 75, 138; inherited, 10–11; lines of, 24; lining up with, 62, 64, 127; not-quite, 21, 43; performative nature of, 96; proximity to, 22, 108; as Swedishness, 21; as Western-ness, 23, 131

Williams, Linda, 51

Wolfe, Patric, 33

working-class: childhood, 74; literature, 75

World War II: contrasting memories of, 77; emotional impact of, 68; in Sweden Finnish literature, 76

Wright, Rochelle, 75

Wyver, Richey, 24

yoik, 57

Zaborskis, Mary, 10, 64

NEW DIRECTIONS IN SCANDINAVIAN STUDIES

Small States in International Relations, edited by Christine Ingebritsen, Iver B. Neumann, Sieglinde Gstohl, and Jessica Beyer

Danish Cookbooks: Domesticity and National Identity, 1616–1901, by Carol Gold

Crime and Fantasy in Scandinavia: Fiction, Film, and Social Change, by Andrew Nestingen

Selected Plays of Marcus Thrane, translated and introduced by Terje I. Leiren

Munch's Ibsen: A Painter's Visions of a Playwright, by Joan Templeton

Knut Hamsun: The Dark Side of Literary Brilliance, by Monika Žagar

Nordic Exposures: Scandinavian Identities in Classical Hollywood Cinema, by Arne Lunde

Icons of Danish Modernity: Georg Brandes and Asta Nielsen, by Julie K. Allen

Danish Folktales, Legends, and Other Stories, edited and translated by Timothy R. Tangherlini

The Power of Song: Nonviolent National Culture in the Baltic Singing Revolution, by Guntis Šmidchens

Church Resistance to Nazism in Norway, 1940–1945, by Arne Hassing

Christian Krohg's Naturalism, by Øystein Sjåstad

Fascism and Modernist Literature in Norway, by Dean Krouk

Sacred to the Touch: Nordic and Baltic Religious Wood Carving, by Thomas A. DuBois

Sámi Media and Indigenous Agency in the Arctic North, by Thomas A. DuBois and Coppélie Cocq

The Swedish Theory of Love: Individualism and Social Trust in Modern Sweden, by Henrik Berggren and Lars Trägårdh, translated by Stephen Donovan

Menacing Environments: Ecohorror in Contemporary Nordic Cinema, by Benjamin Bigelow

The Not-Quite Child: Colonial Histories, Racialization, and Swedish Exceptionalism, by Liina-Ly Roos